from consumer R to connoisseur

## Renaissance Guide to

# Wine &
# Food Pairing

D0032015

from consumer **R** to connoisseur

# Renaissance Guide to

# Wine & Food Pairing

## Tony DiDio and Amy Zavatto

ALPHA
A member of Penguin Group (USA) Inc.

*To my husband, Dan Marotta, for his great patience, love, and support, without which I'd be slinging hash.*

*—Amy Zavatto*


*To my mother, Rose DiDio, who brought me to the table, filled my plate, and revealed the treasures of my Sicilian heritage.*

*To my father, Anthony DiDio, who poured my first glass of wine, nurtured me, and managed to keep my glass full since day one.*

*—Tony DiDio*

# Contents

# Foreword

There are not many books available that give equal consideration to wine and food and the pairing thereof—a subject close to my heart—and it was, therefore, with great pleasure that I got involved in Tony and Amy's book project. I enjoyed hearing about the progression of the manuscript, and the meal that we shared, described in this book, was very special. We tasted myriad wines and considered their matches to the dishes I had created—for me, this was the perfect illustration of the theory that a meal is not just about the food, it is also about the wine. Actually, it is really about the food and the wine—the two cannot be considered separately if they are on the table at the same time.

I grew up on my family's farm just outside of Lyon. Food and wine were always a big part of our family dynamic because, like any French family worth its salt, the meals we shared were always discussed and debated while we enjoyed them. Probably because we farmed, we paid a lot more attention to the quality of the meat and produce we ate than to the caliber of the wine we drank to accompany my mother and grandmother's wonderful meals and my father's homemade charcuterie. In fact, until I started to train seriously as a chef, I really didn't give wine much thought beyond the fact that it came in two basic categories—red and white.

It was only when I went to serve my apprenticeship in a top-notch restaurant that I realized wine was an essential part of any total dining experience. Working with the staff there opened the whole world of wine to me. The chef was interested in the perfect meal that ensued, from matching each dish to the wine that complemented it and vice versa. I was very impressed with the concept that wine and food were considered together in order to create a harmonious meal. It was this period in my life when I started to study wine more carefully and use it as an integral element in my cuisine.

Now that I own my own restaurants, I can really have fun with wine pairings. This is a passion I share with my sommelier, Jean Luc Le Dû. Sometimes we have patrons at Daniel who order their wine first and I plan a meal around their choice; sometimes I plan a tasting menu and Jean Luc has the challenge of finding the ideal wine for each course. Either way, we both know that our working together to create a perfect synergy between food and drink can only enhance the meal our patron is eating. Obviously, the food will taste better and the wine will taste better because we have created a balance between the two, thus raising the customer's dining experience to a new level. The wine and the food are not presented as disparate elements served at the same time; they become partners and create a total dining experience.

Tony and Amy have written a primer for all those who are interested in wine—not just its history, but also the essentials of what I have attempted to describe here—how to create the perfect balance to a meal. I admire the fact that, contrary to many wine experts who lay down the law of what wine should be drunk with what dish and accept no deviation, they offer commonsense guidelines of what goes with what and why, but allow the reader leeway to experiment on his or her own. This proves to me that they are true wine lovers because they know that wine—like anything else in life that one loves—is always looked at from a completely subjective viewpoint. Ultimately, what counts is what you like to drink. In this in-depth book, Tony and Amy help you discover exactly what that is.

Daniel Boulud

In today's world, wines often seem to be judged more by the ratings critics have bestowed upon them than by the actual pleasure they provide at the dinner table. Power and extraction of fruit are the norm if one wants a big score; we sometimes seem to forget that wine is also about finesse, elegance, and its ability to pair well with food. I'm sorry to say, but I do not know of many dishes that work with a wine that has 14.5 percent alcohol and luscious amounts of oak!

Amy Zavatto and Tony DiDio, both lovers of food and wine, met on the sidewalks of Brooklyn while looking for the perfect prosciutto in one of the many great food markets of that fabled neighborhood. Devoted foodies and "bon vivants," they understand the challenges of cooking at home and pairing wines with it. In this book, they show in simple words and examples how to maximize your experience at the dinner table by matching the right wine with a dish. Their combined experience in the kitchen and cellar makes them authorities in the field.

To Amy and Tony, the symbiosis of a great dish with the right bottle amounts to finding the Holy Grail. Their easy yet knowing ways with wine and understanding of the intricacies of pairing food with it are a breath of fresh air. Why, you ask? It is simply because to them, nirvana is in the kitchen and paradise in the wine cellar. Their idea of a great day is to spend the morning at the many specialty food stores that dot New York City and the afternoon cooking up a storm in the kitchen of Tony's Brooklyn flat. Tasting a sauce as it simmers down, they constantly think about the perfect bottle of wine to go with it.

I met Tony about eight years ago upon taking the position of sommelier at Restaurant Daniel. Still wet behind the ears, I was assailed by wine salespersons more eager to make placements than to get me the right wines for Daniel's cooking, and in walked Tony, with a box of delicious cookies from a local pasticceria. We spent the next few hours eating, drinking, and talking about rock 'n' roll, another of our common passions. In Tony, I found a kindred spirit, a man whose eyes shine when he nails the right wine for osso bucco or whatever else is cooking on the stove.

While the understanding of wine often breeds snobbery, Amy and Tony's approach is anything but haughty. They make wine simple because they were brought up in households where wine was a staple of every meal, not a prize served to impress guests. Tony still makes Zinfandel in his basement, just like his grandpa taught him to, and maintains a working garden behind his apartment. Having watched him give wine seminars through the years, I know he has a knack for explaining in simple words the sometimes intricate fundamentals of pairing wine and food. This book is the first one I've seen that does that on paper. It will provide the reader with useful tips and also an understanding of how food and wine work together. Read this, eat, drink, and be merry!

Jean Luc Le Dû

# Introduction

*I only drink champagne when I'm happy, and when I'm sad.
Sometimes I drink it when I'm alone. When I have company,
I consider it obligatory. I trifle with it if I am not hungry and
drink it when I am. Otherwise I never touch it—unless I'm thirsty.*

—*Lily Bollinger*

In America, we tend to put wine into the "special occasion" category.
We drink it as part of a celebration or when we've put great effort into
cooking a scrumptious dinner or when we dine out at an elegant eatery.
This is not to disparage our ways. In fact, we have become a country
that loves, encourages, and embraces creativity of all kinds in food.
Whether it's behind the helm of a stove, dining out at old favorites or
the hottest new eateries, or catching a favorite foodie program on TV,
we've all become more attuned to a world of sights, smells, and tastes
from the kitchen. However, even with such an open-armed embrace
for eating, when it comes to feeling confident about choosing wine, and
successfully pairing it with our food, we still feel a little like the shy
chess-club geek asking the head cheerleader for a dance at the prom.

What we hope to do within these pages is to encourage you to think
of wine not just as something to drink on special occasions, but rather
something along the lines of Ms. Bollinger's sentiment. The occasion
to drink wine is any time you sit down to a meal.

This isn't just about changing attitudes, though. There's another,
even better reason that goes beyond breaking out of old patterns: Wine
and food do wonderful things for each other. Their flavors mingle to
create something that each item on its own doesn't have. They become
more full, richer, and more complex; flavors are accentuated that
might not have been without the benefit of a foil or friend.

We call this book the *Renaissance Guide to Wine and Food Pairing*
because what you are about to experience is a sort of renaissance of
your own. A renaissance by definition is a transitional movement
marked by artistic or intellectual activity. You will learn to think of
wine and food pairing as both—artistic in the sense that you become

free of any preconceived notions or fears you have about the topic and learn to stretch the bounds with your own creative palate; intellectual in the sense that you learn basic, important tools that will aid you in not only knowing a good pair from a bad pair right off the bat, but also when to let that artistic spirit go crazy and break the rules. You will ...

❖ Learn a bit of wine's history, as well as where it comes from and how it's made, to better understand why it tastes the way it does.
❖ Learn the most important thing you'll need to know about wine and food pairing: balance. This applies to the flavors on your palate, on your plate, and in your glass. You will do this by gaining an understanding of the different taste sensations you experience when eating and drinking and how they work (or don't) together.
❖ Be taken blow by blow (or, maybe more suiting, course by course) through a myriad of food and wine possibilities, from poultry and fish to beef and game, to pastas, cheeses, and unusual spices, all the way to that sweet treat, dessert.
❖ Experience wine and food pairing at the table with some of the most renowned and well-respected chefs the world has to offer.
❖ Receive invaluable insight from winemakers and sommeliers.

Our goal is to give you confidence and, through that, freedom—freedom to experiment; freedom to make mistakes; freedom to learn what works, what doesn't, and why; freedom to enjoy wine and food whenever, wherever you like—and, if we have our way, with total, gleeful abandon.

We hope you have as much fun reading, learning, and tasting as we did writing this. May all your pairings be perfect—*cin-cin*.

## Acknowledgments

**Mutual acknowledgments:** For all their great help and support, we would like to thank Joy Tutela, David Black, the brilliant Jimmy Rose, Joseph Delissio, Steve Miller, Jillian Rein and Ed Lauber, Mark Lauber, Rob McNeil, the Italian Trade Commission, Jeff Davis, Michael Bonadies, Matthew LaSorsa, Rick Landy, Nicola Marzovilla, New Zealand Wine Council, Drew Nieporent, Jimmy Canora, Jean Arnold, Bob Sessions,

Paul Draper, Donn Riesen, Bob Lindquist, Jim Clendenen, Daniel Boulud, Pascal Vittu, Rick Moonen, Don Pintabona, Michael Lomonaco, Mauro Mafrici, Charles Scicolone, Michele Scicolone, Jean Luc Le Dû, Johnny Iuzzini, Tom Matthews of *Wine Spectator,* Professor of Viticulture Ann C. Noble of U.C. Davis, Fran Matistic, Hilary Tolman, Alexander Nixon for the beautiful photos, Marie Butler-Knight, Renee Wilmeth, the calm in the storm Mike Thomas, the ever-delightful Christy Wagner, Jennifer Chisholm, and Dawn Werk.

**Amy Zavatto:** Thanks must go to: my dad Michael Zavatto and the lovely and unstoppable Zavatto sisters, Linda, Janet, and Laura; the extended Zavatto family who know a thing or two about a good time at the table; the Marotta family for tolerating my crankiness and for always feeding me; the people I am lucky enough to call my friends who throughout the years have sealed the deal over many a meal and bottle of wine and who kept and continue to keep me going—you know who you are. In the category of best-for-last: Teresa Zavatto and Virginia Zavatto—you are both sorely missed at the table.

**Tony DiDio:** I wish to thank the men and women in my family who brought to life this incredible world of food and wine and encourage my participation in it: Rosa DiDio, Biagio DiDio, Fannie Taranto, Blaise DiDio, Charles J. Cusimano, and Thomas Gambino Sr. Thanks also to my partner in crime and wine, Jimmy Rose. Much thanks for your patience, inspiration, and for just plain being there.

# *part one*

## About Wine and Winemaking

*The Rich and Rugged History of Wine*

*A Primer on Winemaking and Varietals*

*Vintage Words: Interviews with Winemakers
Paul Draper, Bob Sessions, Bob Lindquist,
and Jim Clendenen*

*Becoming Your Own Sommelier*

*Vintage Words: Interview with Sommelier
Jean Luc Le Dû, Restaurant Daniel*

# chapter one

# The Rich and Rugged History of Wine

*Wine is constant proof that God likes to see us happy.*

*—Benjamin Franklin*

You've taken on the task of learning more about wine so you can understand how to better match it with what you eat. But here's a little secret—that's what it's all about, and it's been going on for thousands of years: The quest for the right wine with the right dish.

The history of *vino* is a rich tale chock full of drama and intrigue: plagues, wars, betrayal, lust. It's a story as good as any miniseries (and the names haven't been changed to protect the innocent). But more than just a good story, the history of wine tells us many things: how tastes have changed, how in the past class and society have made wine at times seem more high-brow (and how this same cycle happened all over again in the twentieth century), and—most important—how wine evolved into what it is today.

## When It Began

Wine has been around for an awfully long time—about 10,000 years, give or take. Because searching for the first winemaker and the place where the first vines were grown and vinification began isn't exactly the thing of which archaeological digs are made, researchers tracing the timeline have relied upon everything from tomb paintings to import/export merchant records. This is what they've found …

Think back to those days in school when you were learning about times gone by. One of the things you might not have studied in the G-rated version of history was that wine was a big deal to the ancients. The earliest record of wine production and trade can be traced to the fertile Tigris-Euphrates valley of Mesopotamia. Not only does it appear that wine was an integral part of trade, but it also played a vital role in banquet rituals. So important was it that any formal agreement (which these days would take place with contracts and lawyers present) was considered permanently sealed when food and drink were shared at a meal. (Just imagine if you were held to everything that you've promised while indulging in wine and good food with friends and family!)

But it wasn't until about 3,000 B.C.E. that things got really juicy ...

*The Tigris-Euphrates valley of Mesopotamia, where we have the first records of vines rooting into the soil.*

## From Delta Decadence to Dionysus

Leave it to the builders of great pyramids in the land of golden Pharaohs to turn winemaking into the thing of legends. Although beer was also a popular mass-produced beverage in Egypt, it was consumed mostly by the general public. Wine, on the other bejeweled hand, was the elixir sipped by the socially elite. So popular was the beverage, that some Pharaohs even made it clear in their last wishes that bottles were to be entombed with them to ensure that they had wine to carry them into the afterlife.

The Egyptians, while not the first wine-growing people whom we know of, were the first to record the winemaking process. Records of grape harvesting and wine production have been found on stone tablets and on the tomb walls of the Pharaohs.

Although some wine was imported from Syria, grapevines were plentiful in the Nile delta, where white and black grapes were produced and, usually, turned into wine. (Although the Egyptians were known to make wine from such exotics as figs and dates as well, which was probably the equivalent of what we'd now consider a dessert wine, with its sweetness and high alcohol content.) It seems that the Egyptians made quite a production of the task, growing the vines on trellises and arbors, harvesting the grapes at the precise time, using the old stomping method to get to the juice of the matter, and finally sealing the beverage in terracotta *amphorae*, which later, in the third century B.C., were replaced by a gadget that would remain the aging implement of choice for thousands of years to come: the barrel. These wine pots and barrels were even given labels and marked with the vineyard where the wine was produced, starting another tradition that winemakers still follow.

*Amphorae* are large, usually oval-shape terracotta jars with a narrow, round neck used in ancient times.

5

Now, let's fast-forward a couple thousand years to Greece (oh, how time flies with good wine). As the Egyptians did, the Greeks considered wine the beverage of the socially well-set. At this point, wine was not available to the masses; the less fortunate had to satisfy themselves by drinking diluted vinegar or whatever was left over from a second pressing of the grapes (sort of the ancient-times equivalent of screw-cap Almaden). But as with philosophy, literature, and architecture, the Greeks took it to a whole new level. Each Greek island apparently had its own "varietal," which was traded within Greece as well as with Egypt and the Middle East. Reds were known to come from Thrace, Thasos, and Chios, while whites thrived in Mende. Not so very far off from today, the wines that were the most precious were aged and had a dark color and a strong aroma and taste.

*Although we certainly owe much to the Egyptians for recording their winemaking processes and their innovation in wine storage, it was the Greeks who gave the production of wine "regional" pride and characteristics.*

Wine in Greece played a large role in religious and political rituals, like the *symposion,* where one would consume wine and supposedly become possessed by the gods or the muses and get a little rowdy—an excellent excuse for out-of-character behavior, wouldn't you say?

Wine in Classical Greece was such an important part of the culture, poets, and artists praised it in verse and paint. It even got its own deity in the form of Dionysus, the Greek god of wine.

But more important than odes and class structure and deities, the *process* of winemaking and the importance of wine with a meal really began to take form and set precedents that are observed to this day. In fact (save for the complicated language barrier), a conversation with a winemaker of ancient Greece and a winemaker from, say, modern-day Sonoma might not be so very different. They would each discuss soil and color and climate and age. They would talk about barrels and flavor and longevity of taste (or *finish,* which we'll get to a little later), and how those flavors worked with the food they ate.

The Greek diet consisted largely of barley, beans, olives, honey, grapes, and the by-products of these home-growns (such as, of course, wine!).

So is wine all Greek to you? Well, maybe a little more so than you thought. But as long as we're dwelling in the land of cliché, when in Rome …

## Rome Around the World

Even before Italy was Italy, the people of the land that would become renowned for its *vino* and cuisine knew a good thing when they sipped it.

The Greeks used wine mostly in rituals and business or political deals, and rarely mixed it with dining for pleasure, but the Romans were all about bringing the two together for the pure fun of it. In fact, banquet eating for pleasure (called a *cena*) was such an event in Rome that it practically became a multi-course art form in itself. A typical cena included such delicacies as olives, eggs, oysters, pregnant sow (yes, really—this was quite the delicacy at the time), game, fruit, nuts, and—but of course—various wines to match the courses served.

> To Romans, the natural taste of a wine was less desirable than manipulated forms of the drink. Depending on what the wine was to be consumed with, strange (to us!) flavors were added, like fermented fish sauce, absinthe, garlic, mint, and rose petals.

There were a couple of important developments with respect to wine during the span of the Roman Empire: For one, it became available to the masses. No longer did the average citizen have to drink the leftovers of the wealthy (although the very poor still drank the equivalent of vinegar mixed with water, which was known as *posca*), and in the larger cities a wine bar popped up on nearly every street corner to meet the beverage's popular demand. Cults arose around the Roman God Bacchus (as you likely know, the equivalent of the Greek's Dionysus) and became a celebrated drink among worshippers.

The second important development was the production of wine in other areas of Europe. As the Roman Empire spread, so did vineyards in what is now modern-day France, Spain, Germany, southern Russia, and parts of England. (And as the French and Spanish are particularly known for their excellent wine, this was an integral event in wine history.)

## Dimmed but Not Forgotten

After the fall of the Roman Empire in the fifth century C.E., wine production became the loving responsibility of the monasteries throughout Europe. During these Dark Ages, the Catholic Church gained greater and greater influence in Western Europe, and monasteries spread throughout the countryside—and with them, vineyards.

Drinking water during the Middle Ages in Europe was not exactly the pure, bottled stuff of today. Disease was rampant, and so water was not really considered a viable beverage. Wine, on the other hand, was, and thus became a staple of the average person's diet during Medieval times.

As wine became more and more cultivated by the monasteries, the notion of "good" wine changed. The idea that wine needed to be sweet or flavored—as was the ideal of the Greeks and Romans—changed as wine production grew more sophisticated. The emperor Charlemagne insisted on more hygienic rules for wine production, banning the stomping of grapes and storing of wine in animal skins, which was a practice that had become the norm. Also, different grapes from different regions with varying weather conditions came into the fold, varying the taste influences in the final product even more. England imported wine from Germany and Portugal, and other countries traded their grapey products as well.

The popularity of wine grew so much during this time that by 1264 the king of France planned what may have been the first big wine-tasting event of the civilized world. Immortalized as "The Battle of the Wines" by the poet Henry d'Andeli, this competition of the vines between the north and south of France became a tradition for hundreds of years.

## As Time Goes By ...

During the sixteenth century, wine was still the drink of choice. But as time went on, other quaffs and decent drinking water gave the beverage a little healthy competition. Gin, coffee, tea, Champagne, brandy, and better beer and ale grew in popularity among the masses. But still, wine had become such a part of society that desire for it never fell off entirely.

In fact, by the eighteenth century the wines of the Bordeaux region of France were so celebrated that merchants came from all over Europe to trade for their superior fruit of the vine. The English and the French weren't getting on so well (the result of which was the Napoleonic

9

Wars of the nineteenth century), and the Brits kept importing wine from Portugal, but also added South Africa and Holland to their import list, countries that had a supply of desired goods from the New World like coffee to trade.

> You have two people to thank for bestowing upon us that lovely, sparkling beverage we all love to celebrate with: Champagne (as well as two of the most famous names in the bubbly quaff). A seventeenth-century blind monk named Dom Perignon is credited with inventing Champagne. During the nineteenth century, Nicole Barbe Clicquot-Ponsardin (as in Veuve Clicquot)—a widow— came up with ingenious methods of producing Champagne that are used to this day.

While all of these European advances were going on in wine production during the sixteenth, seventeenth, and eighteenth centuries, there was another glint on the horizon that, early on, may not have seemed like it would be integral to the future of wine, but was more important than anyone could predict. Exploration became the hot ticket and the New World was born.

## New World, New Wine

It was that great man who penned the Declaration of Independence who is largely to thank for bringing wine to the American table by taking greater care in its cultivation. Thomas Jefferson, having traveled extensively in France, longed for wine in his new country. More than being fond of the taste of wine, though, Jefferson felt strongly that lack of wine in the New World was making men resort to stronger spirits, thus sapping their own.

A devoted gardener and naturalist, he saw no reason why, if other European flora could thrive on American soil, grapevines couldn't as well. On his beautiful Virginia estate, Monticello, Jefferson tried and tried to make European vine clippings thrive, but to no avail. He also made great attempts with various indigenous vines, which produced grapes like the Scuppernong of Florida. Although this was more successful than the European vines, the Scuppernong created a quaff that was sub-par, to say the least.

It wasn't until a surveyor and acquaintance of Jefferson's named John Adlum came upon a "new" vine in Maryland that things began to look up. Adlum helped himself to some cuttings of the vine, and with them produced a fruit and wine that would become the first American-wine success story. He sent a bottle to Jefferson, who proclaimed it a fine wine. From then on, Adlum dubbed this vine Catawba after the river in North Carolina near where he grew these hearty grapes.

## California Dreamin'

When pioneering Americans hooked up the wagons and headed West, some of the gold they struck was not just that of the shiny ore siphoned out of riverbeds—it was in the form of fertile land ripe for the growing of grapes.

The Left Coast's first dabbling with wine occurred during the late eighteenth century when some of the state's earliest settlers dotted mission after mission along that scenic, seaside strip that is now the famous Highway 101. To fill the need for Mass wine (and, maybe, a relaxing glass or two at mealtime), these Spanish missionaries cultivated what came to be known as the Mission grape, a red grape that made sweetish wines and was also used to boost the flavor of brandy.

Probably the first vineyard of the Spanish missionaries was at the halfway point between Los Angeles and San Diego, Mission San Juan Capistrano. But the best-known and most successful was Mission San Gabriel just east of L.A. All this was the brainchild of Father Junipero Serra, a Catholic missionary priest, who was the true visionary behind the success of the mission vineyards. His desire for plentiful Mass wine fueled his efforts to establish vineyard after vineyard up and down the California coastline.

Of course, the wines of the missions were small potatoes compared to the industry that they engendered later on. Likely the first person we can look to as the groundbreaker of the California wine industry as we know it was a Frenchman named Jean-Louis Vignes. Vignes had a ranch near the Los Angeles River, and realized that the fertile ground near this riverbed was the perfect place to start a vineyard. He brought plants over from his native France and cultivated what was likely the first successful vineyard in America.

W ith all due respect to California, the first truly successful vineyard in America was actually located in none other than the Midwest. John Adlum introduced the Catawba grape to a man named Nicholas Longfellow, a New Jersey transplant in Ohio. In 1823, he planted the vines on the banks of the Ohio River, and the resulting wines were apparently so good that they won honors in French competitions in the late nineteenth century.

From here on in, Vignes' idea burgeoned a whole new world in winemaking. Napa Valley was put on the map by growing grapes and producing wine that rivaled much of what was coming out of France.

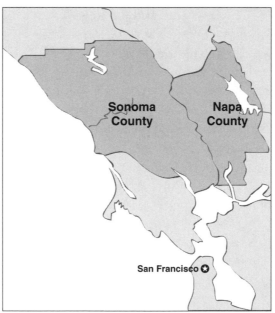

*Although today we think of California, especially Napa and Sonoma, as the spot in the United States that is at the forefront of all things great in wine, its beginnings were much more humble than one might expect as winemaking began there to fill a need in religious rites.*

Just as a vine grows and grows, pushing its winding way until it can go no farther, the history of wine is a twisting, turning tale that craves expansion, yet relies on the strength of its roots—and the presence of a good meal. From Egypt to Oregon, if there's one thing we can learn from all this history and hoopla, it's this: You can't keep a good vine down.

# chapter two

# A Primer on Winemaking and Varietals

*In water one sees one's own face; but in wine one beholds
the heart of another.*

—*French proverb*

Wine has certainly made many a shrewd businessperson lots of money.
But truth be told, nobody goes into this business without a great love
for the final product—if they did, there would be infinite amounts of
mediocre wine, but no great ones. Winemakers put such devotion
and heart into the making of their wares, it would be a shame if you
didn't understand how that ruby-colored glassful you're enjoying with
your steak au poivre made it onto your table.

The way wine is made has certainly changed since the Egyptians and
Greeks discovered that the result of trodden-upon grapes was one of
the most wondrous beverages known to humankind. But at this point
in the twenty-first century, winemakers have the method down to a
very exact science. Modern advances have streamlined some of the
steps and made the results more reliable, but the process itself is fairly
universal from vineyard to vineyard. How does it happen? Let's take a
closer look.

# Juice of the Vine

Even before the presses begin, years of planning go into creating the bottle that winds up on your table. *Viticulture* (the study of grapes) has taught winemakers much about how to make a vineyard thrive and how to protect the resulting products from various calamities in the interim (disease, drought, frost, too much sun, too little sun, wind, overpruning, underpruning, and a million other details). From the time a root is planted to the moment the grapes are harvested, a winemaker has to ensure that all the proper conditions are preserved and come together to produce the desired final product: the perfectly ripe grape.

The basics of transforming grapes into wine are pretty much the same from wine to wine, although there are some differences with particular types of wine (see Chapter Six) as well as slightly different processes for making reds and whites.

You might be surprised to learn that most grape varietals grown for winemaking are grafted (that is, attached) onto an entirely separate rootstock. Just as it sounds, a rootstock is the system of roots that grow beneath the soil. To protect a vineyard from a barrel's worth of disasters, hearty rootstocks—the result of years of research, trial, and expensive error—are available today that are not susceptible to disease, drought, and other factors threatening to a vineyard's lifeblood. And the best part is that any variety of grape can be grafted onto a rootstock, so a winemaker can be assured of the root's heartiness no matter what varietal he or she grows.

## Skin Deep

The first stage of the actual winemaking process (that is, excluding the years of research and work that go into planting, growing, and establishing a vineyard) occurs when it is decided that the grapes are at the appropriate ripeness. When this time is upon a winemaker, the fruit is harvested and pressed. This process is exactly the same for both red and white grapes, but once the crushing begins, the paths diverge slightly.

Red and white wines infuse a whole new freshness to the cliché "Beauty is skin deep." In fact, when it comes to wine, the skin means quite a lot. It is (a) where a wine's color comes from, and (b) where tannin dwells—a natural substance contained in the skin and stems of grapes that gives a red wine that puckery, slightly bracing sensation, as well as aids in the aging process of any wine.

In the case of red wine, the skins and sometimes stems are left in for the next stage of the winemaking process creating a vat full of pulp, seeds, juice, stems, and skins. (It may sound like mish-mash stew, but it actually is so important to a red wine that it has a name: *must.*) All of this floats to the top of the vat and forms something called a cap. Like a great accessory that "makes" an outfit, the cap is what gives a red wine its color, aroma, flavor, and tannin—its real character.

For whites, however, the skins are separated from the juice after crushing and before fermentation begins. Mostly this is done to have as little tannin present as possible. Think about it: white wine even *appears* more fragile than red, and it is; too much tannin in a white wine would ruin its delicate taste and give it a brashness that just doesn't belong.

## From Fermentation to Bottled Libation

The process of fermentation actually begins when the grapes are crushed and the skins come in contact with the mushy inside of the grape, known as the pulp. The process continues in much the same way for both red and white wines—yeast is added to the mixture, carbon dioxide and heat are emitted, and the sugar of the fruit is turned into alcohol. How long this process occurs can differ depending on how much sugar the winemaker desires in the final product. However, with red wine, after fermentation the juice is drained off the skins (also known as free run), and then sometimes put into oak barrels to age and further ferment for anywhere from a few months to years on end. The leftover solids (skins, pulp, etc.) are then pressed to squeeze out any additional wine, which may or may not be used.

Y ou may have noticed that oak appears to be the only wood ever mentioned in the barrel-aging process. That's because it's one of only two used (the other is chestnut-tree wood in Italy, which results in barrels called *botti*). Oak contains certain chemical compounds that other woods do not possess, which are integral to a wine's aging process and final flavor, most notably phenol—a compound that gives off the flavors vanilla, tea, and tobacco. Oak also contains tannins, which is why red wines are aged longer in barrels than whites, as too much tannin in most whites is undesirable.

White wine fermentation happens at cooler temperatures than that of red, because the desired result has more to do with preserving the delicate nature and influences in the fruit, rather than adding tannin or infusing color. In fact, after fermentation most white wines (with the exception of Chardonnays) are cooled down even further until just above the freezing point in order to prevent *tartrate crystals* (sort of like little snowflakes) from forming after the wine is bottled and chilled. Whether or not this cold stabilization is used, barrel aging might be the next step in the process for certain white wines (such as California Chardonnays and white Burgundys).

Both red and white wines may go through a filtering process before bottling; then they are bottled and, possibly, aged before winding up on your liquor store shelf.

## Varietals: The Spice of Life

The culture you grow up in influences whom you become in your life— from what you sound like to your politics to the way you dress to the food you appreciate to a million and one other little details. Your surroundings intricately contribute to the individual you become. It's the same with wine.

The taste of one wine compared to another can be as different as the places from which they hail. From the full-bodied, sun-drenched, fruit-infused taste of a Napa Chardonnay to the delicate, clear, tingly flavor of a Riesling, a wine's personality can be directly traced to the soil from which it sprang and the surrounding area.

Although there are many, many subcultures of grapes and their resulting vintages (some estimate that the number of varietals is as high as 5,000!), only 150 are used for commercial purposes, and of those, we would say 13 are names you see over and over. Why? They are the main varietals of the wine-producing world (or, as we like to call them, the classics).

Classic wines from white grapes include the following:

* ❖ Chardonnay
* ❖ Chenin Blanc
* ❖ Gewürztraminer
* ❖ Pinot Gris
* ❖ Riesling
* ❖ Sauvignon Blanc

Classics from red grapes include the following:

* ❖ Cabernet Sauvignon
* ❖ Merlot
* ❖ Pinot Noir
* ❖ Sangiovese
* ❖ Syrah
* ❖ Tempranillo
* ❖ Zinfandel

That's a lot easier than you thought it would be, isn't it? Already, you can probably think of other wines you know off the top of your head that aren't even on that list, like Gamay or Pinot Blanc (we'll get to those later). But first, we'll take a closer look at the classics and their characteristics. Keep in mind that every winemaker puts his or her personal stamp on a wine, the result being that one Riesling can taste entirely different from another. But there are some general characteristics that each of these wines possesses.

## Chardonnay

By tradition, Chardonnay is known as a full-bodied, dry white wine. However, the fruity notes it also tends to have—pineapple, green apple, pear—can be confusing to the untrained nose and palate (see Chapter Six) and be declared sweet. Chardonnay is usually aged in oak for a short time, which allows it to take on other flavors it is known for: vanilla, toast, and butter. These grapes are hearty and adaptable, which is why you'll find quality Chardonnays from such a variety of places, like California, Burgundy, Champagne, Chablis, and, more recently, Long Island and Washington State. It's also interesting to note that the Chardonnay grape is the only white grape used in the production of Champagne (believe it or not, the other two grapes used are red!).

> Tony is always amused when he sees people wrinkle a nose when offered Chablis. For many, Chablis is known more for being sold by the screw-cap gallon jug than for being a fine white. However, it's made from Chardonnay grapes. Before the name Chardonnay became in vogue in the 1970s, people ordered this bold glass of white wine by the name of one of the regions where it was grown. Thus, Chablis was the term of the time.

## Chenin Blanc

Everyone has that one friend who has the ability to adapt to any situation and thrive or wear anything and look fantastic. This is what Chenin Blanc grapes are like. With their high acidity, they are so versatile that they can successfully be used to create a crisp, dry style of wine, with a mineral-like taste, or a sweeter, fruitier version drawing on flavors like pear or melon. Although Loire produces the most famous wines from Chenin Blanc grapes, California also produces excellent varieties.

## Gewürztraminer

Think of Gewürztraminer as the quiet, seemingly bookish and sweet girl-next-door you knew in high school who surprises you by one day busting out and becoming the next singing, acting, dancing sensation. We often hear of Gewürztraminer being written off as a "sweet" wine, as these grapes are generally harvested late in the season, but its hidden talents lie in its flurry of flavors—spice, citrus fruit, honeysuckle. The best bottles of this low-acid wine come from Germany, Northern Italy, and Alsace.

The German word *Gewürz* translates in English to "spice." Not to be confused with hot peppers or a mean curry, in this instance spice means that the flavors and aroma of a wine made from Gewürztraminer grapes aren't shrinking violets. They are bold and yet harmonious to your olfactory and taste sensations.

## Pinot Gris

You might be more familiar with the Italian name for this grape, Pinot Grigio. This uncomplicated, simple wine has a light, crisp flavor that sometimes has hints of nuts and pear and can even be ever so slightly bitter at times. Alsace and northern Italy had always been the main producers of this wine, but in the 1990s, Oregon became a contender for creating excellent Pinot Gris. And of course, California has a hand in it, too.

## Riesling

Ah, the noble grape (and a big favorite of Tony's). If light could be held in a glass, Riesling would be the physical incarnation of it. This grape produces an entirely refreshing and crisp dry white wine. It favors cool climates, which is why Germany is probably the most famous place of production for it (sometimes it's even called Johannisberg Riesling after the German city of the same name). However, Austria and Alsace have been known to produce fine Rieslings as well.

Tony feels that German Riesling is the most versatile grape for food pairing. The lightness of the body, the great acidity, and the typical low alcohol make this the perfect foil for everything from cream dishes to Szechuan. The 13 wine regions of Germany produce the world's share of great Riesling. It is here that we see "terroir" (the soil and all the influences in and around it) as the major influence on the final product in the bottle. The soil structure and climate are the tools of the great German winemakers.

## Sauvignon Blanc

The Mother Earth of the classic wines. Sauvignon Blanc can be described as herbal, grassy, smoky, and even haylike. True to its earthy, herbal character, Sauvignon Blanc vines are known for their nearly untamable nature (as the word the wine's name comes from—the French *sauvage*—not-so-subtly suggests). If they aren't tended to regularly, they can get entirely out of control. But in the right hands, this wild-child grape can result in a clear, crisp, cut-to-the-chase flavor that's absolutely perfect on a hot summer night. The most famous (Pouilly-Fumé and Sancerre) versions hail from France's Loire Valley and New Zealand, but Bordeaux (which is known for blending Sauvignon Blanc grapes with Semillon to create Sauternes—see the following section) and California are also contenders with this grape.

## Cabernet Sauvignon

Amy likes to compare Cabernet Sauvignon to a really well-made egg-plant parmigiana: It's lovely when it first comes out of the oven, but after a day or two not only do the flavors begin to intertwine, but the acidity in the eggplant and the tomatoes drops, subduing that initial bite and leaving you with something so delectable and perfectly melded, it's almost like a whole new dish. Time is the key. A well-made Cabernet has a similar flavor arc: with age (of course, more than the couple of days in our eggplant parmigiana example), all those berry flavors blend with bell pepper, currant, plum, and other influences to create some-thing that generally only gets better. Bordeaux and California are in-arguably the most famous regions growing and producing Cabernets, but Washington State, Argentina, and Chile are becoming known for Cabernets as well.

## Merlot

Kind of like the quieter, more subdued sibling of Cabernet, Merlot has similar berry and cassis flavors and a floral nose, but is less tannic and mellower than a Cab. Tony likes to think of it as the all-around-complement wine, as its flavors tend to be so subdued that it allows a meal with lots of bold tastes to really shine without any flavor interruption. Over the last decade, Merlot hit a bit of trendy stride in America, and the demand for it became such that a lot of not-so-good versions of it were filling shelves and some wine lists. California and Washington State produce some fine Merlots, as does Long Island and South Africa, but Bordeaux remains the primary and most famous area of quality Merlot.

## Pinot Noir

Oh, for a silky, sought-after sip of this wondrous wine, many folks have had to pay a pretty penny. For years and years, Pinot Noir grapes, with their inconsistent and fragile nature, made this wine quite expensive. But when done well, it is also sublime. The resulting bottled quaff can take on the scent of the earth and cedar, as well as cherries, strawberries, mushrooms, and even chocolate. Burgundy is the most famous (and expensive) area of production for wines of this grape; however, recent years have shown Oregon to be a contender in producing quality bottles of Pinot Noir, as well as California, Champagne, and some areas of New Zealand.

## Sangiovese

The grape that made the red-and-white checkered tablecloth famous, Sangiovese, is the source of that magic elixir often found in the straw-encased glass bottles, Chianti. In Italy, its popularity is equivalent to that of the Gamay grape's in France (see the following). Its herby, black cherry-infused, earthy flavor is also the source of a few other popular Italian wines: Montepulciano, Montalcino, and the newer "Super Tuscan" wines (named after the region from which these grapes hail), which are a blend of Sangiovese, Cabernet Sauvignon, and other grapes.

## Syrah

You may have seen this grape called Shiraz from areas like Australia and South Africa. Potato or po-tah-to, Syrah has a spicy, earthy, woody taste that's complemented by hints of plum and herbs.

## Tempranillo

Hailing from España's famous Rioja region, the easy-going Tempranillo grape has a high acidity and influences of cherry in its younger phases, and, as it ages in oak barrels, can take on a hint of vanilla and dark chocolate.

## Zinfandel

Black and blue and jammy all over, true red Zinfandel (as opposed to the pink-colored white Zinfandels that gained popularity during the 1980s) has a dark berry flavor with hints of chocolate that, especially when aged, can be difficult to discern from Cabernet. Zinfandel grapes and the state of California have had a long-standing love affair since the mid-nineteenth century, producing some of the most consistent, exceptional wines of this kind worldwide.

## More to the Mix

Of course, as we mentioned, there are more varietals. Many more. But as we know you're reading this to learn how to enjoy your meal to the utmost—not become a walking-talking wine encyclopedia—we're going to give you a short run-down of some other excellent grapes that can enhance your dining experience that much more.

*Whites:*

- ❖ **Pinot Blanc.** Amy's husband, the Chardonnay shunner, tends to favor Pinot Blancs. This isn't unusual, as Pinot Blanc is kind of a less in-your-face version of Chardonnay. It has a softer, more easy-going flavor and finish with a faint aroma of apple. Think of it like deciding to pass on that complex, well-reviewed foreign film for a night of Must-See TV.
- ❖ **Semillon.** Behind every great wine is a great grape—or two (or sometimes three). Known more for its complementary blending abilities, Semillon's low acidity and susceptibility to *botrytis cinera* ("the noble rot"—more on this in Chapter Six) seem to

only enhance its natural peach, apricot, and honeylike flavor and aroma. Semillon is most often found growing (and being pressed) in the Bordeaux region of France and in Australia, although the grape is used for blending in California as well.

❖ **Viognier.** A well-defined, full-bodied flavor tinged with peach, honeysuckle, and honeydew melon, the most well-known and well-loved versions of this grape's final product come from about 300 acres in the northern Rhône region of France, but it is also made in California.

*Reds:*

❖ **Barbera.** An amalgam of dark-fruit flavors (think plums, black cherries, raspberries, blackberries), Barbera wines have a high acidity that makes them an excellent mealtime companion. Although the grapes are known for their production in the northwest Piedmonte region of Italy, they are also grown in California.

❖ **Gamay.** You may not have heard of the Gamay grape before, but you've surely imbibed it. When? Likely during the late fall and early winter when Beaujolais Nouveau hits the shelves and, likely, every holiday party you attend. This is one of the only (if not the only) red wine what breaks the room-temperature rule: This easy-to-drink, strawberry/cherrylike wine is actually best served slightly chilled (which is why Amy likes to use it as an ingredient in her sangria).

❖ **Nebbiolo.** The harvesting of the Nebbiolo grapes brings to mind some of the most romantic imagery, as they are picked when the fog is at its thickest in the hilly, truffle-strewn Piedmonte region of Italy (in Italian, *nebbia* means "fog" or "mist"). That mushroomy soil seems to add a hint of truffle to the bold, slightly bitter wines with hints of leather and tar made from these grapes—Barolo, Barbaresco, Gattinara—which generally only seem to get better with time.

Piedmonte has just experienced seven great vintages for wine. From 1995 to 2001, some of the greatest wines out of Italy will come from this region. Barolo, Barbaresco, Barbera, and Dolcetto will reign as Italy's top wines. What about Piedmonte's other treasure, the truffle? Unfortunately for foodies, it's the inverse: Great harvests in the vineyard yield mediocre and expensive truffles. When the harvest is bad, as in 2002, hampered by months of rain and hail storms, the truffles are good. Such a compromise ...

For quick reference purposes (because, as beyond-busy people ourselves, we understand the need for fast answers on the fly), we've provided you with a chart that gives you the grape varietal, the region from which it hails, the wines that are produced from it, and their general dominant flavors and characteristics. Photocopy it, stick it in your attaché, and next time you're lost in the wine store or befuddled from a wine list in a restaurant, use it as your crib sheet. (Of course, we won't leave you in the lurch with only this—in Chapter Four we're going to give you a crash course in becoming your own sommelier!)

| Varietal | Region(s) | Wines | Characteristics |
|---|---|---|---|
| *Whites* | | | |
| Chardonnay | Chablis, Burgundy, Champagne, California | Champagne, White Burgundy, Chardonnay | Green apple, pear, pineapple, citrus nose, creamy texture |
| Chenin Blanc | Loire Valley, Califonia | Vouvray, Savennies | Crisp and clean, with great acidity and mineral qualities |
| Gewürz-traminer | Alsace, Northern Italy, Germany | Gewürz-traminer | Low acid, dry and spicy |
| Pinot Blanc | Alsace and Italy | Pinot Bianco, Crement d'Alsace | Light apple nose, medium body |

| Varietal | Region(s) | Wines | Characteristics |
|---|---|---|---|
| Pinot Gris | Alsace, California, Italy, Germany (Pfalz), Oregon | Pinot Gris, Pinot Grigio | Fruity, medium-bodied, very clean with a nutty aroma |
| Riesling | Germany, Austria, Alsace | Riesling | Made in different styles from dry to sweet, great crisp acidity with aromas of fresh peach and pear |
| Sauvignon Blanc | Bordeaux, California, New Zealand, Loire | Pouilly-Fumé, Sancerre, Sauternes, Sauvignon Blanc | Yin and yang of flavor profiles, from smoky and dry to over-the-top sweet (Sauternes) |
| Semillon | Bordeaux, Australia, California | Sauternes | Fat, rich, intense wine; when blended with Sauvignon Blanc in Bordeaux, creates the long-lived Sauternes floral nose of peaches and young apricots; also does well in Australia when blended with Chardonnay |
| Viognier | Rhône Valley, California | Condrieu, Viognier | Very fragrant when young with sweet peaches and honey-dew melon; produces full-bodied wine |
| *Reds* | | | |
| Barbera | Piedmonte, California | Barbera | This dark and acidic grape makes a very complex wine that is easy to drink |

| Varietal | Region(s) | Wines | Characteristics |
|---|---|---|---|
| Cabernet Sauvignon | Bordeaux, California, Chile | Bordeaux, Cabernet Sauvignon | Aroma of bell peppers and black fruits, this noble grape is full-bodied and can be long-lived |
| Gamay | Beaujolais, United States | Beaujolais, Gamay | Easy drinking, fruity, and light-bodied with hints of fresh strawberry and cherry in the nose |
| Merlot | Bordeaux, California, Washington State, South Africa, Long Island | Merlot | Deep-colored wine with a floral nose and soft taste; less tannic than other reds like Cabernet |
| Nebbiolo | Piedmonte, California | Barolo, Barbaresco, Gattinara, Nebbiolo | Very tannic when young, with aromas of tar and leather; perhaps the most age-worthy grape to emerge from Italy |
| Pinot Noir | Burgundy, Oregon, New Zealand, California, Italy, Champagne | Burgundy, Pinot Noir, Pinot Nero | A slightly sweet taste with aromas of cherries, mushrooms, and fresh-picked berries |
| Sangiovese | Tuscany, most regions of Italy, California | Chianti, Sangiovese, Super Tuscans | This light-bodied grape has moderate to good acidity, with an earthy, herbal aroma and hints of black cherries |

| Varietal | Region(s) | Wines | Characteristics |
|---|---|---|---|
| Syrah | Rhône Valley, California, Australia, South Africa, Washington State | Hermitage, Châteauneuf, Syrah/Shiraz | Dark color with hints of spice, herbs, and plums |
| Tempranillo | Spain, California | Rioja, Tempranillo | This grape has long aging potential; hints of chocolate and cherries; produces soft yet elegant wines |
| Zinfandel | California, Southern Italy, Australia | Zinfandel | With an aroma of spice, sweet blackberries, and hints of chocolate with a potential to age and become quite elegant |

# chapter three

# Vintage Words: Interviews with Winemakers Paul Draper, Bob Sessions, Bob Lindquist, and Jim Clendenen

In our quest to find the Holy Grail that holds all the answers to perfect food and wine pairing, we knew we couldn't amass this tome without going to the true experts: winemakers, sommeliers, and chefs. Who better to discuss the topic than those who live it every day?

The following pages contain interviews with four of America's top winemakers—Paul Draper of Ridge Vineyards in Sonoma, Bob Lindquist of Qupé in Santa Barbara, Bob Sessions of Hanzell in Sonoma, and the ever-entertaining and always frank Jim Clendenen of Au Bon Climat in Santa Barbara. See what they had to say about everything from price to pairing to flash-in-the-pan trends.

## Paul Draper, Ridge Vineyards

It wouldn't be a stretch to say that Paul Draper has tilling the earth in his blood. Having been raised on an 80-acre farm in Illinois, there was no escaping his agricultural destiny. Draper's expertise is one that goes beyond plows and fences, though. He took off for Italy after receiving a degree in philosophy from Stanford and then spent a year at the Sorbonne in France, all the while traveling through Europe to glean all the traditional winemaking techniques he could. After heading southwest and setting up a small winery in Chile, Draper landed in the spot where he has remained since 1969—as winemaker and chief executive officer of Ridge Vineyards.

Tony and Paul met up at Draper's home in Northern California's Monte Bello Ridge to talk winemaking, pairing, and his opinion about the future of wine in America.

**Tony DiDio:** Do you think of food pairing when making wine?

**Paul Draper:** Yes and no. Yes, but only in the general sense that the wine should complement food. It should not dominate it, for example, by being so high in alcohol or so overwhelmingly fruity (read: fruit bomb). Otherwise, no. Just as a chef working with the fresh ingredients allows them to express their distinctive qualities without getting in the way, so the wine grower, working with high-quality fruit from a single site, would try to let its distinctive characteristics come through in the wine.

**Tony:** Any advice to the audience on how to match flavors? Wine first or food first?

**Paul:** If a group of friends have chosen wines to take to dinner—for example, to compare old Bordeaux and old Cabernets—in that case we would choose foods that complement the wines. Otherwise, I choose dishes on a menu that appeal to me and then choose wines that I think will complement the food.

**Tony:** Does price dictate quality?

**Paul:** Only at the lower and lower-middle end of the market. That is, I think it is difficult to find truly interesting fine wines under $18 a bottle retail. Pleasant wines, yes. Distinctive wines, rarely. But on the other end of the scale, I find that very high-priced wines that are $80/bottle or more retail can often be matched in quality by wines in the $30 to $50 range.

**Tony:** What mistakes do people make when trying to pair wine with food?

**Paul:** The only thing I consider a mistake is matching a delicate wine to an overpowering dish and an overpowering wine to a delicate dish. Otherwise, good wine goes with good food.

**Tony:** In the past 10 years, the new culinary trends have embraced Mediterranean and fusion cuisines; have you changed your winemaking style in order to comply with the trends?

**Paul:** I don't intend this to sound arrogant, but if you are making fine wine that reflects a distinctive site, rather than a wine concocted through processing, adding concentrate, or lowering alcohol, and most importantly your customers are continuing to buy it, you have no reason to make wine to fit some fashion in food. The finest Bordeaux of 1884 or 1870 would still be the finest Bordeaux you could make today.

> Paul Draper makes a fine point here: Great wine is great wine, whenever it was made. Top winemakers do not follow trends in the market—they make wines that reflect the terroir and their own passion.
>
> Just because "fusion" may have been the rage for the past five years, we can't see Ridge Monte Bello Cabernet change its style or structure to match to a seared hamachi with mango and pineapple salsa.

**Tony:** I have always said that you brought Zinfandel to a higher plane; that Ridge really made Zinfandel a viable varietal. The style that you have is more elegant sometimes than that of others. Because of that, I tend to drink more of your wines with food than I can with some other Zinfandels. This is not to bash anyone else, it's just a style I appreciate.

**Paul:** When I joined Ridge, here were these Zinfandels made in a very straightforward fashion, as was the Monte Bello, and it was clear that the potential was there. I didn't know much about Zinfandel when I joined Ridge—I joined it because of Monte Bello and the potential I saw there after tasting the 1962 and 1964, which had the complexity and intensity in the direction of great Bordeaux. But what I found here, of course, were a couple of Zinfandels that they had made in the past that I started making right in 1969. I saw this intensity and this complexity, and the potential for it, and really got turned on to the whole idea of Zinfandel. We were, I think, among the first, if not the first, to treat Zinfandel as though it was Cabernet Sauvignon. We were trying to show that if handled as you would handle your Cabernet, it could make a far more complex wine, a higher-quality wine with elegance and subtlety and so on, rather than this very straightforward, rather rustic, earthy wine that the best of it had always been. We knew from these 100-year-old vineyards with low yields just how great the best Zinfandels can be, so we said, well, if it's that good in potential from the vineyards we're dealing with, then let's give it the treatment it deserves. And that was probably something Ridge did that had not been done.

**Tony:** So my question of taking it to a higher plane, or different plane, adding an elegance to it, is that far off?

**Paul:** No, not a bit. We also have our own vineyards. Today, let alone in the last 15, 20 years, very, very few of even the best Zinfandel makers own their own vineyards. Many of them don't have the opportunity to control the farming or to necessarily control whether they can continue to get the grapes.

**Tony:** How much do you buy and how much do you really own?

**Paul:** With our Zinfandel, we own what is now our single largest vineyard, which is Lytton Springs. The eastern half in the early 1970s was the Valley Vista Vineyard. We decided to use the name Lytton Springs because the area was owned by Captain Lytton, who came out to California in the 1860s after the [Civil] War as far as we know. The first maps we have of the area are from about 1873 and show Captain Lytton's property extending from the old Redwood Highway, now 101, all the way west to the bluff of the benches above Dry Creek. So basically what we were doing was buying some of the oldest vines on what had been his property. What we have now is about three-quarters of Captain Lytton's original vineyards. And that is a truly major Zinfandel vineyard, but also a mixed vineyard. It's got Petit Syrah, it's got Carignan, it's got 100-year-old Grenache as well.

**Tony:** It's a great mix.

**Paul:** We keep all the old vineyards, interplant missing vines, and as we take out the non-Zinfandel varietals, we replant them to Zinfandel.

**Tony:** So it still is truly a field blend by nature.

**Paul:** Well, some of the blocks with the 100-year-old vines and the 40-year-old vines are in fact field blends. To define that, that's where a block or parcel is interplanted with various varieties. You can go through that parcel and count the number of Zinfandel vines and count the number of Petit Syrah or Carignan or Grenache, which is what we do every year, but we pick the whole block. So the Carignan, which ripens later, adds a brighter fruit and a higher acid than the Zinfandel, which is fully ripe, and it really complements the Zinfandel. That would be just one example. The Petit Syrah adds spice, adds depth of color, it adds tannins.

**Tony:** And those are being vinified?

**Paul:** They're being vinified together. As with the old farmers back in the nineteenth century who planted them that way, we pick them as a unit and then carry forward the varietal blend of that particular block for that particular tank. As we put together the assemblage we take into account what percent the final wine is from knowing how many vines are in each block. So the old vines, the 40- and 100-year-old, are interplanted that way at Lytton Springs. The younger vines, let's say 30 [years old] to the young vines we plant today, we do not interplant. We plant them as blocks of Zinfandel, Carignon, Petit Syrah, Grenache, and so on. And what it does is to give us the option then to decide whether the wine has improved that year by a small block of Carignon or a small block of Petit Syrah, so it gives us greater control.

**Tony:** So you're really in more control because with a field blend, it's really nature talking more than anything and then with the new blocks you'll see where it goes and if you need a percentage of Carignan or whatever it is, and blend it in or have the option of not blending it in.

**Paul:** Exactly.

**Tony:** But it's funny, talking about how you farm and look after Lytton Springs and how things are harvested, it really goes back to what you said about Cabernet because you have this blend of wines. In essence, it's a Bordeaux style because you have four, five different grapes going into a blend. What about French vines being imported to California— how did that effect the way things are now?

**Paul:** It seems as if when the series of importations came in from the south of France in the 1870s and 1880s, it included Syrah, which apparently arrived about eight years before Petit Syrah and yet it never took off. A number of vineyards were planted and when they died off from the phylloxera attack of the nineteenth century, they were not replanted. So Syrah disappeared from California until recent times.

*P*hylloxera Vastatrix, or phylloxera, is the name of a small plant louse that devastated European rootstocks in the mid-1860s. More than 2 million acres of vineyards were destroyed by phylloxera in France alone. Even with all the experiments with resistant rootstock, though, phylloxera still looms dangerous today. Just as recently as the mid-1990s, phylloxera destroyed hundreds of thousands of acres in California alone.

**Tony:** But why?

**Paul:** Okay, my theory is this: Zinfandel from the 1850s and 1860s was the most widely planted. Until 10 years ago, it remained the most widely planted. Then Cabernet Sauvignon overtook it. So until then, what people were looking for were varietals that would work with Zinfandel, that would complement Zinfandel and make it even better than it was. They weren't looking for stand-alone grapes. Syrah does not work as well as a complement as Petit Syrah.

**Tony:** That's a great theory. Unless there was a great sale on Petit Syrah! *[laugher]*

**Paul:** Right! But really, Syrah just disappeared until very recently.

**Tony:** You work really with a lot of different wines. You make a Chardonnay. You make a world-renowned Cabernet, and I think you'll always be known as a man who put his stamp on Zinfandel. But as we started this conversation before, I've always said I've never had a hard time in drinking Ridge wines with dinner, which I think has to do with the winemaking style you've incorporated, the way winemakers did hundreds of years ago. They utilized what they had, they made the wines to their strengths, and they realized that these wines could not stand alone; that a blended wine is sometimes more interesting than a 100 percent varietal.

**Paul:** Right, but also at Ridge we began to focus on the tactile sensation—the feel of the wine in the mouth. Not just the nose, and the level of fruit, and if it's varietally typical fruit—which was a big California hang-up for years—but basically, what does this wine feel like in the mouth *as* food. I mean, we all know how incredibly important texture is in food. Well, as you know, it is equally important in wine. I think that at Ridge we began to focus on that really early on. And even today, not everyone in California looks for texture, or worries about it, when they're putting out a wine. I think that may well be a major piece of why our wines seem to work with food.

# Bob Lindquist: Qupé

If only Ray Davies knew at a 1972 concert in Santa Barbara that he was doing much more than wailing on his guitar and entertaining the masses—he was sealing the fate of one of California's most respected winemakers.

It was that fateful Kinks concert that got Bob Lindquist fired from his job at a wine shop and subsequently hired as a tour guide at Zaca Mesa Winery. It was there that he met Jim Clendenen of Au Bon Climat Winery (see later in this chapter) and Ken Brown of Byron Winery—the men who would teach Lindquist the processes that would lead him to engender Qupé in 1982. By 1989, things were going so well in his production of the Rhône varietals of Syrah and Chardonnay that he and Clendenen joined forces to open another winery on the Bien Nacido Vineyard in Santa Barbara that produces an average of 25,000 cases of wine a year.

Here, Lindquist talks to us about educating yourself on varietals, his theories on pairing, and learning how to balance your flavors between the glass and the plate.

**Tony DiDio:** This whole book is about balance, balance of wine, balance of food, really balance of flavors. So when you are making wine are you thinking about food?

**Bob Lindquist:** Always. I think one of the hallmarks of our wines are balance. I am kind of a Europhile, Francofile. You know I love European wines; they are made with balance. Balanced alcohol, balanced acidity, not too much oak, not too much power. I mean, there are exceptions to that, but when I make wine, I make it to drink with food.

**Tony:** When people are trying to do food and wine matches, either at home or in a restaurant, what do you suggest they do first? Pick out the food, then go to the wine, or vice versa?

**Bob:** Well, it depends on the situation. If you have a special bottle you want to drink, then you plan around that. Normally it is the other way around. You figure out your menu, or if you are in a restaurant, you pick what you want to eat, and then you follow up with the wine selection. One of the things I like to recommend is to consult with people in the restaurant who might know something about the wine, unless you are sure enough about it yourself. There's nothing wrong with that, I think a lot of people are intimidated to ask the sommelier or ask the waitperson what they think about certain wines. In most better restaurants they know their stuff, and they can describe the flavors. They can describe how big the wine is, how sweet the wine is, or how much acid it might have, or how much tannin it might have, those kinds of things.

**Tony:** Sometimes prices in restaurants really put people off from ordering wines that are anywhere from two-and-a-half to three times the wholesale price. Do you think there is any kind of parity between price and value or quality in wine?

**Bob:** Not really, although there certainly is a "you get what you pay for" aspect to wine, to some degree. [Although] the bargains might be from the lesser-known regions like Tuscany, Alsace, Germany, or Austria, or Santa Barbara County instead of Napa.

**Tony:** Right. And there are enough bargains out there that are good wines. So when you talk about food and wine pairing, what do you think are some of the mistakes a lot of people make with food and wine pairing?

**Bob:** A lot of times they will drink something too young, or too well known, or too powerful. Those are the biggest mistakes, especially in California wines, they can be real powerful, alcoholic, tannin, and they are just young and not ready to drink. A lot of times wines are made to get press and to get scores rather than made for balance, and made for food pairing.

**Tony:** So some of the mistakes people usually make are imbalance of flavors?

**Bob:** Right, like going for bigger wines, or more prestigious wines, or wines that get big scores, rather than wines that have balance and acidity.

**Tony:** What about people who are not reading the *Spectator*? What kind of mistakes are they making? Or what can they avoid?

**Bob:** I think a lot of the casual wine drinkers do not know enough about the different varieties, they may be more oriented toward Cabernet, Merlot, Chardonnay, and not really know Riesling, Syrah, or rosé, for instance. I mean, who orders a rosé? It is all a matter of education, learning a little more about wine, and the wide varieties that are available.

**Tony:** I think there has been a great effort, by Americans, to learn more about food, more about wine. I feel that in the future, even now, people are getting a bit more savvy about wine and food. I remember many years ago I was in Milan by myself at a trattoria, and there were these two guys—I bet probably just civil servants—having a heated discussion about what wine to have: "Should we have a Dolcetto? Should we have a Barbera?" And I thought that was cool. The people were really discussing it, and it is part of their life. Do you think that Americans will ever get to the point of embracing wine as part of the meal? Or do you think that it will always be for a special occasion, or let's open a bottle of wine, we have guests coming over?

**Bob:** It's definitely going to happen. It is just a matter of time and generations. We teach our kids about food and wine, and they teach their kids, and it is just one of those things that is just going to spread and grow. The more we learn about the health benefits of moderate wine consumption, the more that will help also.

## Bob Sessions: Hanzell

In 1973, Bob Sessions joined James D. Zellerbach—founder of Hanzell—as winemaker and general manager of the vineyard. Up to his 2001 retirement, Sessions's keen sensibilities created some of California's finest and much-lauded Pinot Noirs and Chardonnays in the true Burgundian style. The wines are fine and elegant, understated but not without depth. Kind of like Sessions himself.

**Tony DiDio:** Now, your wines traditionally are true Burgundian style— the Pinot Noir, the Chardonnay. And, this is not meant as a disparaging remark to other winemakers in California, but we never think of you as one of those full, blown-out, California heavily oaked, fruit-up-front type of producers. I think the vineyards you deal with at Hanzell have yielded for you some of the great, elegant, Burgundy-style wines that have really fit into food and wine pairing.

**Bob Sessions:** I think that is well put. In other words, the grapes really dictate that, how we make them in a sense. And, yes, making wines like that we more immediately get a sense of pairing food with. This just is going to the earlier process of cold fermentation.

**Tony:** Maybe you don't even think about the food really because it just comes naturally?

**Bob:** It really does. When you are crushing the grapes, and making the wine, and whether it is a white or a red, the whole thing is just doing it as you want it to be done, and looking at what the grapes seem to call for. And I think that, in a sense, I can say that food is somewhat close to the consciousness.

**Tony:** Now, this is interesting, I was talking with Jim Clendenen and Bob Lindquist, my question to them was what really came first; was it choosing the land that you chose because you liked it geographically, or was it a desire to make, in Clendenen's case, Burgundian-style wines, and in Lindquist's case, Rhône-style wines? So my question to you is, once you got to Hanzell, you were making Cabernets there, weren't you?

**Bob:** Yeah. Talk to a lot of people, and they say this isn't the right place [for those wines], but then they taste the wine and they sure like it.

**Tony:** But you are still cooler in climate where you are than, say, St. Helena and Napa Valley.

**Bob:** We are.

**Tony:** I was curious, now you have done a lot of winemaker dinners, and you guys eat out a lot, and one thing we like to talk about in this book is flavors and how to match them—wine flavors to food flavors, and vice versa. What is your advice to the audience in general, if you are going into a restaurant, should you look at the wines first?

**Bob:** Yeah, I do have some thoughts on that. I don't always go in thinking "matching," it's just more like you get a good wine and get a course, but I find that by doing that sometimes you find that a lot of things go with the items you wouldn't think of. But my main advice would be to be bold on matching flavors. Go through the routines of having red wine with steak, and white wine with chicken, but go beyond that, and I think that is what makes it interesting.

**Tony:** Yeah, we found that out with a couple of different wines in the past couple weeks. And we see how a food or a dish or even a spice can change wine, and we've also found out how a wine really changes a particular dish as well.

**Bob:** Exactly. The wine isn't always the changee, it can be the changer.

**Tony:** So you are probably not going to enjoy a Fumé Blanc with a filet mignon. It's a general thing, but just kind of go beyond that and see what the spices are.

**Bob:** But you can take a Pinot Noir and go a lot of different directions with it, [with] different kinds of food. And the same with a Chardonnay, depending on how it is made and what you are matching it up with. I feel a lot of match-ups can be rewarding, but they aren't made because they are untraditional.

**Tony:** Since you have been making Pinot Noir for a few years, have you traditionally used Pinot Noir with food items other than meats? Have you been eating fish with Pinot Noir?

**Bob:** Sometimes I eat fish with Pinot Noir, yes. I think I tend to be thinking Chardonnay with fish and chicken, and tend to think Pinot Noir with pork or beef. But because when you get around our age you've done everything, you know, okay, the world hasn't ended [if] the wine you've got is no good and it's the last wine in your house. A good, full-bodied Chardonnay can certainly lend to the meal what something red would not. And that Chardonnay with a pork chop, or Pinot Noir with some fish, you know a little bit stronger fish, a great salmon, is not going to blemish the enjoyment of that meal.

We're both happy that Bob Sessions talked about "rules" in choosing wines with food. Tony has eaten many times with Bob and his lovely wife, Jean Arnold—another passionate wine professional. Tony swears they've spent more time reading a wine list than the menu, although great attention is always given to what everyone orders food-wise. They want to make sure that the food and the wine complement each other and that delicate balance is achieved. So when Bob refers to "weight," he is talking about how heavy or full-bodied a wine is. Being aware of the weight of a wine makes more sense than whether it is red, white, or pink.

**Tony:** Right. It seems that people are being more open. The whole spirit of this book is "drink what you like to drink with the food that you want to drink it with," but on the other hand, hey, these are some suggestions we're making. Not necessarily myself and Amy, but you and Paul Draper, and Daniel Boulud, and the others who we've interviewed here. We want to encourage the readers to take a couple chances. Maybe you'll enjoy the meal even more!

**Bob:** Be bold. Take a shot.

**Tony:** Yeah, I like that. Definitely, I think that is the most important thing. At some point, you just have to go for it, baby. And see where it goes.

**Bob:** I think to really enjoy wine, you need to let loose a little. Don't think that the rules are rigid or rigorous necessarily.

**Tony:** I don't know who made these rules up!

*[laughter]*

**Bob:** They're good. It's good general advice, and it matters most of the time, perhaps.

**Tony:** One thing we wanted to ask everyone about was prices. Do you think that prices necessarily dictate quality, not only on a wine list, but also in a wine shop? There are obviously some bargains out there from some different countries, but just in general, do you think that price necessarily dictates the quality?

**Bob:** I would say that in general—and I would emphasize that "in general" part—it does. You know some of us in the business, not Hanzell, but others do raise prices automatically just because they can go up. In my mind sometimes the wine doesn't deserve to be raised in price. Some people just do it automatically because they think, oh, with a Chardonnay I can go up this far, and maybe that makes monetary sense. But in general the whole pricing thing is the way to go. I think once you get away from pricing, and get to know wines more, you can probably get some good bargains, and you can also appreciate why some wines are charging $70 or $80 or $60.

**Tony:** But of course prices are going to vary from wine list to wine list, so I don't necessarily think that a $100 wine is necessarily two times better than a $50 wine. Both of us know what things cost, and we also know each restaurateur, each wine shop, has to make their markup, and I appreciate that. They have to do what they need to do, but Paul

Draper, for example, said something like it seems that there are some good wines out there that you can get for $20, $30, $40, but not necessarily very interesting wines.

**Bob:** Yeah. I sort of agree with that. There are some great wines, and adequate wines, but you are not going to get the really interesting, special, great wines at $20. But boy, it's amazing.

**Tony:** You're certainly going to get some good drinkable wines.

**Bob:** I've been in the business so long, and I can look back, where there was a lot of bad stuff out there, and now it's all drinkable. That's great.

**Tony:** You're making two wines—a Pinot Noir and a Chardonnay—and I think both of them are great matches for food, great foils for food. Are your wines, generally speaking, ready to drink upon release or is it dictated by the vintage?

**Bob:** Oh, there's definitely a difference, especially with Pinot Noir on that. The wines, in general, can be drunk at release. But we try to tell people wait until the first of the year or something. In a white wine, our Chardonnay, they should try to wait at least six months. And ideally wait a year. But sometimes the wines are so good, you get the flavors so good, that, even if they are closed, they are still going to be rewarding. There's kind of a borderline here that's come along, and I just sort of keep my fingers crossed; make suggestions.

**Tony:** You hold back the Pinot a little while longer?

**Bob:** Yeah. We do. It's about three and a half years when it's released, and the Chardonnay is about two, so we are holding back a fair amount.

**Tony:** You're going from almost 18 months in oak, in barrel, and then maybe 3 months in bottle, in the Chardonnay.

**Bob:** Yeah. Our current Pinot is 2000, so it's about three and a half years when we release.

**Tony:** One thing we wanted to ask you about is trying to explain tannic acid—tannins in meat, tannins in the casks where you make the wine, and how that tannic acid helps to develop a wine and what does it do to the food.

**Bob:** Well, tannic acid comes in from the skins of the grapes. And you know how it affects the wine as far as the feel of it goes—it actually has a presence itself. It is not just there as a preservative. A little or more than a little bit of tannin in some wines can actually add a balance, a nice balance, to a wine and can offer something to the flavors and other parts of the wine.

**Tony:** Now the play of tannin with food, let's say a steak.

**Bob:** Yeah, I think it can be very useful, very rewarding. I think the tannin can be there with the flavor, help the flavor of the wine, and yet meet and be equal to the strong flavors of a steak. There are some tannins in meat. The tannin breaks down some of the flavors in the meat and helps it marry a little better with the wine that has tannin in it.

**Tony:** Another thing we were curious about—we all travel, and I grew up in a family that drank wine with dinner. And I was encouraged to drink, so it was never really foreign to me, it was part of the meal. In your travels, do you think that Americans are embracing that concept?

**Bob:** I think they are going towards that. I can't see at this stage Americans as a whole accepting wine the way that Europeans do. But, I see more and more people that are discovering wines, and becoming eager to learn more about them. More and more people come that hardly know anything about wine, come over to the house, and I see an eagerness to learn something about wine. So I think there are certain segments of the country that one day might become almost like Europe. I think all the great cities, perhaps every capital in the country and other larger cities, are becoming influenced by this curiosity about food and wine, and I think that once the influence starts, it will never stop growing once that seed is there. Where there is wine, everybody in that winegrowing region will drink it. But while there is wine everywhere here in one sense, there are only a couple areas where there is much of it on the two coasts.

**Tony:** What do you think are some of the mistakes people make? I am sure you have been to at least a handful of winemaker dinners, and if you have total control of the whole thing, I've done it a couple times, I look down and say what the hell was this guy thinking about when he matched this wine with this food, what is he …

**Bob:** I don't know what specific mistakes people make, there are probably hundreds of mistakes. I think the only one I can think of, is picking the wrong weight. I don't think the mistake is in choice of red or white, I think it's weight maybe.

**Tony:** Right, but then again, it's also those contrasting flavors. It's funny, we had a session with Rick Moonen a couple of weeks ago. We did a skate dish. All the chefs we've worked with so far sent me in advance what dishes they were going to make, and the ingredients, and it gave me a couple days to figure out what wines we wanted to bring. I would always bring in at least a third wine, or a fourth wine, that I think, hey, let's take a shot at it. And one of the wines was a Lagrein. It blew us away. It was just a great match, it is a light red wine. It blew Rick away, too! But it's fun, they are out there, there are all those kinds of wines out there.

**Bob:** Yeah, and that's part of …

**Tony:** That's being bold!

## Jim Clendenen: Au Bon Climat

The yang to partner Bob Lindquist's yin, it's fitting that Jim Clendenen is a man who works with forces of nature, as he truly is one to be reckoned with himself. His enthusiasm and overwhelming bounty of knowledge make him seem more like an eager, wide-eyed kid than the seasoned, 50-year-old professional that he is. In fact, Lindquist refers to him as "The Information Man," as he absorbs every sight, smell, and taste like a thirsty sponge. But after being nominated as *Food & Wine* magazine's Winemaker of the Year in 2001, Clendenen certainly has a working method to his madness. Ever clad in Hawaiian shirts, Clendenen isn't afraid to be bold, and not merely in appearance. Here, we got a little of the true Clendenen no-holds-barred thoughts on winemaking, flash-in-the-pan trends, and his love of regionalism when it comes to pairing.

**Tony DiDio:** It's probably your experience in Europe that has influenced your winemaking style, I would imagine.

**Jim Clendenen:** Completely. I went all through Europe with my high-school girlfriend. We didn't have any money, so we headed south where it was warm, and wine was cheap. You could buy a liter of red wine or rosé for a quarter, and drink that.

**Tony:** It's funny how tastes change over the years, but it is really what we are exposed to. I grew up drinking wine at home, so wine was never foreign to us. I grew up watching my father drink wine every night at dinner, my parents would have a glass of wine. I would always help my grandfather make wine, my father make wine—I made wine in the same machines my grandfather did, so it was part of a culture. So many people are not exposed to that, are not exposed to wine.

**Jim:** The second time I went to Europe, I had graduated college and committed to going into the wine business. I spent a lot of time in Spain and France, went to Champagne, went to Burgundy, and that unlocked all the puzzles for me. Every place we went, even Spain, whose wines were pretty dubious at the time, were dirt-cheap. But all designed to go with the foods there. I spent no time in Germany, I could understand somebody working in Germany, and then coming back here and being enamored with the wine collector, the wine club, wine drinking, but not the food and wine pairing aspect of life. Germany is not a food and wine culture. Italy is a food and wine culture. Spain is a food and wine culture.

**Tony:** That is one question I had for everyone. Do you think that we will ever get to a point in this country, or are we moving in that direction, that Americans will embrace wine like Europeans? Do you think we will ever get that way, or are getting closer to that, are we moving further away from that, what do you see?

**Jim:** Currently I see that we are getting further away from that. That is what is frustrating. My biggest objection has been the changing of styles to appeal to novice drinkers, or to appeal to critics, that are no longer food compatible. Nobody can tell me that a 15 percent, 4-gram acid Chardonnay is food compatible. It's not. If you choose to drink it, and you choose to drink it around food, that is your combination. That's your choice, but it's not designed to do that.

**Tony:** Actually, the theme throughout the book is balance. We've been fortunate; we've spent four sessions already with some of the top restaurateurs and chefs in New York—from Daniel Boulud, to Don Pintabona, to Rick Moonen, to Mauro Mafrici from I Trulli [see Chapters Nine, Eleven, Fourteen, and Seventeen]. And it was great, because we all talked about balance. And that is my theme, and my partner Amy's theme, is that we just want to balance it out. We found a lot of times that wine, whether good or bad, draws out something in the food, and the food draws something out in the wine. And that's the fun of it.

About having friends over, and pulling out some good wines, and making some good food. It's just that. It doesn't have to be $50 bottles of wine; it doesn't have to be $100 bottles of wine; it just has to be balanced.

**Jim:** There is no question that acidity is the key thing in food and wine pairing. The length of the wine and the balance of the food, so you can think of having some simple food with some very powerful wine, but for me it just doesn't work. And then there are 15 percent alcohol, very fruity wines, all the things that actually work in wine. Why do a lot of "dirty" wines from Europe taste so good with long-braised meats in the dead of winter? Because they taste a lot better with that food than by themselves. It's a mutual-enhancement type thing.

**Tony:** What about the area where you're growing your grapes? How does that affect the wine?

**Jim:** I was the first person, as far as I know, that celebrated a marginal climate, the idea of a marginal climate in California. I wanted to make wines with high acidity. I was seeing all we didn't have in California: mature vineyards, the right clones, and the moderated growing conditions that allowed us to ripen grapes fully with good acidity. That is why people started coming down to Monterey, and for the fog they started coming down to Santa Barbara. You go from Calistoga to Carneros, and you have made some improvement, but when those people saw the flavors coming out in Santa Barbara they all came rushing down here to buy land for Chardonnay, and ultimately Pinot Noir. [At first] we had bad clones, bad density, way too much warm-climate farming going on down here. Too much water, too much vigor in the vines …

**Tony:** But you learned?

**Jim:** Yeah, we learned. When I worked in Burgundy in 1981, what did the Burgundians have hanging around their cellars, stuff that doesn't sell very well. So I am seeing a lot of 1977 whites, a lot of 1980 reds, a lot of 1972 reds and whites, whites that wouldn't finish malolactic. To them they weren't even wines, they were total failures. And then you look at them 18 years later, and they have gained body, they have gained depth, they've gained balance. They have come into harmony, where the weaker elements have surrounded the stronger elements, so the body of the wine surrounds the acidity. The flip side of that is what is happening now, in American wine, and we have the experience of having something that seemed like it had balance, and then looking at it three years later and finding it was totally disgusting. You know Chardonnays turning the color of iced tea, Zinfandels that have 16.5 alcohol, and now they are gassy and funky and going through changes in the bottle, and if they aren't that, you just take a sip with food, and all of a sudden you get this wash of alcohol.

**Tony:** Yeah, it's a weird time in wine. I think younger people who I come in contact with are at least open to learning. You know when I sit down with them and say, hey try this with this or this. A lot of them really like the jammy, fruity Shiraz, though.

**Jim:** Yeah, and it's not bad if it's a step in getting people to drink. [Some winemakers] are into that, making wines that they consider delicious, that don't have the balance.

**Tony:** If they don't have the legs, it will never go 10, 15, 20 years—those wines won't last. Joey Delissio, from the River Café, the sommelier there for the last 22 years, 15 to 20 years ago he was the guy who really introduced American wines to New York City. He started doing older Chardonnays, he introduced me to older Chardonnays 15 years ago, and now he is hard pressed to find any that are really going to age, because the balance isn't there, the acidity isn't there. It was the old Montelenas that had it.

**Jim:** Absolutely and they got barbecued. But you can make wines with great acidity, that age well, that are more generous when they are young. That is the French way, I mean, the 1986 Batard Montrachet tastes great in 1989, the 1989 tastes great in 1992, and that tastes even greater in 2010.

**Tony:** What about prices right now? Prices are crazy.

**Jim:** It just reflects lack of interest in any kind of harmony at the table. If you understand where wine belongs, and how you are supposed to consume it, there is no justification for young wines to have that kind of price. A young wine shouldn't have any merit, and if you are having a young wine that is delicious, so as to be consumed right now, but has the same value as a 1964 Latour, or a 1947 LaFleure, then it's an argument that I won't accept. But it is an argument that is constantly made to me by critics. The problem is when you have a wine that's

$125 when it is released, and $300 at auction a week later, the smart people are reselling it, because they triple their money, and getting out.

**Tony:** It's interesting. So there is no correlation between price and taste.

**Jim:** There is no correlation between price, taste, and utility, and what you and I are talking about is balance and utility. The wine will taste great with a particular dish, or you can take a mediocre wine with the right dish and make it better. Why the food and wine culture has been temporarily derailed is that the wines that are praised the most, that are being judged the highest quality, are wines that are specifically the ones that are too expensive, and not at all food compatible. Chardonnays that are golden when they are bottled are not likely to become meritoriously developed and golden when they are 25 years old, they are just brown and dead. Red wines that are black are very unlikely to be stable enough to age and become more complex and better, so then you have to drink them when they are oaky, woody, tannic, and effusively fruity, and what do you serve with that?

**Tony:** There's nothing to serve with that.

**Jim:** How many times have you heard, "This wine is so great you can even serve it with burgers."

**Tony:** Yeah, it's about the only thing you can eat with that! Now, you are so closely associated to Burgundy, the Burgundian varietals. Was that your selection because it was a matter of taste, or was it geography? In other words, saying, "Hey, I landed here, this is the land I bought, this is what goes with it." How did all this happen?

**Jim:** It all happened for me because I went to work in Burgundy, and I was trying to unlock some questions in America. You try to find a place that Burgundy varieties fit the soil. But in retrospect for me there is no question that I really wanted to find a place for Pinot Noir, and Chardonnay, and I was really lucky that this area had the possibility to make it work.

**Tony:** One thing in this book we've really stressed is, when possible, regional pairing. When I am in Italy I want to drink *locale fresca;* when I am in France I want to drink *vin de table.* This is it.

Tony has referred to Paul Draper as the Godfather of red wine and Bob Sessions as the Dean of American wine. Surely Bob Lindquist and Jim Clendenen are the Young Turks of Santa Barbara County. They both make wine and live with a great passion, and you can tell it in our interviews with them as well as in the bottles they produce. Be it Bob's Hillside Syrah or Jim's La Bauge Pinot Noir, both men demonstrate a lust for life and a passion to make great wine ... and they certainly succeed.

**Jim:** That is the other thing that comes with a maturing palate. A lot of people are trying to get experience. That was one of the things I wanted to talk about when I mentioned regional with food and wine tasting. There was a period of time when I first went to Italy that I would cherry-pick a Barolo off the list in Bari, or if I was in Lazio, or if I was in Friuli. After a while I realized that some regional varieties like a Cabernet Franc that is made by a serious winemaker, or Picolit, or Torgiano, by itself tastes funky in America. But where it originates from paired with the food of that area goes brilliantly, and then that is what you have to figure out. We don't have to do that as much in California because we don't have regional cuisine quite as well-stated. But to a certain extent in California, we have made a statement for lightly cooked national ingredients. We don't have a climate that demands long-stewed, long-cooked, long-braised foods, like you have in New York, and a lot of friends of mine like to cook. When you have those foods, sure, drink a bigger, richer wine, but when you have lightly cooked things ... My wines are so popular in Asia and in Hawaii, because we have acidity and we have brightness, and they go very well with lightly cooked food. You have the same thing in California. But when you start seeing these practitioners of California cuisine at Spago or Chez Panisse, and all of a sudden they are doing 15 percent alcohol wines, it is stupefying.

**Tony:** Places where there are 400 Zinfandels on the list. It's like, hey, forget what everyone wants, you can also educate, and this is what we are all missing. I Trulli restaurant, one of my favorite restaurants, they have guts—their whole list is Italian, their food is Italian, there is nothing else that goes with it. I brought Draper there, I brought Don Riessen there, I brought Don Weaver there, I brought everybody there, and they love it because you can sit down, and you can drink regionally. You can have something from Friuli, and something from Alto Adige, and you feel at home.

**Jim:** The obsession with these high-scoring, completely inappropriate at the table wines is just pandering to a new kind of client that is not going to be a long-term client.

*chapter four*

# Becoming Your Own Sommelier

*One not only drinks wine, one smells it, observes it, tastes it, sips it, and one talks about it.*

—*King Edward VII*

When either of us is dining out with our chef friends or other cohorts in the food industry, we don't relinquish our menus and ask someone else to choose our meals for us. That would be ridiculous, wouldn't it? All the fun in dining out is choosing the food, consulting with your fellow diners—and then, of course, selecting the wine.

But when it comes to that last task 'round the dinner table, Tony has found an interesting recurring phenomenon. When dining out with his "nonwine" friends or family, time and time again he is elected to choose the beverage that will be consumed during the next two hours. But why? The obvious assumption is that, as someone who works in the industry, he's the best man for the job. Ah, but within that last sentence lies the word that is the key to this situation: *job*. Selecting a wine should be fun, not work—and it most definitely shouldn't be intimidating.

If you're having a cocktail, do you ask someone else to pick it out for you? Of course not. Maybe the juniper taste of gin isn't to your liking, or "fruity" drinks leave you feeling overloaded with sugar, or scotch is just too harsh for your palate. Whatever your taste, you feel fairly secure in the knowledge of what you like and what you don't.

This is the basis from which you should view, and enjoy, your wine-choosing opportunity.

If elected to choose the wine when dining out or at home, your job is to select wisely and enjoy the task at hand. By increasing your wine knowledge you should be able to feel comfortable reading the list, selecting the wine, and pleasing your fellow diners. After all, as the adage goes, "Life is too short to drink bad wine."

There was a great article in *Gourmet* magazine by Suzanne Hamlin that posed the following question: Why do they give out a food menu to each person, yet the table itself only gets one wine list? Presumably, most people in attendance are drinking. You have to guess that one or more of them has an opinion or a preference on what they want to drink.

Tony's dear, late friend Pat Cetta, owner of the famous Spark's Steakhouse in New York, took care of that problem. The massive menu, with the food on the first page and the wine list on the next three, is to this day handed to everyone at the table. Pat's passion was wine, and his legacy the innovation of including all diners on the choice of wine.

Short of this, you shouldn't be shy about asking for multiple wine lists when dining out. At the very least, there should be one or two extra handy that you and your fellow diners can share and have fun picking and choosing from.

It's time to step up and become your own wine expert. This doesn't mean you have to assume an attitude, adapt a vaguely European accent, sniff every cork, and expect a tip from your fellow diners. The modern sommelier is usually a young, enthusiastic person dripping with wine knowledge and ready to please. And when they're not available? Tag, you're it!

## Building Your Wine Knowledge

Increasing your wine knowledge is a lifelong process. It's not something you can accomplish overnight or by taking one class or by reading one book or magazine article. Part of the root of the Latin word for wine is *vin,* which means "life." This is how we want you start looking at wine and learning about it—it's not an overwhelming chore, there's not going to be a test at the end of this chapter. It's just one of the wonderful components of dining that makes it—and life—that much more enjoyable.

Learning about wine is fun, it's rewarding, and it's profitable. When we say profitable, we're not talking about money in the bank, per se. But the more you know about wine, the better your chances of picking the right wine for a great price. This is true in both restaurants (where the markup on a bottle can be as high as 200 or 300 percent) and at the local wine shop. And learn this now: Price does not necessarily dictate quality. The more expensive wine is not always the better wine.

## How Wine Is Priced

Many factors may determine the price of a wine for a consumer: (1) cost of grapes, (2) providence or track record of that wine, (3) vintage, (4) start-up costs of a new winery, (5) good old-fashioned greed. Not all producers grow 100 percent of their own grapes. In fact, most are purchased from a grower. The price is determined usually around harvest. Prices can be steep during a great growing season when demand is high.

Estates such as Château Latour in St. Lambert, Bordeaux, Diamond Creek in Calistoga, Napa, Domaine Leroy in Meursault, Burgundy, and a litany of others have a track record of producing great wine year after year. These wines command a high price annually.

Although a winery will more than likely set the price for its product, vintage sometimes plays a part in dictating the price that you pay. The 1999 vintage of Cabernet from California was considered a stellar year—prices either went up or steadied at a price close to 1997, another great year. The same holds true for any other viticultural areas. The demand for 2001 German wines will drive up the prices as well, and the list goes on.

If a Napa winery had bought land to plant grapes 15 years ago, they would have paid for prime location anywhere between 20K to maybe 50K per acre. Today, the average price of existing vineyards or land runs about 150K per acre on average. Start-up costs are expensive, and then you have to farm the land, plant, build a winery, and pray for great weather.

And there are no geographic boundaries for greed. A winery can, out of nowhere, receive accolades and great scores from wine critics, and bingo, the next vintage of that wine will most likely go up in price. We in the wine trade have experienced at least 10 great years of wonderful wine, good steady prices, and interesting finds from New World countries. That's why we say price does not determine quality. Great finds are out there from Spain, southern Italy, Chile, Argentina, South Africa, and so on. There is also a lot of wine you wouldn't even want to cook with. You get what you pay for, but sometimes you get less.

## Reading Up on Wine

The least expensive way to gain knowledge about wine is to read. Start with your local paper, as most of them have a wine column at least once a week. Make sure you pick up the paper that day and look over the column. Most of these writers suggest wine or give their opinions. Take the suggestions and experiment with the choices. You are the best critic.

> *The Wall Street Journal* has an excellent column on wine every Friday in the Weekend section called "Tastings" by Dorothy J. Gaiter and John Brecher, a husband-and-wife team who write frankly about wine without pretense or attitude. Check them out!

Aside from newspapers, numerous wine magazines are available to the public that aren't for experts only. *Wine Spectator* leads the pack in content with a keen eye on wine criticism and lifestyle coverage, followed by *Wine Enthusiast*, which also does a great job of keeping abreast of what's going on in the world of wine. Also, there's some great wine coverage by such magazines as *Saveur, Bon Appétit, Gourmet, Food & Wine,* and *Wine & Spirits.* Each of these offerings has not only information on what's hot with particular grape varietals and winemakers, but also pairing suggestions (usually with recipes), which is a great way to learn right in your own home. Invite some fellow wine enthusiasts over, try to re-create the recipe together, and drink the recommended wine with it. It's a fun, interactive way to learn about wine, food flavors, and why they do or don't complement each other.

Of course, there are books. Walk into any local bookstore and you will find enough books that, if read cover to cover, will turn any tee-totaler into an enthusiastic master sommelier. Peruse the wine section of your local bookstore and pick what catches your fancy. Remember, this is supposed to be fun—not the SATs. Of course, if it's hard for you to decide, we have some suggestions for some wonderful wine references to start with:

- *The River Café Wine Primer* by Joseph DeLissio (Little, Brown & Company, 2000)
- *The Wine Bible* by Karen MacNeil (Workman Publishing, 2001)
- *Windows on the World Complete Wine Course: A Lively Guide* by Kevin Zraly (Sterling Publishing Co., 2002)
- *The World Atlas of Wine* by Hugh Johnson and Jancis Robinson (Mitchell Beazley, 2002)

And don't forget the web. See Appendix A for a short list of top wine sites.

All reading and no drinking can get pretty boring, though. You want fun? Well, this is how to really begin: Let's start drinking.

# Educating Your Palate

With all apologies to the Bard for paraphrasing, to thine own taste buds be true. The best wine knowledge you can get doesn't come from a book, but from educating your palate.

Having the book knowledge is the first step. The second is knowing what you like and dislike. This takes time. Being in the wine and food-writing industries has afforded us the luxury of tasting far more wines than we can remember. Yet this is the key to being your own sommelier: tasting, tasting, and more tasting. We're not advocating selling the farm, quitting your job, and becoming a candidate for the Betty Ford Clinic. (Certainly not with the price increases in wine in the last few years—you'll need that job!) But you do need to make tasting wine a priority.

## Find the Right Wine Shop

There are many good wine shops out there, but how do you know which one is best? Of course, a good wine shop should have a good selection of wines from varying countries and regions in a range of prices. The staff should be knowledgeable and eager, as well as able to answer questions about winemakers, varietals, vintages, and trends. That's pretty obvious. Quite simply, though, the best wine shop is the one you trust and the one that has employees or an owner with whom you have a rapport. Tony loves his local wine shop, Heights Chateau in Brooklyn, for that very reason, as well as Sherry-Lehmann in Manhattan, where all the salespeople have a vast knowledge of wine.

*Although sense memory is an important aspect of wine and food pairing, so is taking notes. Amy and Tony practice what they preach at the home of Don Pintabona.*

Just like when you go to a restaurant, when you enter a wine shop you should have an idea of what you're looking for (what you like, what you're not fond of) while being open to suggestions. Be sure to tell them what you like to drink, what you don't like, and a price range you are comfortable with. Buy two or three bottles in the same category, sit down with some friends, and let the fun begin. Everyone will have an opinion because everyone's palate is different.

> Take notes on the wines you like as well as the wines you could live without. That way, when confronted with a wine decision in a restaurant, you'll be able to look at the wines that are familiar to you on the list and ask yourself, "Did I like it or hate it?" and make the choice that's best for you. Keep a separate notebook just for your thoughts on wine so it will be organized and easily accessible.

The better wine shops want to suggest good wines to you because they want you as a customer. The right rapport with a salesperson makes experimenting all the more fun.

## Wine Classes

We are strong advocates of wine classes and formal tasting, but be sure the price is right for you. Good classes can break the budget of a novice drinker and sour your taste for wine (and we can think of few things more tragic in the culinary world). There are so many great teachers out there, but how do you know which one to choose?

First off, read the course description of the class—does the course seem interesting to you? Does it sound like it's going to be all talk with some tasting, or more sipping than soliloquy? A good wine course should be a balance of both lecture and tasting. You need the book knowledge as well as the taste knowledge; however, you also must create a sense memory for wines: What they taste like, smell like, what color they are, and how they finish on your palate.

Seek out advocates of the course you're looking into. Get a friend's reaction to it or, even better, your local wine shop's opinion. They usually know all the teachers who are offering courses in the community and can give you the skinny on where you'll learn and where you're just tossing money out the window.

## Start a Tasting Group

This is a great social and educational way to gain more wine knowledge and sense memory. The more people tasting, the more opinions you'll have on the wine. You should start small, with four to six people. If you can't drum up interest among your friends and family, ask at your local wine shop if they know of any tasting groups in your area. Meet once a week or even once a month. Pick a theme (like area of production, varietal, vintner, California vs. France, etc.) and a price range, and divide up the jobs of who is shopping and who is hosting. Everyone should have the chance to shop for the wine as well as choose the category. Once the group has found its legs, you can experiment with more expensive wines and even blind tasting.

Blind tasting is a great way to test your sense memory with wine. You would be surprised at some of the remarks people make about a wine when they can't see the bottle or have any knowledge of its year or origin. Guessing a varietal is one thing, guessing an appellation or vintage, well, that can get pretty heated! After sticking with your wine-tasting task for a while, you'll be happy to see how much you can get simply from smelling the aroma and tasting a sip. But be careful about falling into the trap of regional snobbery when it comes to wine. If you find yourself uttering things like, "Without the right parentage, how good could it taste?" stop right there. Who's to say a New Zealand Pinot Noir is not as good as a Nuits St. George? This kind of thinking will only prevent you from experiencing some great wines. Pull the cork, taste it, and enjoy—that's what building wine knowledge is all about.

If you and the members of your group have the tenacity to keep things going, you'll be surprised by how endlessly intriguing the topic of wine can be. As soon as you are comfortable with Burgundy, Bordeaux, and Sonoma, all of a sudden South Africa and New Zealand wines get hot, and here we go again. Each year new wines emerge on the scene, raising the bar and putting pressure on all wine students to increase their wine knowledge. Wine writers and critics are also affected with the conundrum of how to judge wines from New World countries that haven't been on the market. They need to study the climate, soil conditions, and winemaking process of these new areas. How do you critique wine without any history or criterion to judge it? Simple—pull the cork. That goes for the pro as well as the novice.

Building wine knowledge and sense memory is a lifelong avocation. Finding new wines from different appellations is what makes wine simultaneously fun and endlessly fascinating. And it beats the heck out of collecting stamps (all apologies to our philatelic friends out there).

You would have been hard pressed to find a good New Zealand, South African, Chilean, or Argentinean wine in the States 10 years ago. Now the shelves are full of them, with emerging appellations such as Marlborough, Hawkes Bay in New Zealand, Stellenbosch in South Africa, Montez from Chile, and Achaval-Ferrer from Argentina. Importers such as George Galey and Andre Shearer have led the way by introducing these wines into the American market.

## Reading a Wine List

With all the wine options out there—red, white, rosé, sparkling, dessert, port, etc.—how does one come to an opinion on wine? Simple: Pull that cork and try it. People constantly want to know what the best wine is. The answer is easier than you'd think—it's the wine you like to drink. We could tell you that a 1995 Le Montrachet from Domaine Leflaive is flawless, and you could wrinkle your nose at it and say, "Next!" The bottom line is that what you like to drink is what's best. We are merely suggesting that certain wines go better with certain foods, and together they should create an experience that's pleasant and bring you back for seconds.

With all that said, we now come to the moment you've been waiting for: How do you read a wine list?

Every restaurant is different, of course, and every list has its quirks. But a list should generally be organized by types (i.e., red and white) or by country.

We tend to drink wines we are comfortable with—names that are familiar or ring true. If you're in a fish house and open up the wine list and find nothing but Bordeaux, a big Zinfandel, and Australian Shiraz, what's up with that? Not that some of these wines won't work with the food, but it seems odd to have all the powerful wines matched with fish. Tony just ate at a Peruvian steak house that was loaded with floral Austrian and Alsatian wines, all about six years old, and a smattering of Italian whites. Hello? Did anyone know that Chile and Argentina make some great wines? The quirky lists are out there—if you find yourself confronted with one, use your budding knowledge of pairing to make the best selection you can.

The list should reflect and complement the cuisine of the restaurant. If you're going to a fish house, expect a list dominated by whites, with a smattering of reds. Conversely, a steak house, by tradition, will most likely have a hefty list of Bordeauxs, California Cabernets, and Italian reds, with a bit of white. Again, people drink what they like, so who's to say a Chardonnay is the wrong wine with steak? If you like it, it's not.

Good wine lists have three characteristics: balance, size, and depth.

- **Balance.** Same amount or approximate amount of red to white, country to country. The list should complement the cuisine.
- **Size.** A great restaurant will have a wine list that reflects the size and variety of the menu. However, a short menu doesn't necessarily mean that options and variety are sacrificed. Even a short wine list should contain a good mix of red and white varietals. The list should address and reflect the range of flavor as well as the size of the food menu.
- **Depth.** Depth should be reflected by the sommelier's journey through a country's wine regions, and his or her final selections for the best wines to reflect the cuisine. Depth allows the customer the freedom to choose the right wine and not be intimidated by a one-dimensional list. It gives you choices within the varietals as well as among the varietals.

One great innovation in wine lists as of late is the grouping of wines by their weight—light body, medium body, and heavy body. This kind of list is great for the beginner who might not recognize names of producers (or even varietals) because it helps them to find the right balance by matching the weight of their wine to the weight of their food. It's sort of like Grrranimals for wine and food pairing. Dan Perlman of AZ restaurant in New York put together his wine list in just this way, so as not to stagnate his list by region and to make the list more user-friendly for his patrons.

What follows are excerpts from two different wine lists. The first one is from I Trulli restaurant (see Chapter Seventeen), which is regionally based and shows you how European wines are generally listed. The other is from River Café sommelier Joseph DeLissio's comprehensive list of California vintage wines. Take a look at how each of these is set up to note the differences in listing styles.

One thing you should notice about this list is the depth. Although it is a regionally based wine list, there is something for everyone here price-wise. The number on the far left is the bin number, which is how the sommelier or waiter knows which wine you want and where to find it in the cellar; the next name you see is the name of the wine; after that is the vintage year; and, finally is the name of the producer. So in the last wine shown on the list above, 6040 is the bin number, Sagrantino di Montefalco is the name of the wine, 1996 is the vintage, and Arnaldo-Caprai is the producer. To the far right is, of course, how much the bottle is going to cost *you*, which on this list goes from least to most expensive within a region. And since for most of us price is generally at least part of the deciding factor, this is a very convenient feature of this list.

## Campania

| | | |
|---|---|---|
| 3715 | Aglianico *Sannio* 2000, I Normanni | 28.00 |
| 3725 | Gheppio Rosso *Aglianico* 2000, Mustilli | 27.00 |
| 3735 | Cesco di Nece *Aglianico* 1998, Mustilli | 35.00 |
| 3745 | Lacryma Christi del Vesuvio 2000, *I Normanni* | 24.00 |
| 3760 | Furure Riserva 1997, Marisa Cuomo | 55.00 |
| 3770 | Taurasi *Selve du Luoti* 1998, *Feudi di San Gregorio* | 62.00 |
| 3780 | Taurasi 1997, Terredor | 65.00 |
| 3782 | Naima 1998/99, De Conciliis | 79.00 |
| 3785 | Vigna Camarato 1995, Villa Matilde | 82.00 |
| 6015 | Naturalis Historia 1997, Mastroberardino | 135.00 |
| 6020 | Montevetrano Rosso 1999, Montevetrano | 150.00 |
| 6022 | Terra di Lavoro 1998, Galardi | 150.00 |

## Abruzzi, Molise, Lazio

| | | |
|---|---|---|
| 3910 | Montepulciano *D'Abruzzo Riparosso* 2001, Illuminati | 22.00 |
| 3940 | Montepulciano *D'Abruzzo Binomio* 1999 La Valentina | 80.00 |
| 3945 | Montepulciano *D'Abruzzo* Toni 1999, Cataldi Madonna | 85.00 |
| 3950 | Montepulciano *D'Abruzzo* Riserva *Zanna* 1998, Illuminati | 50.00 |
| 7020 | Montepulciano *D'Abruzzo* Riserva *Zanna* 1993, Illuminati 3.0 Liter | 295.00 |
| 6028 | Montepulciano *D'Abruzzo* Riserva 1985, Emidio Pepe | 175.00 |
| 6029 | Montepulciano *D'Abruzzo* Riserva 1983, Emidio Pepe | 180.00 |
| 6030 | Montepulciano *D'Abruzzo* Riserva 1979, Emidio Pepe | 275.00 |
| 3955 | Ramitello 1999, Di Majo Norante | 23.00 |
| 3960 | I Quattro Mori 1998, Castel De Paolis | 40.00 |
| 3970 | Colle Picchioni Vigna del Vassallo 1997/99, Paolo di Mauro | 55.00 |
| 3980 | Mater Matuta *Syrah Blend* 1995, Castel del Giglio | 80.00 |
| 7030 | Colle Picchioni Vigna del Vassallo 1988, Paolo de Mauro 3.0 Liter | 300.00 |

## Umbria

| | | |
|---|---|---|
| 4000 | Rubesco Riserva 1990, Lungarotti | 65.00 |
| 6035 | San Giorgio 1990, Lungarotti | 100.00 |
| 4010 | Calanco Rosso *Sangiovese/Cabernet* 1999, Le Velette | 52.00 |
| 4015 | Rosso di Montefalco 1998, Terre de'Trinci | 26.00 |
| 4022 | Rosso di Montefalco Riserva 1999, Terre de'Trinci | 36.00 |
| 4031 | Sagrantino di Montefalco 1998, Terre de'Trinci | 48.00 |
| 4032 | Sagrantino di Montefalco 1997, Terre de'Trinci | 57.00 |
| 4035 | Sagrantino di Montefalco Special Release 1997, Terre de'Trinci | 80.00 |
| 4040 | Sagrantino di Montefalco 1996, Arnaldo-Caprai | 75.00 |

We love drinking wines that reflect and complement the food we are eating. Charlie Scicolone, the wine director of I Trulli restaurant in New York City, has put together a great list of only Italian wines from the 21 regions of Italy to complement the superb Italian menu created by chef Mauro Mafrici. This way you can eat and drink like an Italian and experience their culinary way of life.

## The California Classic
### Cabernet Sauvignon/Blends

| | | |
|---|---|---:|
| 1997 | Tapestry, Beaulieu Vineyards, Napa Valley | 110.00 |
| | Château St. Jean, Cinc Cepages, Sonoma County | 160.00 |
| | Château Montelena, Napa Valley | 175.00 |
| | Dalle Valle, Napa Valley | 600.00 |
| | Beringer, Quarry Vineyard, Napa Valley | 175.00 |
| | Heitz Wine Cellar, Bella Oaks Vineyard, Napa Valley | 125.00 |
| | Harlan Estate, Napa Valley | 265.00 |
| | Jarvis, Napa Valley | 195.00 |
| | Opus 1 Mondavi/Rothschild, Napa Valley | 310.00 |
| | Screaming Eagle, Napa Valley | 1,500.00 |
| 1996 | Château St. Jean, Cinq Cepages, Sonoma County | 265.00 |
| | Dalle Valle, Napa Valley | 240.00 |
| | Togni, Spring Mountain Napa Valley | 145.00 |
| | Araujo, Eisele Vineyard, Napa Valley | 425.00 |
| | Insignia, Joseph Phelps Vineyards, Napa Valley | 250.00 |
| | Château Montelena, Napa Valley | 185.00 |
| | Shafer Vineyards, Hillside Select | 320.00 |
| 1995 | Beaulieu Vineyard, Georges de Latour, Napa Valley | 188.00 |
| | Ridge Monte Bello, Santa Cruz Mountains | 240.00 |
| | Harlan Estate, Napa Valley | 720.00 |
| | Dalle Valle, Napa Valley | 290.00 |
| | Dalle Valle, *Maya*, Napa Valley | 665.00 |
| 1994 | Grgich Hills, Napa Valley | 780.00 |
| | Bryant Family Vineyard, Napa Valley | 800.00 |
| | Jordan, Alexander Valley (magnum) | 325.00 |
| | Harlan Estate, Napa Valley | 780.00 |
| 1993 | Ridge Vineyards Monte Bello, Santa Cruz Mountains | 220.00 |
| | Dunn Vineyards, Howell Mountain, Napa Valley | 160.00 |
| | Dalle Valle, *Maya*, Napa Valley | 660.00 |

## The California Classic *continued*
### Cabernet Sauvignon/Blends

| | | |
|---|---|---|
| 1992 | Beaulieu Vineyards, Georges de Latour, Napa Valley | 165.00 |
| | Dalle Valle, *Maya*, Napa Valley | 540.00 |
| 1991 | Beaulieu Vineyard, Georges de Latour, Napa Valley | 170.00 |
| | Heitz Cellar, Martha's Vineyard, Napa Valley | 270.00 |
| | Harlan Estate, Napa Valley | 620.00 |
| 1990 | Dunn Vineyards, Howell Mountain, Napa Valley | 260.00 |
| | Caymus Vineyards, Special Selection, Napa Valley | 670.00 |
| | Ridge Vineyards, Monte Bello, Santa Cruz Mountains | 380.00 |

Obviously, for us, an American vineyard wine list is easier to read. The River Café's wines are grouped together by grape (in this case, Cabernet Sauvignon and Cab blends), which is usually the American way of listing wine. Within that category, it goes by year, vineyard name, location, and then price. Now, why are these wines on this particular list so expensive? While the River Café offers a wide price range of wines, as any good list will, this particular section is a reserve list of hard-to-find and rare California wines, the result of years of collecting by sommelier Joseph DeLissio. In fact, DeLissio is credited with being the first East Coast sommelier to really pay attention to the vintage quality of California wines.

In becoming your own sommelier you must read each wine list and gather as much information as possible. As your wine knowledge increases, these tasks become perfunctory. The list should provide you with all the necessary information in order to pick out the wine you wish to drink:

1. **Type of wine.** Most lists read like a book. Chapter One, Champagnes and sparkling wines; Chapter Two, white wines; Chapter Three, reds. Pretty short book. The better lists are broken down by varietal—i.e., Chardonnay, Sauvignon Blanc, Riesling, etc.

2. **Vintage.** Tony is often asked whether the vintage of a wine matters. Well, it does. This is when climate and wine knowledge come into play. The vintage is determined not only by weather at harvest, but the climate conditions all year round, especially in the spring during flowering and bud break. Knowledge of vintage can help determine a great wine choice. However, don't become a slave to a vintage chart. Use it judiciously, more as a

guide than a bible. Not everyone can remember that 1982 was a great year for Bordeaux, but 2002 a disaster in Piedmonte, so that's why we included the following vintage chart to help guide your choices.

Certain wine critics dubbed the 1998 vintage from California one to avoid. Following the much-hailed 1997s, the 1998s paled in comparison. This is not necessarily true, though. Not every California wine is subjected to the same climate conditions. If it's raining in Sonoma, it could be bright and sunny in the Central Coast.

3. **Regions.** By increasing your knowledge of wine-producing regions, you're increasing your ability to choose the better bottle for you. It's true, certain regions grow particular grapes better than others. We are of the opinion that certain grapes should grow only in their region of origin, but not everyone would agree. For Tony, Sangiovese is born of Tuscany and should stay there. However, many of his winemaker friends have tried growing it in California. The outcome is usually good wine, but not possessing the varietal qualities of a true Tuscan Sangiovese. Still, you'd be hard pressed to say that Chardonnay grows best in Burgundy, with Sonoma and Napa in the running, as well as half of the world's other regions. Pinot Noir, the dominant red grape in Burgundy, is producing some great wines in Oregon and now New Zealand. The list can go on, but—believe it or not—this only helps you in your choices.

4. **Price.** Prices of wines vary from restaurant to restaurant. There should be some kind of correlation between entrée prices and wine prices. We were in a restaurant recently where the entrée topped off at $24 and the least expensive wine was $40—we drank beer. Lists like this one discourage the consumer to drink, and believe us, there are plenty of great wines that could appear on any list at $20, $25, or $30, and make a profit for the restaurant. The prices should also be as diverse as the wine list. The range should go from reasonable to wherever. The list should be inviting and encourage you to drink.

# Wine Spectator

## 2003 VINTAGE CHART

(Updated January 2003)

Vintage charts are, by necessity, general in nature. Vintage ratings listed here are averages for region and year. For current vintages and exceptional older years, you will find our score and drinkability rating. A score range indicates that most wines of the vintage were not yet released at press time.

| 100-Point Scale | |
| --- | --- |
| 95-100 | Classic |
| 90-94 | Outstanding |
| 85-89 | Very Good |
| 80-84 | Good |
| 70-79 | Average |
| 60-69 | Below Average |
| 50-59 | Poor |

### WHITE WINE AND CHAMPAGNE

| Vintage | Score | Drinkability |
| --- | --- | --- |
| **FRANCE/ALSACE** | | |
| 2000 | 90-94 | Drink/Hold |
| 1999 | 87 | Drink/Hold |
| 1998 | 90 | Drink/Hold |
| 1997 | 89 | Drink/Hold |
| 1996 | 92 | Drink/Hold |
| 1995 | 90 | Drink/Hold |
| 1994 | 91 | Drink/Hold |
| 1993 | 87 | Drink |
| 1990 | 93 | Drink/Hold |
| 1989 | 96 | Drink/Hold |
| | | |
| **FRANCE/BURGUNDY WHITE** | | |
| 2000 | 90 | Drink/Hold |
| 1999 | 88 | Drink/Hold |
| 1998 | 88 | Drink/Hold |
| 1997 | 88 | Drink |
| 1996 | 95 | Drink/Hold |
| 1995 | 93 | Drink/Hold |
| 1994 | 87 | Drink |
| 1993 | 82 | Drink |
| 1992 | 89 | Drink |
| 1991 | 85 | Drink |
| 1990 | 92 | Drink |
| 1989 | 92 | Drink/Hold |
| 1986 | 92 | Drink |

| Vintage | Score | Drinkability |
| --- | --- | --- |
| 1985 | 94 | Drink |
| **FRANCE/CHAMPAGNE** | | |
| 1996 | 90-94 | Drink/Hold |
| 1995 | 92 | Drink/Hold |
| 1994 | 82 | Drink |
| 1993 | 87 | Drink |
| 1992 | 84 | Drink |
| 1990 | 97 | Drink/Hold |
| 1989 | 90 | Drink/Hold |
| 1988 | 95 | Drink/Hold |
| 1985 | 96 | Drink/Hold |
| 1982 | 94 | Drink |
| 1979 | 91 | Drink |
| **FRANCE/SAUTERNES** | | |
| 1997 | 92 | Drink/Hold |
| 1996 | 89 | Drink/Hold |
| 1990 | 97 | Hold |
| 1989 | 98 | Hold |
| 1988 | 93 | Hold |
| 1986 | 90 | Hold |
| 1983 | 95 | Drink/Hold |
| **GERMANY/RIESLING** | | |
| 2000 | 82 | Drink/Hold |
| 1999 | 90 | Drink/Hold |

| Vintage | Score | Drinkability |
| --- | --- | --- |
| 1998 | 89 | Drink/Hold |
| 1997 | 88 | Drink/Hold |
| 1996 | 89 | Drink/Hold |
| 1995 | 88 | Drink |
| 1994 | 86 | Drink/Hold |
| 1993 | 89 | Drink/Hold |
| 1992 | 88 | Drink/Hold |
| 1991 | 85 | Drink |
| 1990 | 97 | Drink/Hold |
| 1989 | 92 | Drink/Hold |
| 1988 | 93 | Drink |
| 1983 | 93 | Drink |
| | | |
| **CALIFORNIA/CHARDONNAY** | | |
| 2000 | 88 | Drink/Hold |
| 1999 | 94 | Drink/Hold |
| 1998 | 85 | Drink/Hold |
| 1997 | 96 | Drink/Hold |
| 1996 | 97 | Drink/Hold |
| 1995 | 97 | Drink |
| 1994 | 95 | Drink |
| 1993 | 88 | Drink |
| 1992 | 93 | Drink |
| 1991 | 92 | Drink |
| 1990 | 92 | Drink |
| 1986 | 91 | Drink |

## Take the Guesswork Out of Buying Wine

Each issue of *Wine Spectator* magazine points you to the top wines, the best values and the most exciting producers. Our popular Buying Guide features ratings and tasting notes for more than 500 new releases, in every price range.

To subscribe to *Wine Spectator*, visit us online at
**www.winespectator.com** or call **800-752-7799**

*A vintage chart gives you important information about how good a year was (or wasn't) for a particular wine, thus helping to guide you through what could seem like endless amounts of information.*

# How to Read a Wine Label

The road to being your own sommelier takes many twists and turns. Here is one side trip that will lead you down the path of better drinking: reading a wine label.

Either in a restaurant or in a wine shop, the wine label will give you enough information without having to buy the bottle and drink it yourself. Vintage charts, sense memory, and knowing the hottest appellation in South Africa helps when choosing a wine, but reading a wine label gives you more information about the juice in the bottle than any vintage chart.

When stranded in a restaurant without the help of a sommelier or a knowledgeable waitperson, ask to see the bottle before making your choice. Even we have found ourselves not knowing or recognizing the wines just from the list. Ask for the bottle and start the investigation.

It's safe to say some labels are easier to read than others, especially if they are in your native tongue. When they're not, it can seem a little complicated. There is a key to deciphering wine labels that aren't in English, and it has to do with classification. As you will see by the example of wine labels from Germany, America, Italy, and France, each country classifies its wines differently. We're going to start with the hardest—or the one that seems the hardest. What do you do when the list is heavy with German and Austrian Riesling without a friendly Chardonnay in sight? Well, pass the spaetzle, ask to see a few bottles of wine that you recognize from the list, and get to work.

## Reading a German Wine Label

The German terroir has dictated which grape it produces well and that grape is Riesling. We have already talked about the attributes and versatility of this grape. Now we want to make it easier for you to choose one you like.

Germany's climate does not assure the winemaker proper maturity by the end of August or early September, as it does in other areas.

This cool and somewhat severe climate in northern Europe stresses the vines and presents somewhat of a challenge to achieve the proper sugar levels at harvest time. Because of this natural phenomenon, the grapes experience a longer "hang time" in order to achieve the proper brix level (see Chapter Six). Therefore, the quality of German wines rests not solely on appellation, but also on level of ripeness.

Here's an example of a German wine label:

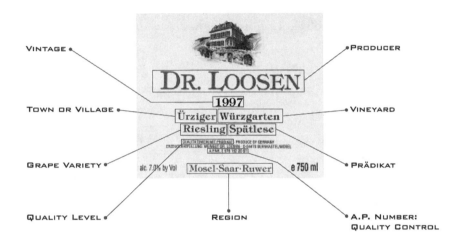

We can tell a lot about this wine just by looking at the label. First of all, the producer's name is prominent, on the middle or top of the label. Recognizing a producer's name takes study and years of tasting. However, if you follow our lead and write down the names of wines you like and don't like, it will go a long way to helping you navigate the seemingly tricky German wine labels, as well as help you to recognize a name and the way a particular producer's wine tasted more quickly.

We talked before about vintage. It's hard to make a blanket statement and condemn a whole year based on the opinion of one or two people. Knowing vintages helps, but it's better to trust in the name of a producer whose wines you have enjoyed in the past (and that goes for any wine—German, American, French, Italian, Chilean, etc.).

Unless you are a great student of German geography, knowing the name of the town or village may not help you in choosing the wine, as it does with French or Italian wines, for instance. What's more important to us than the village, as far as German wines, is knowing the grape varietal and the prädikat, or style of the wine (sugar content, color, bouquet), with German wines.

Although with a German wine label, learning the names of the villages or towns might be quite an undertaking, you can familiarize yourself with the *region* of origin. In the case of Dr. Loosen and the Mosel-Saar-Ruwar region, that's where a lot of our favorite Rieslings come from. Knowing the regions or origins of wines is important for improving your wine knowledge. So if you taste a German wine that you like, write down the region of origin as well as the producer's name. When it comes up again, you'll remember that the wine you tried from that region was to your liking.

Regions play a large part in determining which grapes grow best where. In our conversations with Jim Clendenen and Bob Lindquist in Chapter Three, we learned that their commitment to the Santa Barbara growing area was based on climate, soil, and what grapes grow best in that particular region. Since both winemakers are dedicated to Burgundy- and Rhône Valley–style wines, it's a logical move to shy away from Cabernets and Merlots from that region of California. It's the terroir that dictates what grapes grow best in what regions. As far as German wines go, the Mosel-Saar-Ruwar region means Riesling.

For us, these are the most important items to remember when reading a German wine label:

1. The producer's name
2. Grape variety
3. Prädikat, or style
4. Region of origin

These four things should guide you through any wine list or wine shop. Not including vintage on that list doesn't mean we are diminishing its importance. We are merely saying that many good producers make very good wines in marginal years. Be more comfortable with a producer with whom you have a track record, a grape varietal you enjoy drinking, a style of wine that fits your culinary needs, and a region that you feel produces wine you want to drink.

## Reading an American Wine Label

American wine labels are, of course, a bit easier to read but do not provide us with as much information as a German wine label. For instance, a California wine bottle usually states the name of the grape, the producer, and vintage.

Here are two examples of American wine labels.

Again, not as detailed as the German label, but a lot easier to read. The Miner Merlot also states the vineyard where the grapes are from and the Judd's Hill merely tells us the type of wine, origin, and vintage. If all the grapes came from a single vineyard, it would most likely be on the label as well. Single vineyards bring more money to the producer as well as prestige. Vineyards such as Stagecoach (as in our Miner example here), Gary's, Camp Meeting Ridge, and Lytton Springs have a track record of great vintage year after year. These wines are sought after by collectors and consumers upon release. Putting these names on an American label is just like having a Grand Cru status in Burgundy. Read it on the label, and you can bet you are about to drink a little bit better that night.

With American wines, knowing a little something about the climate can go a long way. For instance, you may have enjoyed a great Pinot Noir from Sonoma, which is indeed a fine area for Pinot. For the most part, with warm days and fog protecting the grapes until late morning, as well as cooler evenings, climatically it's a great case for Pinot Noir grown in Sonoma Valley, especially if you taste a few like J, Flowers, and Hanzell. Looking farther south toward the Central Coast, the marine influence on the grapes is completely unique. Calera, Testarossa, and Tally Vineyards in Arroyo Grande are committed to grapes that grow better in cooler growing areas.

Learning these few facts can help you pick out a better wine to enjoy tonight with dinner. Also be aware that not all of California is blessed with 365 days of sunshine. Again, be cautious and take a quick glance at that vintage chart.

There are no guarantees of quality just because the label has a single vineyard designation. It simply tells us where the grapes are from. Are we asking you to disregard wines made from multiple vineyards? Well, if we did, you would be missing a lot of great wines. By gaining more wine knowledge, especially by learning to extract the important information off of a wine label, you may avoid some clunkers and enjoy some really good juice.

On an American wine label, these are the most important items to remember:

1. Producer's name
2. Vintage
3. Type of varietal
4. Appellation (i.e., Sonoma, Willamette Valley, etc.)

## Reading an Italian Wine Label

Italian wines are named after a town or region; for example, Barolo from Piedmonte or Chianti (the region) in Tuscany. Learning what grapes make these wines is another study.

*Parle Italiano?* No? Not to worry, Tony is conversational and has traveled throughout the Italian wine regions for 20 years. Being able to converse in Italian doesn't guarantee you'll be drinking like a king, but knowing the regions, grapes, and producers doesn't hurt.

Italy also has its own governing board, the *Denominazione di Origine Controllata e Garantita,* or DOCG. This usually appears below the name of the wine (see the following figure). These laws protect the heritage as well as the quality of these wines. A country such as Italy with a long history of winemaking must be able to protect this tradition in order to promote the quality of its wines.

Unlike the American label that tells you the type of grape, the Italians name their wines after the region or town. Here is a Chianti Classico from Badia a Coltibuono, a great name in Chianti for 800 years.

(Now that's tradition!) We know only from building our wine knowledge that the main grape in Chianti is Sangiovese. This name does not appear on a label (nor does Pinot Noir appear on the Chambolle-Musigny Premier Cru label from Burgundy). For Italian labels, learning your regions will go a long way.

On an Italian wine label, the most important things for you to pay attention to are the following:

1. Producer's name
2. Vintage
3. Type of wine (i.e., Chianti Classico)
4. The government stamp (DOCG) so you know that the grapes were grown correctly
5. That it says "Product of Italy" so you know the grapes in the wine are from Italy and not other countries

## Reading a French Wine Label

The French also classify their wines by region and by vineyard. Burgundy, however, has always proved to be a challenge, even to the educated consumer, with 30 miles of perhaps the most expensive hills and vineyards in the whole wine world. The Côtes de Nuits in the northern section has eight villages planted in almost all Pinot Noir. To the south, the Côte de Beaune is composed of 20 villages. Burgundy is another book in and of itself (in fact, there are many great books on Burgundy in print). Some of the great food and wine pairing come from this area. With Pinot Noir used for its red wines and Chardonnay for its whites, the Grand Crus and Premier Crus are perhaps the finest expression of these two grapes. Grand Cru is what the French government designated over a hundred years ago as the best site in a particular area for the grapes grown in a particular wine, like a Les Clos in Chablis or Montrachet in Burgundy. A Premier Cru (or first cru) is the next step down from a Grand Cru, although in many cases they aren't too far behind their more esteemed siblings.

Here is a label of red Burgundy from Joseph Drouhin, winemakers since 1880 and fine producers of both reds and whites.

Maybe you recognize the name of the producer—if not, the wine's origin (Bourgogne in Burgundy, i.e., where Pinot Noir is grown) should tell you a bit more. Premier Cru, another description, should indicate that some interesting drinking is in store.

Many European governments regulate the wine business by imposing standards to guarantee quality. In France, if you call a wine a Champagne, the grapes must all come from the Champagne region—they must be produced there, aged for a certain amount of time, etc. You will find on a bottle of French wine the words *Appellation Contôlée* or AOC. This is the guarantee from the government that this wine has followed the strict rules that the government has set out to uphold tradition and to guarantee quality.

A Chablis (i.e., Chardonnay) that bears a village appellation is fine from a top producer. When the label bears the magic words *Les Clos* (which translated means enclosed, or in this case, a vineyard enclosed or walled in), a Grand Cru vineyard in Chablis, you are guaranteed a Chablis from perhaps the finest vineyard in the region. So many producers have relied upon great vineyards to make their wines.

With French wine, the following are the most important items to consider when reading a label:

1. Type of wine (i.e., Côtes du Rhône, Châteauneuf-du-Pape)
2. Government approval (i.e., AOC)
3. Producer's name
4. Where the producer is from
5. Vintage
6. The label should say "Product of France" so you know the grapes are from France and not a blend from other countries

## Enjoying the Task at Hand

By becoming your own sommelier, it is your job to gather as much wine knowledge as you can. Read newspaper articles, books, and magazines. Look at the wine list in the restaurant, ask questions of the waiter or captain. Read the wine label and try to see how much information about the bottle you can gain before opening it.

*Tony in his wine cellar.*

Above all, enjoy the task at hand. Make friends at your local wine shop, go in with an idea of what you like and want, and give them a budget or comfort zone of what you wish to purchase. If you don't recognize the wine from a list, ask to see the bottle and practice some old-fashioned label reading. Last, don't forget to record your impressions about each one: what you liked about it, what you hated, and what you ate with the wine.

Wine and food pairings are a lot of fun, whether alone or with a bunch of friends. There is nothing better than a great meal, lowly hamburgers included, matched with the right wine.

*chapter five*

# Vintage Words: Interview with Sommelier Jean Luc Le Dû, Restaurant Daniel

*There are no 100 percent rules in food and wine matching.
There are days you just want to enjoy what you just want to enjoy.*

—*Jean Luc Le Dû*

The sommelier may well be one of the most misunderstood occupations in the food world. This isn't because many people confuse what they do in their day-to-day operations, but because many diners fear that you need to know what you're talking about in order to summon the sommelier when ordering wine in a restaurant.

Nothing could be farther from the truth.

Not only is the modern-day sommelier there to help guide you in your choice of wine, but he or she is also there to help you pair your meal and your wine with the best possible results in mind. After all, these people spend an awful lot of time absorbing wine knowledge—it's no fun keeping it to themselves. They desperately want to share it.

And share it Jean Luc Le Dû did—with us (and, therefore, with you). Le Dû, the venerable sommelier of Daniel in New York, is likely one of the most respected sommeliers in the country (it's not everyone who wins *Wine Spectator*'s Grand Award or who gets a nod for "Outstanding Wine Service" from the James Beard Foundation). Le Dû moved to New York in 1985 from his native Brittany in western France, where he worked as a captain at Bouley. From there, he moved on to Daniel. When the position of sommelier opened up, Boulud was so impressed with Le Dû's wine knowledge that he offered him the job. Since then, they've become a pairing to be reckoned with.

Here, he talks about how wine has changed over the last half-century, how these changes have affected what you drink and, of course, how it matches with your food, as well as the role of a sommelier today. Tony pulled up a chair in the predinner rush calm of Daniel's dining room with Le Dû and talked *vin*—all for your eavesdropping and imbibing pleasure.

**Tony DiDio:** My first question is where do you see the role is of a modern-day sommelier?

**Jean Luc Le Dû:** The role of the modern-day sommelier hasn't changed too much from the old-day sommeliers. Which was first to stock a cellar with wines that can be drunk in their youth or age, and also to be on the floor and guide customers with pairing their food and wine together. It is the techniques of cooking and the way the wine is made today that have changed more than the role of the sommelier. Because the way the wine is made today is very different than the way wine was made 50 years ago. I think that has changed a lot, how you pair your food and wines together.

**Tony:** What do you mean when you say that cuisines have changed? We've seen in this country that there has been a great emphasis on Mediterranean cuisine, we have seen a great influence of fusion, we've seen a lot of Asian dishes coming into play, even in the most modern French restaurants, or modern American restaurants.

**Jean Luc:** It's interesting, because it seems that food and wine have taken two totally opposite roads in the last 20 years. Cooking has gotten lighter and more complex. I think in dishes people are using ingredients they weren't using 20 years ago. On the contrary, wines used to be made in a more rustic style; today they are made in a very extracted style. They are made in a much bigger style than they were 25 years ago. So really, both food and wine have changed very much.

**Tony:** Do you taste a lot of wines before you choose them, or do you know the winemaker's style?

**Jean Luc:** Well, you taste a lot of wines. You do know the taste, the way a winemaker works. You have an idea when you get to this stage what kind of wines you are going to get, because you know the winemaker, or you know the estate. But we do taste very often. We taste about 10 to 15 wines a day.

**Tony:** Is it necessary to taste every wine? Let's say, I don't think Château Latour has really changed their style in the last 50 years, or have they?

**Jean Luc:** I think they have. I think with a lot of the Châteaux, it's not maybe changing their style, but just the organization of the wine facilities these days. Things that were allowed and not allowed before. Like 30 years ago, 40 years ago, the way the famous 1961 vintage was produced, people had to throw big beds of ice onto the fermentation tanks.

**Tony:** Oh, in order to slow down the fermentation.

**Jean Luc:** To cool down the fermentation, yes. Today you don't have to do that. You have a method that allows you to do things a different way. So when I say the wines are made differently, in a more modern way, doesn't mean necessarily they are made in a way to be more accessible to a new clientele. It's just technique is so much better today than it was 40 years ago, so you can make cleaner wines.

**Tony:** Right, I find that, too. But I mean, you go to Burgundy a lot more than I do—have you found the cellars are changing? Are they cleaner? Do you see any changes from five, ten years ago?

**Jean Luc:** They are definitely cleaner. The technique of making Burgundy has definitely changed. Maybe the technique of making Burgundy has changed in a different way than making Bordeaux, if I may say so. Because as much as in Bordeaux you make wines today that are more concentrated, and more supple when they are young, they are easier to drink when they are young. I think the wines from Burgundy, and maybe you can say the same thing for the wines of Barolo and Barbaresco, have gone through a change in a slightly different method, a lot of the great winemakers have gone back to the techniques used 50 years ago. Which was not the case in Burgundy 20 years ago; you could have said there were not many great ones produced, because I think the techniques of making wine there were pretty lackadaisical. People would not look at what their neighbor was doing, and everyone making wine was really in a closed world. And when I went today a lot of the younger generation has been to school together, they look at what their neighbor does, they are really interested in winemaking techniques. And I think the modern techniques to make wine in Burgundy has been to go back to the way wine was made 100 years ago. There is a lot more attention to detail: very low yields, no pesticides, no herbicides, nothing like that.

**Tony:** When I was in Burgundy two summers ago, I met with Phillipe Drouhin, and Phillipe is really in charge of the estates and vineyard management. He was telling me that he was trying to get all their vineyards, whether it was the ones they own, or the vineyards they manage, to go biodynamic, and to go as organic as possible. So it's a slow process. You are kind of reverting back to what was done before.

**Jean Luc:** Two hundred years ago they were doing biodynamic without even knowing it.

> *Biodynamics* is a method of organic agriculture that views a farm, vineyard, et al., as a living whole. It emphasizes low impact on the environment and building soil fertility, and is carefully tailored to the particular property.

**Tony:** Right, they didn't know. One thing I think people are interested in is when you approach a table, do you basically talk about wine, or are you also talking about food?

**Jean Luc:** It is always a combination. Well, not always, but in most cases, it's a combination. When you get to a table and there is a customer who has been studying the list for some time already, of course I engage in a conversation about wine. But one of the first questions I would have would be to inquire if they've ordered already and what kind of food they have ordered. So it is always a combination of food and wine.

**Tony:** Do most sommeliers do that? Were you trained to do that, or is it instinct? I'm just curious.

**Jean Luc:** I would think most sommeliers do that. Daniel has always trained our staff, when they start, to make sure that the end result of the wine ordering is to try to find a bottle that matches as closely the type food they've ordered. Which doesn't always happen, but this is our goal.

Does a sommelier need to be certified in order to call him- or herself this? Not exactly. Way back in the time of kings and courts, sommeliers were wine stewards for the noble of birth. Today, a sommelier is a wine steward to the masses with the responsibilities such a job entails. Of course, a sommelier must have a bottomless depth of knowledge of wine, as well as the burning desire to learn more as the industry changes. He or she must also be a historian, be up on the latest trends, have savvy business skills (how else could you know you're buying a vintage wine worth holding on to or merely a flash-in-the-pan?), and have cellaring skills; of course, charm doesn't hurt either. But do you need to have a degree or pass a course in order to call yourself one? No. However, a few organizations will certify you as a sommelier. One such organization is called the Court of Master Sommeliers, and being admitted to this organization (which requires taking and passing three levels of sommelier-based courses and then being invited to join the Court) is a great honor and distinction in the world of wine.

**Tony:** What are some of the questions that you ask a diner? How do you determine their taste? Do you basically ask them what they like to drink?

**Jean Luc:** Well, you try to inquire about what style of wine they like to drink, the country of origin. For some people it is very important to drink an American wine, or a French wine, or a Spanish wine. Basically try to find out their taste, and then after that try to pair their taste with the type of food they are choosing, depending on the region, depending on the grape varietal, things like that. There are not only 18 percent alcohol Zinfandels, there are also delicious 13 percent alcohol Zinfandels. Pinot Noir can be made in many different fashions, from a light Volnay that is going to be very light in color, that is going to be a little flowery, that is going to be a very elegant style of wine, to a Martinelli Pinot Noir from the Sonoma Coast, that is a much more massive, spicy style of wine. So many grapes can be made in different fashions.

**Tony:** And how do you determine the budget of the person? How does that come about, or doesn't it come about? Do you point and say, "Are you comfortable with this, or this"?

**Jean Luc:** You try to establish a dialogue with the customer, trying never to mention the price. At Daniel, we have a wine list that goes in price from $24 to $7,000 a bottle—the range is very, very wide—so of course, you try to determine the budget of the customer without ever trying to make them feel uncomfortable. We try not to ask the question. Sometimes the customer will point to a bottle on the wine list that is in his price range, but not necessarily the bottle he wants, but it is the price range he is looking for. And that is always a good example. Or what I try to do, when speaking with a customer, is once I've determined what kind of wine I think the person would like, I try to choose two or three propositions in different price ranges, and that person is going to point me to the price range that they desire to go to. And then after that they can elaborate, or change the bottle or something like that.

**Tony:** Yeah, because it is a delicate situation.

**Jean Luc:** It is a delicate matter, because sometimes they are there to impress somebody, but they are on a budget and they might not want the rest of the party to know they are on a budget. They might be on a company or a business account, which happens a lot in a restaurant like Daniel, and they just don't want to be over budget.

**Tony:** Now, Daniel is a four-star restaurant—my favorite restaurant in America, honestly—and the wine list is a stellar wine list. It won the *Wine Spectator* Grand Award, it has been written up in all the food and wine magazines. Do you find that the pressure is on every night in order to pick out the right wines for people? When I am there as a diner, I can see that there are people there expecting a lot from that experience. Do you feel that pressure or do you just go about and do what you do?

**Jean Luc:** I don't think it's pressure. I wouldn't call it pressure. Of course, like you say, people come to a restaurant like Daniel with very high expectations and deservedly so. They should have high expectations; it *is* a four-star restaurant; it *is* supposed to be one of the best restaurants in America. I don't feel pressure because I think it is pretty excellent, it is really interesting, because here we are in a great restaurant with amazing food. The variety and the range of food Daniel can create in this restaurant is very wide. It's not like we are selling only one type of thing; Daniel has many different facets to his cooking that he shows off in the restaurant. And I've been blessed with a budget that allows me to have a very comprehensive wine list. So actually, I don't feel pressure. I almost feel like a painter: You can mix all of your colors together, and it is what a wine list like that is. Because we really have the occasion to visit many countries, and there are so many different types of tastes and aromas in the wines, that instead of pressure I think it is elation. It is actually a lot of fun.

**Tony:** That's good to hear. It's also got to be exhilarating to be in that atmosphere. You get people with great sophisticated taste, and you get people there for the first time who probably never come back, only because they live in Iowa, or they live in India, and they are just there because they heard great things about it. Now, because you are a Grand Award–winning wine list, Daniel becomes a destination not only for the food, but for the wine. So do you get a lot of people coming in for your wine list? Do you get to meet a lot of those people? Do you feel they are coming specifically for that combination of the food and the wine?

**Jean Luc:** We do get that type of clientele, the wine collectors, the wine amateurs, people for whom the wine is as important as the food, some for whom sometimes it is even more important than the food. Yes, we do get that kind of clientele.

**Tony:** I know you guys do great tasting menus; I've had a few over the years. The interplay you have with the chef is interesting. Do you have a menu specifically for food and wine? Let's say a chef's tasting menu with wine?

**Jean Luc:** Yes. When there is the chef's menu, Daniel will prepare the menu and then the waiter will bring me the order, and I will look at it and put wines that I think will go well with all of those dishes.

**Tony:** I am always interested in the interplay between you and Daniel. Daniel has told me usually you'll come in and say, oh, they have ordered this wine, what do you want to do with the menu?

**Jean Luc:** It works both ways. Like you said, some people will first order the food and then want to add the wine that's paired with it. But some people … come to the restaurant, and even before they have ordered their dinner, they will decide, oh, I would like a bottle of Chassagne Montrachet, I would like a bottle of Gruner Veltliner. So I will go to the kitchen and see Daniel and either tell him what kind of wine the customer has ordered, or if the bottle is open, take a little bit to Daniel so he can taste the wine. And together we can decide, "Oh, this would go well, and this would go well," to make a good decision about the food and all the ways it can work with the wine.

**Tony:** You guys take food and wine seriously. Obviously, it shows when you walk into Daniel. Do you feel that you are an educator, at points in the night?

**Jean Luc:** Absolutely. First of all, people go to restaurants for many different reasons. Some people go to a restaurant for dinner; they don't want to be bothered at all by the waiter or the staff or anything. They just want to order their food and have their meal delivered. And I suppose with those people, you do not want to spend so much time at their table because you do not want to alienate them. You want them to have their time alone; this is the reason they came to the restaurant. Some other people, on the other side—you might call them foodies— go to a restaurant and the world of the food business or restaurant business is very interesting. For them they love wine, they are passionate about wine. Any time they can gather some information from some- body they will do that. When you go to a table, and see customers like that, it is always a real pleasure to share knowledge. Educate a little bit without being pedantic, without being overzealous. But I think as far as the role as an educator is—it's not being an educator, it is just sharing the passion you have about wine. I have learned as much from customers, because there is always something that you do not know. When you engage in a conversation about something that you love, which in this case is wine, they are always very happy to share their knowledge, too. Which sometimes, in some areas, can be deeper than yours. A sommelier has the role of educator, but the sommelier also should always know where he stands. And never impose on a table.

**Tony:** That actually goes into my next question. What happens, when you approach a table of three or four, and everybody orders filet of sole and tuna tartar. They're eating very light and very acidic food, let's say, and all they do is order bottles of Bryant Family Cabernet. Do you ever say, oh, would you maybe want to try something else, or do you just let them do what they want to do? If they are ordering the food, and you think the food and wine match is the food and wine match made in hell, do you ever impose, or do you just let them drink what they want to drink?

**86**

**Jean Luc:** Well, I usually mention something.

**Tony:** Like, "What, are you crazy!?"

*[laughter]*

**Jean Luc:** Yeah, something like that.

**Tony:** Something subtle.

**Jean Luc:** Something very subtle just to let them know that maybe in regards to the food and wine matching, they may enjoy something different that would work better with those types of dishes. But making the decision of the wine is up to the customer, and if they decided to drink Bryant Family, this is their wine. It wouldn't be the first time. It has happened to me, where I really just wanted to taste the wine even though it didn't match whatsoever with what I was eating that night, just because I wanted to taste the wine. There are no 100 percent rules in food and wine matching. There are days you just want to enjoy what you just want to enjoy.

**Tony:** Exactly, and that's the whole theme of the book: balance and enjoying choices. The whole thing is really trying to balance flavors between food and wine, and ultimately drinking what you enjoy. But, the other thing is, give us a chance to give you an alternative choice of wine.

**Jean Luc:** Absolutely. When you are speaking with a customer, you know it's all right to suggest that a Sauvignon Blanc would work really well with that style of dish. Give him another view to it, and if you see that person is like, well, I really want a big, fat Cabernet Sauvignon with that, this is that person's wine.

**Tony:** That's the philosophy—you guys say, hey, here's a suggestion. People who come to Daniel for dinner are usually a good mix—very sophisticated, not so sophisticated, first time there, long-time returning diners, etc. But you see a lot of Americans. Do you feel that Americans are beginning to embrace wine a bit more, or do you see that it is still part of a celebration; something you only drink once in a while?

**Jean Luc:** I think they are drinking wine more and more. It's hard to say, because the tone in New York City is not really an example of the rest of the United States, as far as wine drinking. But I think the American customers are very sophisticated and drink wine more and more. And I think just the fact, for example, that the government is admitting that drinking a couple glasses of wine a day is good for you. It sends a clear message to the rest of America that wine enjoyment shouldn't be prohibited like it was for a while in this country. So I think more and more people are opening up to wine and drinking wine on a more regular basis.

**Tony:** A couple winemakers had gone in different directions with this question. Clendenen thinks we are going the opposite direction, they are drinking wine for all the wrong reasons. He was kind of bashing all the trophy wines. And that people are drinking those wines for the wrong reasons, or even buying them, and holding on to them for the wrong reasons. So he doesn't see that they are becoming an everyday thing as it is in Europe. But, I mean, you are looking at a tradition, let's say in Italy or in France or in Greece or Spain, of wine being part of the culture for 500 or 600 years.

**Jean Luc:** It doesn't mean that a customer isn't a sophisticated customer if they have been drinking wine for 500 years!

**Tony:** Ah, but I'm not saying sophisticated, I am saying it is becoming part of a culture. I'm having dinner, I am going to have a glass of wine. Whether it's an 1983 Diamond Creek, or a Gallo jug wine. It's not a sophistication, I am saying it's part of the culture. When I go to Italy, I want to drink *locale fresca,* I want to drink wines that they produce locally. I don't care the level of sophistication that they have, I want to drink what they're drinking in Alba that day. And when I go to Burgundy I want to be drinking Burgundy, or Bordeaux, or whatever— I want to be part of that culture.

**Jean Luc:** Well, I think then, yes, the level of sophistication of Americans is getting higher. I don't think that it has reached what they do in Europe, where it's very natural for someone to have a glass of wine with dinner. But I think it is becoming more ingrained in people's psyche to drink wine on a regular basis. I don't think it's as ingrained as it is in Europe yet. Now on the level of knowledge, and sophistication, I think Americans are very interesting as a group because, once they get into something, they really want to learn a lot about it. When you go to Europe, people will know the wines from their region, but they have a hard time looking at the big picture of their whole country. And people from Burgundy don't care about people from Bordeaux, and people in Bordeaux have no idea what is going on in the Loire Valley, whereas in America they are more interested in learning globally about wine, what's happening in the wine world. So I think maybe they are more interested, or more curious than their European counterparts. The American clientele is very interesting, because they are always asking questions and want to learn. They are really a fun clientele to work with as a sommelier.

**Tony:** Okay, the last question is about stocking a cellar. Is food ever a part of it? When you are buying wines, are you thinking of filling in or expanding your list, or is food a player? Are there wines that maybe you avoid, or are there wines that you embrace?

**Jean Luc:** Well, when I stock the cellar for the restaurant I don't think I necessarily think about the food that is being served in the restaurant. I have been there for a few years and I know Daniel's cooking and I guess it's almost second nature for me to buy the wines that I think work well with his cooking. This is a reason why, for example, we focus very heavily at the restaurant on Burgundies, or wines from the Rhône Valley, because when we are talking about French wines these are wines that I know historically go with his cooking. There are wines that we avoid at the restaurant. Wines that are too heavily oaked we avoid at times because they tend to cover the subtlety of the cooking. I think it applies to other types of cooking besides Daniel. I think in general, wines that are too oaky tend to detract from the food.

# *part two*

## Learning About Flavors

*Sweet Flavors*

*Salty, Sour, and Bitter Flavors*

*Savory Flavors*

*Vintage Words: Interview with Daniel Boulud,
Restaurant Daniel*

*chapter six*

# Sweet Flavors

*Dining is, and always was, a great artistic opportunity.*

*—Frank Lloyd Wright*

If you sat down at a table and a dish of smoked salmon and chocolate ice cream was set in front of you, you wouldn't think twice about raising an eyebrow. You wouldn't even have to taste it to know that these things absolutely, unequivocally *do not* go together. And if you did venture a few bites on a dare, you likely would be able to come up with a few good, solid reasons why not. We're willing to wager that within those reasons, you would find one common thread: balance.

When considering food and wine pairing, balance is the key to a satisfying, successful eating and drinking experience. When you create or order a meal—a really good meal—whether it is haute French cuisine or down-home American fare, there is balance to what's on your plate. All the flavors might not be the same, but they work together. And you certainly don't need to be Amanda Hesser or Wolfgang Puck to know this. There's a method to the mingling.

This concept isn't lost on you. In fact, like us, you're probably very comfortable within the epicurean world. You know what you like and what you don't like. What food item tastes exquisite to you with one thing, but is lost on another. It's the same with food and wine. In fact, it's the same *within* winemaking. A good wine is a balance of flavors. One or two may be predominant over the others, but there's a chemistry at work there that's been (most of the time) well thought out way before it is bottled and corked and boxed and shipped to your local wine shop.

On the topic of matching the right wine with the food on your plate, and vice versa, many of us can get a little uncomfortable. To many a seemingly sophisticated, food-loving adventurer, the world of wine may as well be a foreign language of strange characters and odd terms. In fact, it *is* a little like a foreign language. The description of a wine can sound more like a conversation about the Rockettes than a bottle of Chardonnay: "It's leggy and bright, and has a long finish."

Think back to when you were in a classroom learning French or Spanish or Russian. When the professor first breezed into the room and cheerily said "Hola!" you felt your stomach tighten and you began to squirm in your chair. In those first few lessons you found your brain working like a verbal calculator, trying to translate what was said and what you read before you lost the gist of the conversation. But then, as the days rolled on, it became easier. You didn't have to think so hard about it all the time and the words began to trip off your tongue with less and less arduous plight. You adapted. You learned. Maybe you even began to have fun with this new, wonderful language.

Food and wine pairing isn't so very far removed from this experience. But the wonderful news is that—really, honestly—it's much easier than translating a Gabriel Garcia Marquez novel into English. Much, much easier. That's because you already have the necessary equipment: your nose and your tongue. This is all you need (well, save for a nice wine glass, a few good bottles of vino, and a healthy appetite). You just need a little bit of training to fine-tune your gear.

In the next few chapters, we're going to look at flavors and the balancing of them. You're going to learn how to take the already sophisticated palate we know you possess and use it for the next logical step in dining: food and wine pairing.

## How Sweet It Is

As we mentioned before, balance is important not just between what you eat and what you drink, but also within a wine itself. One of the most confusing concepts in wine-speak is one that seems simple enough to grasp: the notion of sweetness. You think, "Well of course I can tell the difference between a sweet wine and a dry wine. That's the easy part."

the business like to say. Terroir is not only the soil, but the growing conditions particular to the area of land where the vines are grown. In Tony's opinion, the terroir is what gives a unique character to the wine being raised from that particular patch of soil and the unique influences surrounding it. The dirt is the difference. There is also the climate around the vineyard to consider, the fluctuating weather of the region, the time of day the grapes are harvested, and a whole vineyard's worth of additional influences.

When a winemaker creates a particular wine, the end result is very manipulated. How it turns out is generally not a crapshoot. And as far as the sweetness of a wine goes, there's a particular logic at work.

## Building Brix

Before we get any further into what sweetness is or isn't, we want to give you a little background on where the sugar content in your bottle comes from. As we just said, there's a lot that goes into creating a particular wine. From the climate to the type of grape and a variety of features in between, a winemaker has to consider many factors to come up with exactly the product he or she envisions. Sweetness is no exception.

When winemakers measure the ripeness of a grape and need to figure out the acidity versus the sugar content in a wine, they measure something called *brix*. Simply put, brix is the level of sugar content within a particular kind of grape, as well as the must (that is, skins, pulp, seeds, and stems) and wine product in general, and indicates the grape's ripeness, or sugar level, at harvest. To give you an idea of what this means from one wine to the next, a Chardonnay will have a brix level somewhere around 24, but a Moscato d'Asti will have a brix level of 36, give or take. This is measured using a small gadget into which the grapes are put and crushed. The sugar content is measured and the winemaker is given a brix reading for this particular crop of grapes.

When the grapes are at the desired brix level for the particular wine being made, the vinification process begins. The grapes are crushed, yeast is added, and fermentation begins. As the yeast eats away at the sugar, alcohol content begins to form. Then, the process is stopped, the juice from the fruit is extracted and pressed, and a second fermentation begins.

A major determinant of sugar content in a wine is the timing of the harvest. The longer a grape remains on the vine, the sweeter it gets. In colder climates like the Piedmonte region of Italy, the more sugar a winemaker requires, the longer the fruit will remain on the vine. But in areas like Sonoma or Napa, the weather is warm all year long and a vintner needs to be careful about how long the grapes remain unharvested. In fact, when a grape is ready in this corner of the winemaking world, harvesting usually occurs in the early morning before the sun is at its strongest and ripening will continue at an accelerated rate. Most wines with a higher sugar content are harvested later in the growing season. (In fact, if you look at certain bottles, it will even say on the label "late harvest.")

*Late Harvest* is an indication on a wine label that the wine in question has been made from grapes that have lingered on the vine and were picked much later in the season than others from the vineyard. Therefore, the sugar content (brix) is going to be significantly higher than what is used in most table wines. Usually, late harvest wines are considered dessert-style.

## First Tastes: The Anatomy of Your Tongue

Recently, Tony had some friends over for drinks and he was serving wine. One guest sipped the wine and said, "Oh, I really like this. I prefer sweet wines to dryer ones." This is a comment Tony has heard time and time again. The wine, in fact, was not a sweet wine— although it was a German Riesling, it had a fairly high acidity. What the guest was savoring was the fruitiness of the grapes used.

Amy hears this often from her husband, Dan, too. She loves to have Chardonnay on hand, but Dan doesn't enjoy drinking it, claiming the wine is "too sweet!" But is it sweet? Well, yes and no.

When we are children, the first "taste" we usually learn is that of sweet. It's the one that hits your tongue first and gives you that quick, satisfying "mmmmmm" without much work. This is why, for a child who is likely to have had less experience with food and is learning to appreciate many different flavors, sweet is so alluring. And, if you think about it, as adults many of us turn to sweet when we're feeling down or, sometimes, even elated. When we want instant gratification, it's a chocolate bar or ice cream or pastry that we grab.

*The highlighted area shows where on the tongue sweet flavors are experienced—right at the tip.*

As you can see from the darker shaded area in the drawing, the taste buds at the very tip of your tongue are those that register sweetness. So it's no wonder you might get a little confused—it's the first thing you experience when you take something in, after all. And as wine is made from fruit, there's going to be some amount of sugar lingering around there—it's how much that can be a tiny bit perplexing.

Again, there are wines that do contain a higher sugar content: some Riesling and Gewürztraminers, port, certain rosés, Moscato d'Asti. But with other wines, you may well be confusing the essence of the fruit with sweetness. The fruitiness of a wine captures the essence of the entity—maybe it's pear or peach, possibly fig or berries.

Now, let's take this one step further—what if what you have on your plate contains fruitiness or a sugary influence? Maybe you're about to dive into a plate of sweet bay scallops with the tangy influence of ginger and lime, or a decadent flourless chocolate torte. Then what?

Later in this book, we will take you through various different kinds of cuisines and help you learn how to pair the essence of what you taste in a particular wine with, say, pork loin stuffed with fig or filet of Dover sole with a cream sauce. But for now, we want to get right down to the bare-bones nitty-gritty. For each taste we deal with in the following chapters—sweet, salty, sour, savory—we're going to give you a little exercise with various wines to practice training your palate and learning how to understand what balance is and why it's vital to the success of a truly good dining experience.

## Taste the Difference

We have performed this exercise on our own just for fun on several occasions. In fact, if you have a companion who's game, ask him or her to join you. Not just for the company, but because while one of you might taste one particular aspect of the food and wine combination, the other might be able to describe something else that you aren't picking up on. In addition, having to describe what you taste to someone else forces you to think a little harder about the experience, and therefore deepen your understanding of why particular combinations work or don't.

For this exercise, you will need a few items:

* Four or five bottles of wine (we recommend buying half-bottles if they're available from your local wine merchant for our purposes here). Try using these:
    1. Hanzell Chardonnay (1999)
    2. Chalk Hill Semillon Botrytis (1997)
    3. Cascinetta Moscato d'Asti (2001)
    4. Inniskillin Icewine Riesling (2001)
    5. J.J. Prum Riesling Spätlese (1999)
* One wine glass for each wine
* A wine bottle opener (of course!)
* A dish of something sweet (try currants or raisins)
* A dish of something salty, such as prosciutto or lightly salted nuts (avoid items like potato chips, though—for our purposes here the food item should taste salty, but not be overpoweringly so)
* A dish of something savory (try a cheese like Edam or Majon)
* A dish of something sour (try squeezing lemon onto a slice of cantaloupe)
* Plain, unsalted table crackers

- A glass of water
- An empty glass (for spitting out the wine, which for this exercise we recommend—you're going to be doing a lot of sipping and you'll need to keep your wits about you!)
- A pen and the "Wine and Food Evaluation Chart" in Appendix D.

> Spitting out wine when tasting can be a little messy until you get used to it—don't be put off if your technique isn't seamless at first. Just keep a napkin handy and make sure that you hold the cup or glass under your chin and try to spit it in a single, fluid stream (as opposed to the way you expel your toothpaste when brushing your teeth!).

Set your glasses in front of the wine bottles so that you won't get confused as to which wine is which when you're tasting (begin with any wine you wish).

First, write down the name of the wine you're beginning with. Swirl your wine in a slow circle in the glass and take a long whiff. Then take a small sip and hold it in your mouth while breathing in through your nose (the air you take in aerates the wine and brings out the flavors in it). When you do this, the wine will gurgle a little on the front of your tongue. Hold it in your mouth for 10 to 15 seconds, and then spit it into your "spitting" cup.

Now, write down what you smelled and tasted. Don't be too self-conscious about the words you use. If the only thing that comes to mind is "sweet," try to think about what kind of sweet: Do you taste honey? Pineapple? Try your best to identify the flavor and aroma and write it down next to the wine's name. At first, you may well have trouble attaching a word to the flavor you've tasted, so here are a few terms that might help you get started:

- Apricot
- Peach
- Apple

- ❖ Petroleum (Really! To some female readers, you might also recognize this as "new Barbie smell.")
- ❖ Sea
- ❖ Hibiscus
- ❖ Honeysuckle
- ❖ Geranium
- ❖ Berries (strawberries, raspberries, blackberries)

Of course, it takes time to train your nose to pick up or separate one nuance from another, so don't feel pressured to detect any of these scents. If you just smell flowers, write "floral aroma"; if you taste fruit but you're not sure what, write "fruity." Don't forget other sensations, though—tingly, lip-smacking, thick (like when you have medicine and it coats your mouth a bit). These are all good observations and, believe it or not, important to figuring out the balance within the wine and between the wine and what you eat.

Now we're going to add the food items into the mix. Take another small sip of the wine, hold it in your mouth for a few seconds, and spit it out. Now, take a bite of the sweet item (if you've used our suggestion, the currants or raisins). What do you taste? Can you still taste the essence of the wine? Is the food item complementing the wine and bringing out the flavor of both, or is one overpowering the other? Write down what you experience.

Now, take a sip of the water to cleanse your mouth, and begin again with the same wine and a different food item, writing down what you experience after tasting it.

Once you have completed trying all four food items with the first wine, move on to the next wine. In between wines, make sure you take a sip of water and have a few bites of the table cracker to neutralize your taste buds. Follow the same process with each wine, writing down what you taste initially, and then what you taste when you have the wine with each food item. (If you are doing this exercise with a friend, your companion should be doing the same thing simultaneously. Try not to say aloud to each other what you taste until after you've completed the exercise—just write down your respective responses to the wine and the food with the wine.)

*Balance* is the mark of a good wine. When all flavors and influences in a wine—from the acid to the sweetness to the tannins and fruit, as well as the influences brought on by the *terroir* (the ground the grape is literally grown in as well as the surrounding influences in the area)—blend harmoniously to create the proper balance of taste in a particular kind of wine.

## A Little Knowledge Is a Delicious Thing

Now we're going to give you a little help. (Don't read this part until you've finished the exercise—no cheating!) What follows is a description of the wines you just tasted and what you may have noticed when pairing them with the sweet, salty, savory, and sour items above:

- ❖ **Hanzell.** A classic Chardonnay with a developed nose of green apples and a hint of honey. The fruitiness in this balanced wine can marry well with a dish of Nantucket Bay Scallops sautéed in butter or a novello olive oil. The acid in the wine will cut through the butter and bring out the fruitiness in both the wine and the scallops. You likely enjoyed this wine best when you tried the currants or the cheese. When you ate the salty and sour items, though, did you find the foods overpowered the flavor of the wine?
- ❖ **Chalk Hill.** Great balance and finesse, this wine has aromas of apricot and honey, and an undertone of hazelnuts and dried fruits. What a perfect match for a mixed-nut tart, where the sweetness in the wine is tamed by the toastiness in the nuts.
- ❖ **Cascinetta.** A floral wine with a nose of fresh-cut apples and ripe pears, marries well with a delicate, creamy cheese and ripe tomatoes. The acid in both the wine and the tomatoes are paired to perfection. The cheeses you ate were probably the winners here. But you also might have enjoyed it with the cantaloupe and lemon. The prosciutto was likely too overpowering, as were the dried fruits.

❖ **Inniskillin.** A dessert in a glass, this rich wine has fresh straw-berry and ginger aromas. It's best drunk alone, or paired with a simple biscotti. In this case, you probably discovered that the powerful taste of this wine stunted the flavors of currants and cheese, and seemed entirely wrong with the prosciutto. How-ever, you may well have enjoyed it best with the lemon and can-taloupe combination.

❖ **J.J. Prum Riesling.** A wine of great depth with a nose of flow-ers. It is, in Tony's opinion, the most versatile wine made. Its low alcohol and great *acidity* prove to be the best match for food. We love this wine with dried, smoked meats or sausages that have both spice and heat. The prosciutto was your winner here, wasn't it? However, you may have second-guessed your taste buds when trying this wine, as it likely paired well with each item. (See, you weren't confused—you were correct!)

*A*cidity is the level of acid in a wine. Acid occurs natu-rally in fruits and vegetables. Where wine is concerned, the acid in a grape not only adds a refreshing, tingly taste, it also helps to balance out the other influences in the wine (like sweetness) and helps the wine to age well.

## The Sweet Life

What you learned in this exercise was an important lesson in balancing sweetness with other flavors. Sweetness varies from bottle to bottle—an Inniskillin is going to bowl you over with its sugar content, whereas the Prum Riesling has enough acidity in it to balance the sugar the wine contains, enabling you to pair it with many types of food.

What you've learned in the previous pages is that sweetness isn't just a blanket term you can toss upon any wine. You've learned where it comes from and how it winds up in your bottle, as well as why certain wines may have more and others less. Most important, you've learned that because levels of sugar vary from wine to wine, they call out to be paired with other flavors—and not necessarily the same ones. Balance is the key to creating the sweetest sensations of all.

# chapter seven

# Salty, Sour, and Bitter Flavors

*Sweet, sour, bitter, pungent—all must be tasted.*
*—Chinese proverb*

*A meal without salt is no meal.*
*—Hebrew proverb*

If there's a concept that becomes readily apparent when you begin to concentrate on how food and wine interact with each other, it's that *complementary* does not necessarily mean the flavors are alike.

Flavors can be friends or they can be foils. When flavors are friends (that is, they are similar in taste or nature, and therefore easy on the tongue), they run parallel to each other. It's as if one is the wave that that the other rides upon, allowing both flavors to merrily roll along on your taste buds. For example, truffles and Barolo is a match made in heaven (or, in other words, the Italian countryside because the truffles and the wine come from the same place, and thus have the same *terroir* influences). However, there are other flavors that are so starkly different that they challenge each other; they bring the essence of that sensation to the forefront, where it might get lost in a different pairing. These flavors are foils. Like an Oregon Pinot Noir and grilled salmon. You might instantly think, "Oh, red with fish—that doesn't work." But the tannic (although, in this case, less tannic than other reds), acidic nature of the wine complements the fattiness of this particular fish by cutting through the thick, tongue-coating sensation so you can really taste the essence of the food. And on the reverse, the fatty nature of the fish can stand up to a wine with tannins and acid and therefore allow the nature of the wine to shine through as well. It's a clear-cut case of opposites attracting and making a great couple.

In Chapter Twenty, we talk about the Asian culture's theory of yin and yang in food as well as life; being polar opposites can bring balance to the plate. While opposites don't necessarily attract, they can bring out the best in each other.

And so it is with salty, sour, and bitter flavors. These flavors tend to get a bit of a bum rap, though. Speak them aloud in conjunction with a dish, and we'd bet the listener wrinkles his nose and moves on to the next selection. But as we'll see in this chapter, each is not only necessary but absolutely enjoyable, as well as an integral part in the balance of flavor.

## How They Work

We've said it over and over in these pages: The secret to pairing is balance, balance, balance. We started to see in Chapter Six how balance comes into play. Maybe when you sip a Riesling the first thing you experience is the fruitiness of the grapes and the sugar content from them, but then, as the flavors hit your tongue, the various sensory elements contained in that little sip begin to show up.

Because sweet has immediately pleasant connotations, it may somehow seem easier to think about in terms of pairing than trying to figure out salty, sour, and bitter. But actually, we could argue a case for the opposite. Sweet can be tricky. Too much of it, and your eating and drinking experience can feel more like eating a candy bar and washing it down with maple syrup. Yick. It's actually easy to temper sweetness with, for instance, the addition of a salty, sour, or bitter element (and vice versa, of course).

## Salty

Salt plays an interesting role with food. In diet- and health-conscious America, salt is looked upon as a kind of evil, which is why you see so many products advertised as low-sodium or salt-free. However, save for those with very serious medical conditions, we're proponents of the "everything in moderation" rule. Too much of anything can be bad. (Certainly, too much wine can not only overpower a meal, it might make you forget it entirely.)

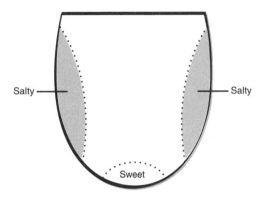

*The shaded area shows where salty flavors are experienced on the tongue. Next time you eat a bag of salty chips or pretzels, notice how close to the front and the sides of your tongue get that zing of salt first before you taste anything else.*

As you can see in the diagram, salt is the next sensation that hits the taste buds after sweet (yet again showing us why we all go right for the ice cream or the potato chips when we crave instant guilty gratification!). When you've eaten a handful of salty nuts or chomped on some crispy seasoned French fries maybe you've noticed that you get that tingly, sharp sensation close to the front and on the sides of your tongue—that's the salt, baby. But salt is much more than a mere guilty pleasure. This tiny little crystallized nutrient acts as a palate-opening agent. Used judiciously, it brings out the natural flavor in other foods (of course, if used in ridiculous abundance, it beats any other flavor sensations into salty submission). Let's take filet mignon. Although it's a very desirable cut of meat because of its tender nature, believe it or not, it is also one of the less tasty cuts because of its low amount of marbling (that is, fat). Add a little salt, and suddenly the flavor of the meat becomes as apparent as its incredibly buttery texture.

The United States is one of the leading producers of salt in the world; in 2001 we churned out nearly 30 million tons. Historically, it has been used as a preserving agent (think duck confit and baccalà, dried, cured codfish), currency, and the source of many an idiom. One of the most famous, "Back to the salt mines," actually refers to the punishment received by Russian prisoners—being sent to very undesirable salt mines of Siberia to work.

But salt isn't just found in the shaker. Certain cheeses, olives, cured meats, seafood, soy sauce, etc., are all salty items—and certainly the kind that you could conceive of consuming with a glass of wine.

Try this experiment. Bite into a Granny Smith apple. What does it taste like? What sensations do you get? Slightly sour, maybe a little bitter, crisp, with undertones of sweetness. Put a little bit of salt on a slice of the apple and take a bite. The salt tames the bitterness and the sour taste and allows you to experience more of the sweet in conjunction with the other sensations.

Experimenting with different flavors can be educational and fun. When we think of salty foods like olives, cheeses, and pork products, Spanish wines come to mind. Go to the cheese store and pick up some Manchego cheese and a few slices of Serrano ham, or try some parmesan and prosciutto di Parma. (Talk about the salt mines!) We suggest a good, inexpensive Cava—Spanish sparkling wine—like Paul Cheneau, or a sherry, either fino or Manzanilla style. Nibble and sip away. Pay attention to what the sweetness in the Cava and the floral qualities of the sherry do to the salty foods. Don't forget, Spanish wines are great buys. We picked up a La Gitana Manzanilla for $11 and served it with a slight chill. The Cava cost less than $10 and worked great with both the hams and the cheeses, as well as the olives.

Salt does interesting things to wine, too. Of course, wine itself is not salty. A wine that has strong bitter undertones (like, for instance, a young, highly tannic Cabernet Sauvignon that hasn't had the aging time to mellow) is eased by salty food. The bitterness is toned down and you can more readily taste the fruit in the wine.

On the other hand, wine can also give a welcome reprieve to super salty foods. Wines with strong acid that haven't been oaked are the best foils for the salty taste. The classic example: Chablis and oysters.

## Sour

Sour by any other name is acid. Whether it be in the tartness of vinegar on your salad, the generous squeeze of lemon on your cherry stone clams, or the astringent nature of a tomato, that pucker-up sensation can be pleasurably tart, refreshing, tangy or ... eye-tearingly, cheek-suckingly, tongue-tinglingly sour. But as we learned earlier in this book, food and drink without acid adds up to nothing more flavorful than a pile of three-day old gruel.

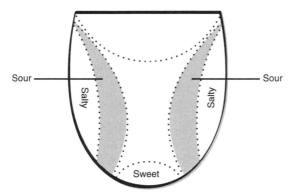

*As you can see from the shaded areas toward the center and back of the diagram, sour flavors tend to linger on the tongue.*

Take a look at our tongue diagram again. Sour is tasted toward the center and back of the tongue. In other words, it's one of the last sensations you pick up on, and therefore, one of the more lingering sensations of a taste experience. So taming the acidic nature of a dish or a wine is the key to keeping things pleasurable as opposed to puckerable.

Acid can wear both the hat of the friend and the hat of the foil—and because of this, it can interact with wine and food in complex ways.

An acidic wine paired with acidic food tends to be a good thing. Why? On the one hand, if a dish has a high amount of acid, it may well *need* the backbone of a highly acidic wine to properly complement and, in effect, mellow its forceful nature. Without the backbone of acid in the wine, highly acidic food will completely overpower what you drink (and therefore, ruin the balance). On the other hand, a highly acidic wine will overpower a dish that lacks the same kind of backbone. For instance, if you drank a highly acidic, tongue-smackingly tannic Cabernet with a lightly herbed grilled chicken and a plate of steamed green beans, you'd lose all the flavor of the food because it would be entirely overpowered by the wine's highly acidic nature. The chicken may be delicious, but you'll walk away from the meal saying, "It was so-so."

There is one caveat with regard to tangy, citrusy foods: You need to match the level of acidic intensity in order for a match to truly be complementary. In other words, a dish high in vinegar or citrus accents will need a more acidic friend in its wine than, say, a dish that's made with a few cured olives.

Acidic wine paired with rich food (and vice versa) is a foil made in heaven. Foods that are naturally rich with fat or oil, or pumped up with oil or butter in the process of cooking, can be beautifully balanced by a wine with a high amount of acid. A classic example of this would be one we used earlier in this chapter—salmon (fat and oil) with Pinot Noir (acid and tannins).

But what if the dish itself is fatty *and* acidic (for instance, a balsamic glaze on your pork roast, sauerkraut with kielbasa, or pickled onion with skate like Rick Moonen makes for us in Chapter Eleven)? Will the addition of extra acid on the food change what "works" as far as wine goes? The answer is yes, but you shouldn't let that intimidate you. Here, it actually opens up your choices even further. The reason lies in the flavor influences at work here. For instance, that addition of the extra tang can still work with a high-acid red in the instance of the pork and balsamic combo because the meat is fatty enough to withstand the acid in the wine and the balsamic. However, balsamic is also a little bit sweet, which plays off the fruit influences in the wine as well. Now, if you were more in the mood for a white wine, that balsamic glaze also just allowed you to enjoy the crisp, clean flavor of a Sancerre, a Riesling, or even a Champagne. Why? Because, while alone the pork wouldn't necessarily complement these wines, the acid of the vinegar tames the fatty nature of the pork and allows you to enjoy a fruitier wine (which would go great with the polish sausage, too, for the same reasons: sauerkraut = sour; sausage = fat).

## Bitter

Bitter is the poster-flavor for foils. The more bitter your food, the more bitter a highly tannic wine will taste. For example, that tongue-tickling bitter sensation you get from spinach will take the tannins in a Cabernet and run amok with them in your mouth. Not so nice.

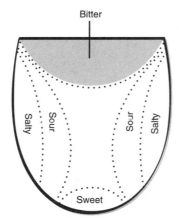

*The shaded area at the back of the diagram shows where bitter flavors are tasted on the tongue. As you can see, bitter is the last taste you experience, so proper pairing is important (otherwise, that's all you'll taste!).*

As you can see in our tongue diagram, bitter is tasted on the back of your tongue; it's the last sensation you get, so it's the last sensation you'll remember. That's why wines with a high amount of tannin and foods that are especially bitter don't leave the best sense-memory in your mouth. Bitter and bitter don't cancel each other out, they team up to wash away all the other flavors that may have been in the dish or the wine and leave you clicking your tongue against the roof of your mouth and scrunching up your nose.

However, this is not to say that bitter is bad. Bitter isn't bad—bitter is good. Bitter balances opposite flavors. It's just a prime example of how stability among flavors is of the utmost importance when wining and dining (as opposed to whining and dining, which is exactly what would happen if you didn't take our advice here). It also isn't a completely unbending rule, though—tannic wines and food with bitter elements aren't necessarily always a bad match. In this instance, salt can come to the rescue and tame the bitter elements, keeping other flavors of a dish from being overpowered by that end-all, be-all, back-of-the-tongue issue. Remember our experiment with a Granny Smith apple in the salty section of this chapter? The salt tamed the bitterness and allowed the fruit's flavor to come to the surface (or at least not linger on the back of the tongue).

When we talk about food and wine pairing, we tend to mention only the main courses—steak, fish, pork, etc. Sure, they are the lead actors, but what about the supporting cast? That lovely spinach, those delectable mushrooms, or that fresh broccoli. Serving them alongside the main event will also change the nature of the dish—so what wine will go with it?

We set out to see which wines go well with the supporting cast of characters. Some simple steamed spinach, arugula, and French lentils. We had a bunch of wines opened and, among them, kept going back to the ones that exhibited earthy and mineral tones. As Rick Moonen points out in Chapter Nine, there are tannins in spinach and we need a wine to step up to it. We loved two wines that worked with this trio of side dishes: the Jean-Marc Brocard Chardonnay Kimméridgien 2000 and the Argyle Pinot Noir 2001. Both wines exhibited a great deal of earthiness and typical qualities of the terroir, with a good balance of acidity.

The arugula, though it is bitter and spicy, worked great with the mineral qualities in the nose of the Brocard Chardonnay, which is a wine that is fresh and doesn't see any oak aging. The spinach and lentils were great with both wines. We loved the nose on the Argyle Pinot, and predicted that the cherry and almost mushroom aromas would do well with these side dishes, and they did.

The addition of salt aside, though, as a general rule of thumb, go for more fruit-forward (that is, wines in which the first aroma and taste you experience is an incredibly strong, very big fresh or even cooked fruit sensation), fuller wines to complement foods with a bitter edge—charbroiled meats, picholine olives, arugula, spinach, and the like. When the wine itself is highly tannic, think in terms of rich, even fattier foods—salmon, pancetta, pork loin, et al.

But, not so oddly, one of the single most common errors in identifying the taste of wine is to umbrella all flavors that aren't of a highly acidic nature under the label "sweet." (And anything that isn't fruity or with a higher sugar content under the term *dry*, but we'll get to that in the next chapter.)

When it comes to finding complementary flavors among what you imbibe and what you eat, remember one important concept: It's all about that same balance we were discussing earlier. And within a wine itself, when we're talking about sugar or lack thereof, you're going to learn in this chapter that not all sweetness is created alike.

Although sugar content is something that happens naturally within a fruit, there are other ways—natural and manipulated—that sweetness is added to a wine. For one, under certain conditions a mold or fungus called *botrytis cinera* (or "noble rot" as it's been dubbed among winemakers) can sometimes attach itself to grapes, piercing the skin and causing them to shrivel, thus deeply concentrating the sugar, acid, and flavor or the grape.

In the case of port or brandy, neutral spirits may be introduced during the fermentation process to stop the yeast from eating the sugar, and thus keeping the flavor at a higher sweetness.

Another method is to add residual sugar to a wine. If the resulting wine is too acidic, this may be added. However, some low-end winemakers add extra sugar to their products, in the same way it is done to orange juice or peanut butter, to produce a sweetness that doesn't occur on its own.

True, there are wines that are of a sweeter nature due to their higher sugar content—some Riesling, Port, Sauternes, and Moscato D'Asti, for instance. When you sip these, the first thing you may well notice is the sugar in them. But is that it? Is that all you notice? Well, of course not. If it were all about sugar, we all might as well pop open a bottle of cola with dinner and call it a day. The taste of a wine is influenced by many things. Yes, sugar content or lack thereof is one of them— but there's also the earth that it's grown in, or the *terroir*, as those in

# chapter eight

# Savory Flavors

*He who distinguishes the true savor of his food can never be a glutton; he who does not cannot be otherwise.*

—*Henry David Thoreau*

When food is the topic of conversation, savory is a word you hear tossed about quite a bit. Savory dishes, savory tarts, savory sides. But what precisely is meant by *savory?*

It's a little hard to come up with a word that encompasses what savory is. It's not exactly a particular sensory element that can be detected on a portion of the tongue, like we saw with sweetness in Chapter Five. You wouldn't be likely to find it on the dessert menu (although, of course, in *haute cuisine,* anything's possible—wait until you see what Jean Georges pastry chef Johnny Iuzzini made for our food and wine pairing in Chapter Twenty-Two!). And yet, if someone said to you, "Oh, I had this savory potato dish with my supper last night," you would be able to hone in on the direction of flavor that this person was speaking of.

Within that arena of flavor, savory can be many things. It is … Thanksgiving stuffing accented by thyme, fennel, and sausage. It is smoked Gouda cheese on sourdough bread with a slice of chorizo. It is chicken rubbed with butter and rosemary. It is an egg, olive, fried onion, and potato frittata with fresh oregano. It is a pizza with mushrooms and meatballs! Starting to get the picture? More often than not, something with a savory quality is many things, but those influences tend to have an earthy, warm, highly seasoned quality that makes you want to stop all conversation and just eat (or, you might say, savor?).

Savory isn't just a way to describe food—it's actually an herb in its own right. There are two types of the savory herb: summer and winter. Both are sort of a flavor cross between thyme and mint (summer savory is less potent and slightly milder than its cold-season named sibling), and physically resemble a combination of the sage and basil plants. Think of it as earthiness and sunshine combined.

Turn your attention now to wine to take this flavor-explosion concept of savory one step further. When you taste, say, a Pinot Noir, you might find many influences at work: plums, chocolate, mushrooms, cherries. Quite an array of flavors. You might go so far as to call it … savory. Even within a wine itself, savory sensations exist. After all, a great winemaker is like a great chef: He or she must take nature's raw materials and turn them into something that allows each contributing item to sing on its own and yet become a whole new experience when put together. Food and drink that are savory meld their myriad flavors yet allow you to detect each of them. Maybe they aren't always each readily apparent, but as with instruments in a song, sometimes you need a few listens before you can hear what the maestro has created in all its complex glory.

This leads us, of course, to one question: How do you find a wine that can take all the components of a savory dish and bring them into perfect harmony, and vice versa? As attractive as a multi-dimensional dish or wine can be, they can also seem a little intimidating. With all those intriguing flavors at work, how does one come up with the "right" eating and imbibing combination?

## The Zen Approach to Culinary Complexities

Before the sweat begins to bead on your forehead, it's time to remind you once again of the mantra of this book: Drink what you like. As many sommeliers may tell you, sure, there are some perfect-pairing guidelines out there for you to follow, but there isn't some all-encompassing chart that they reference. They try to discern what you like, think about what food you're ordering, and then use their knowledge of wine flavors and styles to make a match that will, hopefully, only improve upon your meal.

When a dish is savory, a few particular points come into play:

- ❖ Acidity
- ❖ Knowing the general flavor qualities of your favorite wine(s)
- ❖ Balance

## Acid Test

Acid is backbone. It is structure. It's the big, strong anchorman at the end of the tug-of-war rope who prevents his teammates from landing in the mud. This is what acid does—it keeps all those carefully chosen and nurtured elements in a wine from becoming one, big, muddy mess.

Food, of course, contains acidity too, but the levels of it are a little more malleable. For instance, when you pinch a lemon quarter atop your trout, you're upping the acidity. When you add balsamic vinegar to a sauce, you're giving the final taste an acid boost. Grape jelly on your buttered toast? Acid!

When you squeeze a lemon wedge on a piece of warm grilled salmon, that lemon tames the richness of the fish and brings out and heightens the sweetness and brininess at the same time. This small amount of acid has added a nuance to the dish.

Ceviche is an example of how a lot of acid totally changes the character of the dish. A new piece of yellowtail tuna subjected to an overnight "bath" of lemon and lime basically cooks in the refrigerator. That much acid has transformed a raw piece of fat yellowtail into an explosion of flavors in your mouth. It changed the composition of the fish and added a trio of flavors: fish, lemon, and lime.

With savory foods especially, acid in wine is a star player. Without acidity, a wine can be as disillusioning and disappointing as those lovely desserts you see twirling around in a gleaming, revolving diner case: They look great, but their bland, tasteless nature is a terrible letdown.

With wine, too-low acidity makes the beverage flabby, bland, utterly uninteresting. However, with the right acidity, all the flavors and influences swirling around in your glass are allowed to do their thing. Acid makes flavors pop. It encourages a wine's influencing essences to perform their own arias, as well as mix perfectly as part of an ensemble cast.

If you remember from Chapter Five, the acidity level is greatly determined by where a grape is grown and, subsequently, when it's harvested. Warm-weather spots like Napa or Sicily have a challenge to face when getting their wines to the appropriate acidity level. The heat in these climates allows for a speedy ripening process, thus winemakers run the risk of high sugar, low acid if they don't watch their vineyards like hawks. In places like Piedmonte or Burgundy, the weather is colder longer; even in warmer weather, the mornings are chillier than in, say, Sonoma. Therefore, the acid levels remain high (and it's more of a challenge to get the sugar levels where they belong).

What does acid taste like exactly? It's more sensation than flavor. For instance, you know what it feels like to dive underwater, have a gust of springtime wind blow against your skin, shiver from the chill of a cold snap, sigh at the warmth of the sun on a hot afternoon. Can you taste these things? No, of course not; but you know what they feel like. As far as acid goes, the concept is similar. When a wine contains a low acidity, you might find yourself wanting to use words like plump, smooth, gentle, or velvety. When the acid is higher? It's tangy, biting, tingly, crisp.

It is, of course, possible to have not enough acidity or too much in a wine. What do these sensations feel like? Without enough acidity, a wine feels flabby, out of shape, muddy, and indecipherable. This might sound odd, but it's a little like sucking on a sponge (and who wants to do that?). If the acidity is too high, the fruit will be overpowered by the biting, too-tangy acid level—as will whatever you are eating with it. Too much acidity is like a dictator overruling everything that gets in his way.

With all this in mind about acidity, the question remains of what level of acidity is best with complex, savory foods.

You need enough acid in the wine to counter and complement what's in the food. For example, a ceviche drenched in lemon and lime would kill a fat, fleshy Napa Chardonnay. But a Sancerre or New

Zealand Sauvignon Blanc has the right acidity to cleanse the palate and allow you to taste the food.

A great tomato sauce needs a balanced acid-driven wine or you just won't taste the wine at all. Barbera from Piedmonte is great for such a dish because it has a rich, seductive fruit up front, but a great backbone of acid to cut through the tomatoes and spices, thus enhancing the flavor of the dish.

It wouldn't be a stretch to say that Barbera could be found more often than not on most Piedmontese dinner tables. Why? There are a few reasons. For one, the Barbera grape is naturally high in acid and therefore makes the wine dependable to that end. And in a land where highly acidic foods are the norm, a wine that can stand up to them is required. It's also the most widely planted grape in an area that produces such stunning classic wines as Barolo and Barbaresco. However, unlike the latter two that require aging to really come into their own and ease their highly tannic nature, Barbera doesn't require tons of barrel time to be ready for consumption. It is often called a rustic wine—if you pop open a bottle with a rabbit cacciatore, as we do in Chapter Thirteen with chef Don Pintabona, you'll understand why.

## Waking Up the Senses: Flavor and How to Describe It

In Chapter Four, we showed you how to become your own sommelier by upping your wine knowledge, learning how to read a wine label, and, in the end, understanding that selecting wine is just as much fun as figuring out what you'd like to eat. But learning a little about the basic qualities of wines and how to suss them out can be a great asset when dealing with complex flavors on the plate.

With savory dishes, of course, flavor is a large part of the balancing act. Understanding not only what's on your plate, but what flavor influences are in your glass is important as well.

We've talked about *terroir,* climate, and locale as factors in the final flavor of a wine. What we need to cover now is how to identify and describe these flavors.

Ann Noble, a professor of viticulture at the University of California, Davis, saw a need for clear descriptions of the aromas and flavor influences in wine. To do this, she created the Aroma Wheel. The wheel is arranged in three circular tiers: there are very general terms of description in the center, more specific terms in the middle, and the most specific terms on the outer tier.

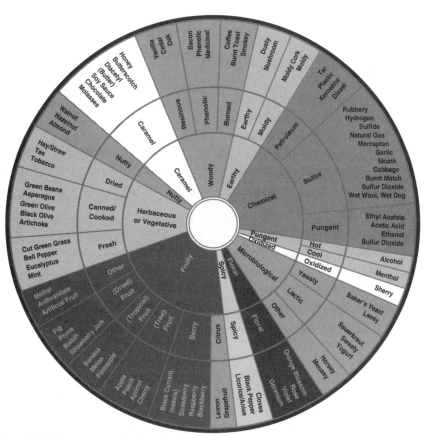

*Ann Noble's Aroma Wheel is an excellent tool to use when you can't find the words to describe the aromas of a wine. To get your own full-color, interactive Aroma Wheel, visit Professor Noble's site at wineserver.ucdavis.edu/acnoble/ waw.html#get.*

As Noble points out, these terms aren't the only way to describe wine, but are generally speaking the most frequently encountered aromas and flavor influences that one will come across when dealing with wine.

What's helpful about this is that when you learn to better describe the wines you like, you'll be able to more readily (and logically) opt for the best one for the dish in question. For instance, let's say the wine in question could unequivocally be described as fruity. Okay, that's a start. Dig a little deeper, though—what kind of fruit? Is it tropical in nature? Berrylike? Citrusy? Of an earthy dried-fruit nature? Each of these is fruity, and yet when you take it to the next level of description you've got some very different aromas. Some that might work with that rosemary-rubbed chicken, and some that might not. And then, if you go farther on Noble's Aroma Wheel, you can get even more specific. If it's berries you detect, are they strawberries or blackberries? If it's tree fruit, are you picking up cherries or apples (two very different influences)?

In addition to the Aroma Wheel, Professor Noble also created a great exercise to help wine enthusiasts better train their sense of smell for both red and white wines. Just as we performed the tasting exercise in Chapter Five to learn how the sensation of sweet can change depending on what flavor combinations you try and how to understand when flavors work together and when they don't, we'd like you to try Professor Noble's exercise to sharpen that sense memory we talked about in Chapter Four. For both versions of the test, you'll need a base wine (i.e., an inexpensive version of red and white; you could even go screw-cap jug—really!) and about 30 glasses or cups. For the wine testing, you'll need to round up the following items.

*For white wine:*

* A few drops brine from a can of asparagus
* A small piece bell pepper (don't leave in too long)
* A drop vanilla extract
* A drop or two butter extract or melted butter
* One whole clove (don't leave in too long)
* A teaspoon-plus fresh (preferably) orange and grapefruit juice mixed together
* A teaspoon-plus peach or apricot juice
* A teaspoon-plus pineapple juice
* A few tablespoons honey
* One bottle, or half-bottle, California Chardonnay for its buttery, oaky aroma and flavor

121

- One bottle, or half-bottle, Sauvignon Blanc (from Sancerre or New Zealand, preferably) for its "vegetative" aroma and flavor
- One bottle, or half-bottle, Riesling from Germany or Alsace

*For red wine:*

- A few drops brine from a can of asparagus
- A small piece bell pepper (don't leave in too long)
- A drop vanilla extract
- A drop or two butter extract or melted butter
- One whole clove (don't leave in too long)
- A few drops soy sauce
- A few drops molasses
- A spoonful mixed berry jam or some crushed, mixed fresh berries (blueberry, blackberry, raspberry, for instance)
- Two to three teaspoons strawberry jam, preferably one that's been sitting in your refrigerator for a bit.
- A few pinches artificial fruit (such as Kool-Aid or some other package-mix drink)
- A twist fresh black pepper
- A few drops anise extract (this is generally found in the spice section of any average supermarket)
- One bottle, or half-bottle, cool-weather California Central Coast, Oregon, or Burgundy Pinot Noir
- One bottle, or half-bottle, Cabernet Sauvignon
- One bottle, or half-bottle, peppery Zinfandel

Start by pouring about 2 ounces per glass of the inexpensive wine (nine glasses for the white, 11 glasses for the red). To each glass, add only one of the ingredients listed. (Be sure to give each a whiff to make sure you can smell the ingredient—if you can't readily detect it, add more to the wine; if the smell of the ingredient is too strong, add a little more wine.) Cover each glass with a piece of plastic wrap to hold in the aroma and not combine with the others in the air. Next, label each one with its predominant flavor (you can write this on small pieces of paper and tuck it underneath the glasses or even tape it to them). Finally, pour out the "real" wines (the Chardonnay, Sauvignon Blanc, Pinot Noir, et al.) into separate glasses.

Start the exercise with the white wines. First, take a whiff of one of the "real" wines. Then, smell the doctored wines. Try to find the aroma or aromas that match what you smell in the "real" wine. (Be sure to use the aroma wheel if you can't quite come up with the right term to describe what you detect, and don't forget to write down what you learned!) When you're done with the whites, move on to the reds and perform the same exercise.

It's a little involved, but this exercise is a wonderful way to learn how to differentiate between one aroma and another, as well as detect gradations of aromas and flavors within certain overarching terms, like floral, fruity, or earthy. By training your nose, you're creating a great recipe for perfect pairing.

## Balancing Act

In Chapter Seven, we talked about balance—balance on the plate, balance within a wine, and balance between what you drink and what you eat. That's a vital topic for savory flavors, too. The previous two topics we discussed here—acidity and identifying aroma and flavor— are vital components in that all-important ideal of balance.

In fact, one of the things you'll notice over and over in our "Vintage Words" chapters is that the wine that comes up the winner in the pairings is the one that strikes the best balance. With savory foods, that means allowing each flavor to sing as part of an ensemble cast— no one flavor stands out too much more than the others because the wine allows each one to be distinct and yet complementary.

Balance of flavors is especially important when trying to match a wine with a savory dish. Remember, don't overpower the dish with too big of a wine and make sure the wine stands up to the food. For instance, when we sat down to dine with Michael Lomonaco of Noche, he made us a rich and savory shepherd's pie with lamb, beef, fresh thyme, carrots, and potatoes so buttery, they were nearly the color of spring jonquils. We tried several wines with this dish: a Chianti, a Zinfandel, and—the unlikely underdog candidate—a Chardonnay. Although at first it seemed that maybe the acid and the spiciness of the Zinfandel would have the backbone to stand up to this savory dish, really all it did was compete with it like a jealous foe. What did work? Each of the other two actually held up quite well, but the Chianti, with its generous earthiness, made the meat sing. And the buttery, oaky-flavor Chardonnay did wonders for the thyme, the potatoes, and the vegetables, really giving this dish the balance it needed.

So it stands to reason that, as far as balance with savory food goes, wines like Amarone, over-oaked Shiraz, and young tannic Cabernets will add nothing. If anything, they'll only detract from the flavors because these wines don't like being part of the ensemble cast—they like to be the star. Lush, fleshy wines such as Syrah or Grenache, either from France or America, are a better choice. Northern Italian Merlots, Pinot Nero, and Lagrein are savory in themselves and would add another dimension to the dish.

Red or white, understanding that complexity warrants some thought in order to successfully weave together the flavors of your dish and your glass is the key to a successful dining and imbibing experience. Understand your flavors, know what kind of acidity you're dealing with, and use common sense to find the balance.

# chapter nine

# Vintage Words: Interview with Daniel Boulud, Restaurant Daniel

*[A meal] is really about the food and the wine—the two cannot be considered separately if they are on the table at the same time.*

*—Daniel Boulud*

The patrons nestled into the dining room of Daniel were none the wiser to our great culinary caper one particularly blustery and snowy winter night in Midtown Manhattan. While they eagerly perused menus by the warm, golden glow of the wrought-iron chandeliers, hungrily anticipating an incredible meal at one of New York's ultimate dining spots, little did they know that chef extraordinaire Daniel Boulud had been kidnapped—by us.

Okay, not *exactly* kidnapped; more like tempted into a tasting tryst.

Daniel Boulud, you might say, knows a little something about pairing flavors on a plate, and, from there, matching them to the perfect wine. Boulud grew up on the family farm in Lyon, France, smack in the middle of Burgundy and Rhône—two of France's most renowned wine-producing regions. From a young age he was surrounded by the fragrant aromas of his grandmother's cooking, as well as the wine his family made at home.

By the age of 14, he headed out to become a chef's apprentice, and the rest, as you may well know, is epicurean history. Boulud's accolades seem to know no bounds—his restaurant Daniel was recently awarded the coveted fourth star from *The New York Times* food critic William Grimes; he was named chef of the year by *Bon Appétit;* he won *Gourmet* magazine's "Top Table" award for Daniel; he has his name on three of New York's most respected eateries; and he opened a fourth in Palm Beach in the summer of 2003.

As far as wine goes, Boulud takes it very seriously. "We believe in a good wine program. The restaurant is young [10 years old]. A wine program is something you nurture. It doesn't have to do with throwing a lot of money around, but I'd say we increase the list by 10 to 15 percent each year. Although Daniel is a French restaurant, the cuisine and the wine represent New World thinking here. Because of that, I have the freedom to experiment." Experimentation, of course, is probably one of the most important things you can do in wine and food pairing. If a restaurant does not try different combinations, they won't know the best way to complement their cuisine or their wine list. It is, of course, the same for an enthusiast—if *you* don't experiment, you won't know if and why a combination works well. Boulud knows this personally and professionally.

That experimenting frequently has Boulud putting his head together with Daniel sommelier Jean Luc Le Dû. "With Jean Luc, it's a combination. Sometimes I ask what a table ordered for wine and I will skew the dish toward this [flavor]. Or sometimes he asks me what are you going to prepare and he'll pick the wine this way, especially when he's doing a pairing menu. We work very closely together."

> Daniel Boulud's second restaurant in New York, Café Boulud, was not the first with this name. The original was in Lyon, France, and belonged to his great-grandparents. In fact, in the kitchen of Daniel is a gigantic black and white photo of this progenitor to Boulud's American beginnings, in which his grandfather as a child sits at a gigantic table with other family members sharing a meal and, of course, a good bottle of wine.

*Executive chef Alex Lee during service in Boulud's pristine kitchen.*

Boulud was more than enthusiastic about our little experiment with flavor and came up with a tasting menu that would cover all the flavor sensations we've discussed in the previous chapters—sweet, savory, salty, sour, and bitter—and then sampled several different wines with each course to see why certain flavors worked, and why others didn't. (The sacrifices we make for our readers—we're practically saints!) Our friend Jimmy Rose, a playwright and wine enthusiast, joined us for our meal, and we all gathered in Boulud's "skybox"—a private room off his office that overlooks the stunning and pristine kitchen of Daniel, where we could enjoy the pairings and watch the movements of a great restaurant in action. The final result was this:

# Course I

Foie gras terrine with fennel confit, dried apricot compote, anise walnuts, and a Sauternes gelée
"Chaud-Froid" of peppered foie gras confit with port wine, endive, and pear
J.J. Prum Wehlener Sonnenuhr Spätlese, 1999
Inniskillin Icewine, 1998
Schloss Saarstein Riesling Auslese, 1997

## Course II

Tuna tartar seasoned with wasabi and crisp cucumber and radish topped with Sevruga caviar and a Meyer lemon coulis
Marinated hamachi tuna with fresh fennel bavarois, shaved fennel, pink grapefruit, and avocado
Herb crusted "Bouchot" mussels with Speck ham, parsley, and a saffron cream
Triennes Viognier, 2000
Pojer and Sandri Traminer Aromatico
Miner Family Vineyards Viognier, 2000
Exp Viognier, 2001

## Course III

Carolina shrimp with caramelized cauliflower, a curry cream, and ginger–golden apple chutney
Roasted bay scallops, crushed butternut squash with amaretto crumbs, and an almond emulsion
Domaine Girard La Garenne Sancerre, 2001
Marcel Deiss Engelgarten, 1998

## Course IV

Pan roasted codfish in a clam and smoked haddock chowder with white root vegetables and parsley
Jean Marc Brocard Chablis Grand Cru Vaudesir, 2000
Joseph Drouhin Domaine de Vaudon Chablis, 2000

## Course V

Roasted lobster with a light parsnip "mousseline" crispy lardoons, and a civet sauce
Joseph Drouhin Chambolle Musigny Premier Cru, 1999
Miner Family Vineyards Pinot Noir, Gary's Vineyard, 2000

## Course VI

Braised pork belly with lentils, seasonal root vegetables, porcini, and black truffle jus
Vietti Barbera La Crena, 1998
Turnbull Syrah, 1999

## Course I: Savory Yet Sweet Foie Gras

We began our culinary adventure with two very different kinds of foie gras. The terrine, with its layer of fennel and fruity accompaniments had a refreshing, light taste to it that was surprising for a foie gras. The foie gras confit took on a more traditional role, its rich, fatty flavor enhanced by the port wine reduction but softened slightly with the gentle additions of endive and pear. Both dishes contained a sweetness (one from fennel and one from fruit and port); however, each was very different—quite a challenge for wine and food pairing. Four wine glasses were set in front of each of us. The first contained J.J. Prum Wehlener Sonnenuhr, Spatlese, 1999 (a Riesling); the second an Auslese from Le Sloc Paulilles, Banyuls, 1998; the third a rich 1998 Inniskillin Icewine from Canada; and the final selection a 1997 Schloss Saarstein, Riesling Auslese. Each of these selections fell to the sweeter, fruitier side of wine, but some (like the icewine, for instance) are obviously much sweeter than others.

**Tony DiDio:** First of all, thank you, Daniel.

**Amy Zavatto:** Yes, thank you!

*[glasses clinking in toast]*

**Daniel Boulud:** Thank you so much. Best wishes for this New Year.

**Jimmy Rose:** It's a wonderful way to start.

**Tony:** I think the way to do it is everyone taste on their own.

**Daniel:** *Voilà.*

**Amy** and **Tony:** *Buon anno.*

**Daniel:** The foie gras terrine with the first wine is wonderful, eh?

**Tony:** That's the J.J. We've got two Rieslings. This one's a Spätlese from J.J. Prum. And the second is an Auslese, so a little bit higher sugar content. Picked a little bit later. I think for the foie gras confit I would go for the Banyuls. For the terrine, the J.J. Prum. To me, for that terrine, the J.J. Prum has a great acidity and works very well with that. Acid is the friend of both wine and food. This rich terrine needs a wine with acid to cut through the fat, wash the palate, and taste both wine and food. A fat or flabby wine without a significant amount of acid would fall flat.

**Daniel:** Yeah, [the J.J. Prum Riesling] has almost an almondy smell. It has a very sweet nuance, but very floral also. But the foie gras with confit and the gelée of port wine and pepper, that definitely goes with the icewine.

**Tony:** Well, you know, I think the Spätlese is more the match, but the Auslese brings out a lot of fruit and depth in the foie gras. Both of them I think are working very well.

**Daniel:** The Spätlese is the right one.

**Tony:** I think that it's more elegant and more balanced. But Auslese is just by nature a little fatter, but it does bring out that fruit …

**Daniel:** … in the foie gras!

**Amy:** I like the Spätlese with the terrine. The acids are great.

**Jimmy:** When you put endive with the foie gras confit, my wine matches change. The sharpness changes which wines I like better. I like the Banyuls with the port wine foie gras, but when I had it with the endive, the icewine was better because it matched the sharpness added by the endive.

> With icewine, harvest occurs at the pinnacle of winter. The best grapes are naturally frozen on the vine and hand picked. During the pressing, the water remains as ice crystals, which are easily extracted from the juice. What remains are a few precious drops of a sweet liquid, which are the foundation of this intriguing wine.

**Daniel:** Me, too! I have a little cabbage oil on it, it gives that line of flavor behind on the endive, the smoky, cabbage-y, black-seed oil, that's why with the Banyuls it's wonderful because it really cut it up [the full, rich taste of the foie gras].

**Jimmy:** With the fennel terrine, I agree with you when you talk about the Alsatian wines, the acidity, they're just so elegant and crisp, kind of like how the flavor of the fennel is so clean. These wines match it—the cleanliness of the flavors.

**Tony:** It's not bad for a Canadian wine, huh?

**Daniel:** It's very good. Another problem with the foie gras, for example, is the sweetness is not totally smooth. Like the Sauternes, for example, you really have a perfect balance. Too sweet of a wine with a foie gras is not always the right match.

**Amy:** But I like the icewine because it brings out the rich flavor of it even more. It's oddly complementary.

**Daniel:** Exactly, very much. Perfect!

**Jimmy:** It really contents your tongue because it's so rich and the texture is so smooth.

**Tony:** I'm going to try it later with cheese, but I think icewine is the better match for the port reduction foie gras. Jimmy is making the extreme sacrifice by the way because he's a …

**Daniel:** He's a vegetarian! I know.

**Jimmy:** Yeah, but I ate the foie gras. In the presence of the king, you must eat!

**Daniel:** The prince obeyed!

## Course II: Pucker Up

For our second course, Daniel went to the sour end of things by adding citrus fruits into the mix. Tuna tartar delicately seasoned with tangy wasabi and crisp, paper-thin cucumber and radish slices topped with Sevruga caviar was given a faintly tart influence of a Meyer lemon coulis, while the marinated hamachi tuna with fresh fennel *bavarois*, shaved fennel, and avocado puckered up with a delicate slice of pink grapefruit. Where did we look for the proper wine pairing? France, Italy, and California, of course: France's Triennes, Viognier, 2000; Pojer and Sandri, Traminer Aromatico from Italy, 2001; and California's Miner Family Vineyard, Viognier, 2000.

**Tony:** We're going from right to left. The Triennes Viognier, the Traminer, the French Viognier, and the American Viognier. I was telling Daniel this morning that the Pojer and Sandri Traminer is harvested at about 2,000 feet up.

**Jimmy:** Wow! Now that is a food white wine. High acidity.

When Jimmy mentioned that the Viognier was a "food white wine," he was talking about the backbone of acidity a wine made in a cooler environment would be likely to have. If you remember from Chapter Seven, we talked about acidity and how acid with acid is a great combination. The dishes Daniel made for us here contained acid from the Meyer lemon and the grapefruit, and therefore needed to be paired with a wine with greater acidity.

**Amy:** Look at the color of the Triennes Viognier as compared to the others. It's almost a little green.

**Jimmy:** Lots of citrus.

**Amy:** Exactly! I think we're on to something here.

**Jimmy:** You're also getting not so much citrus fruit as citrus blossom, there's more of a floral citrusy flavor here. Have you ever smelled a lemon blossom? It's quite a perfume.

**Tony:** Is that wasabi?

**Daniel:** Yeah, but not as spicy as Nobu! I can't kill the caviar with a wasabi, so it's just underneath. … I'm ashamed to say but the Italian wine is very good.

**Amy and Tony:** Hey!

**Amy:** Those are fightin' words, Daniel! You've got a Paisano and Paisana here.

**Tony:** Were you being defensive about the French wine or the American wine? *[laughter]* I know what you mean, though. First of all, I love the nose; it's nice and floral. That's what's working with the cucumber and radish, as well as the Meyer lemon.

**Daniel:** Absolutely. It's really charming, it's really sexy, it's very flattering, this wine.

**Tony:** Jimmy, start with the nose here. The nose gives you a hint of what you're going to taste in this glass. You've got a lot of flower, and there's a zest right in the nose.

**Jimmy:** The wine in the center, the French, I'm getting not so much a licorice, but an anise flavor. Also some light herbal qualities.

**Daniel:** With the fennel used with the hamachi tuna, it's very nice. With the Meyer lemon, the Traminer is wonderful.

**Tony:** You know what, that wine [in the center] is not doing anything for me.

**Daniel:** Exactly, I'm sure it's very drinkable and refreshing as a drinking wine, but married with food it lacks focus.

**Tony:** How does everybody feel with the Miner family Viognier, the last wine, with the tuna tartar with the caviar and the Meyer lemon?

**Amy:** That's the match that gets me.

**Daniel:** It's California style—there's a lot of fruit inside. Miner is not a 100 percent Viognier, no?

**Tony:** Actually, it's 96 percent Viognier and 4 percent Chardonnay.

**Daniel:** It's a blend, uh? It gives it more character.

**Amy:** It is really close to a Chardonnay flavor. Very full—it almost allows the flavors of the fish and caviar and the lemon to float on their own so you really experience them.

**Daniel:** You don't have the nose as much of the Viognier on the Miner.

**Tony:** You get a very ripe, rich wine.

**Jimmy:** I'm getting a lot of peach.

**Daniel:** Viognier is known for having that. Peach is a flavor that we attribute to that.

**Jimmy:** The second Riesling, the 1997 Auslese—smell that and then smell the Miner Viognier. They're very similar.

**Daniel:** That's the sugar! Now, we're going to keep the same wines to see if they work with a savory dish, the mussels and saffron.

**Jimmy:** The Miner Viognier, I see it going with a toasted grain, like a barley. It needs something a little more earthy.

**Daniel:** Yeah, exactly. This wine has a much more bright and crisp flavor.

**Whole table after tasting the mussels:** *Mmmmmm!!!*

**Daniel:** So this is mussel soup. We talk about sweet spice a little bit, like fragrant sweet, rich, a little bit golden, and yet a little briny from the mussels. Now the last Viognier is the surest, versus the other one, which would distort the food.

**Jimmy:** Chef, this is wonderful.

**Amy:** Yeah, I kind of forgot there was wine on the table!

**Tony:** What do people like for the wine?

**Jimmy:** The Miner.

**Daniel:** The Miner, I feel. Taste it with the toastiness of the crumbs, it has a little garlic inside, it's not floral, it's briny and it's a little grassy, and with the saffron gives sort of this richer finish.

**Tony:** It comes together like a bouillabaisse.

**Daniel:** Yes. So you want something a little dry, a little less floral.

**Jimmy:** Is there oak in the Viognier?

**Tony:** Yes, probably.

**Jimmy:** I think that's a big difference.

**Tony:** In the Traminer there's none. That makes it friendlier and easier to drink here.

> Does the word *Traminer* sound familiar? That's because you've heard it before—as part of *Gewürztraminer*. Traminer is a town in Alto Adige, Italy, that at one time was part of Austria—where they first raised the grape.

**Jimmy:** And the oak in the Miner (Viognier) helps cut through the saffron cream, I think.

**Daniel:** So what is the verdict?

**Amy:** Both of these feel too sharp for me. The Traminer and the Triennes Viognier.

**Jimmy:** Well, I think the Italian one is sharp because of its high acid. I'm sure it's cold up there.

**Tony:** Oh, it's very cold up there.

**Jimmy:** So it's not as ripe.

**Daniel:** This is an example of the food overpowering the wine. Whereas sometimes the wine sort of matches or overpowers the food.

**Jimmy:** I am still thinking that the Miner family, though, does have some attributes that go really well with this dish.

**Daniel:** At the beginning more, but now that I'm finished I still feel that overmaturity from the wine. The Miner is a little overripe.

**Tony:** I think the best match is the French Viognier.

**Daniel:** Thank you! Thanks to the French! It was more acidic, though, and a little better for the mussels with the sweet and briny flavors of the dish.

## Course III: Sweets from the Sea

Fish has to be one of the most misunderstood edibles ever to grace a table. And as you'll see in Chapter Eleven when we interview Rick Moonen of RM, it's much more versatile than most diners realize when it comes to flavors and pairing them with wine. What Daniel wanted to emphasize with this particular course was sweetness—the sweetness of the fish, and the sweetness of the accoutrement ingredients that went along with it. Not to mention what wine would match such a thing? We were presented with the challenge of roasted bay scallops.

The distinction of bay and sea scallops is one worth noting. Sea scallops have a much larger, disclike shape and have a hint of sweetness in the meat. Bay scallops, however, are very small, tater-tot shaped, and much sweeter than their larger sibling of the sea. Bay scallops are not always that easy to find and it wouldn't be a stretch to say it's rare to see them on a menu. Many of the areas that were once bursting with bay scallops have fallen on hard times because of strange phenomena in the waters, like the brown tide in Eastern Long Island. Amy, who grew up in Shelter Island, New York, remembers when she was young how on the first day of scallop season much of the school would be absent, as they were all out in the bay harvesting the small mollusks.

**Daniel:** There's a little bit porcini, almonds, Amaretto, and almond cream with the butternut purée. … I don't think the Sancerre is matching the food too well.

**Tony:** It's a bit austere. I thought it would be a little fatter with a little more fruit. I think we went to the Gewürz more for the flavor.

**Daniel:** It's funny how those wines are very good also with very simple food; it cannot be too complex.

**Tony:** There are actually three grapes in the Engelgarten. It's 70 percent Riesling, but there's also Pinot Gris and Pinot Auxerois. You know what? Let it warm up a little, and then go back to the scallop dish.

**Amy:** It's almost right, but it's not quite right with the sweetness of the scallops. I had an impulse to go back to the icewine because I wanted something to bring out the sweetness of the fish, but the icewine, in this case, is too thick, too sweet for the dish. There's no balance.

**Tony:** I like the Miner family Viognier with the scallops. It's the food that changes the wine in this case, but the wine, I think, undercuts all that sweetness. It's the sweetness in the dish that brings out the fruit of the wine. It's interesting how it changes. Actually, I think it would be perfect for the shrimp. The Sancerre, though—it's a great Sancerre, but it's too austere. … The Deiss wine [Engelgarten] has great acidity to it, akin almost to a German Riesling. There's Riesling in here, but you smell this wine and you're thinking more of Germany than you are of Alsace. Alsace wines are little bit fatter. This wine to me is really what's bringing out and taming the myriad of sweet flavors in this dish—the scallops, the squash, the amaretto. And the dish taking out the sweetness of the wine.

**Daniel:** I don't know, maybe it's because the sugar carries; the scallop is already naturally sweet, plus the squash. I was afraid the dish was too sweet for the wine.

**Tony:** For me, the sweetness in the dish brought out the fruitiness in the wine. Drinking the wine by itself, it's almost austere. It's got a low sugar content. But drinking it, I thought it tamed the sweetness in that dish and I just thought it was a nice match. It opened up after a while, also.

**Daniel:** But it's typical of Alsatian wines.

**Tony:** I find that Alsace wines are really richer and bigger than their German counterparts just from the terroir.

**Jimmy:** It seems that there's a curve or an arc where the levels in the wine and food are synthesizing and they match and are doing well together, but then all of a sudden you hit a point where the complexities are too complex for each other, and now you need simple and complex. They break off and one has to be more simple.

**Amy:** Although the interesting thing when I go back to the Traminer from the last course and taste these scallops with that, they became closer and more in sync with their individual flavors when you tasted them together. When you taste them separately, they seem extraordinarily different, but once you put them together, you taste all that fruit in the wine. And the sweetness of the butternut squash takes a slight bow and isn't too sweet anymore. It's perfect.

**Jimmy:** But imagine if you had a 1995 Grand Cru Chardonnay from Burgundy with that squash and scallop dish. It's complex and complex— it would be too much! You've got that sweet lily flavor, and the caramel and vanilla, and thickness, and then you've got the sweetness of the bay scallops and the squash and it's like, yikes! The exception to this rule right now, though, would be the foie gras confit and the Inniskillin from our first course, because those are extremely complex, but simple in their complexity. They're both so rich.

## Course IV: Smoke Gets in Your Wine

Our fourth course was an interesting exercise. At first glance, we thought, "Okay, we've got briny and smoky flavors here—a Chablis with its mineral qualities is the answer!" But … which Chablis?

**Daniel:** Basically, this dish is a little smoky and briny.

**Jimmy:** The Chablis we have here combined with the smokiness of the chowder tastes like an oyster.

**Daniel:** Absolument! Careful, when you drink Chablis you get emotional! *[laughter]*

**Jimmy:** The fruit in the Chablis—and I never think about Chablis as being anything except full of mineral—the fruit comes out. The smokiness draws the fruit out.

**Tony:** But this is exactly what we talked about in the last dish, that the food drew something out of the wine. And sometimes the wine draws something out of the food. That's the fun part about food and wine pairing.

**Jimmy:** It's like synthesis. You're synthesizing two things, and there's a whole new flavor invented that is not in either the food or the wine, but together they create it.

**Daniel:** The Brocard Grand Cru, that's nice with this.

**Tony:** In their cellar, they have a wall that's exposed and it's all chalk. You can go in and take out fossilized scallop shells and mussel shells. That's what you're getting in that nose. The mineral and terroir, which is all chalk. In Germany, it's that slate taste, but here it's the chalkiness, which is a different kind of mineral.

**Daniel:** Yes, it's much more refined.

**Tony:** I think this is the wine—the Grand Cru. It's the best pair so far.

**Daniel:** Yes, I agree. It adds depth. The thing about these two Chablis is that one is a little more greenish, a little more young. Less ripe. Even though they're both 2001, one feels younger.

**Tony:** There are different levels in Chablis, which is why this is interesting to me. The highest level is the Grand Cru, it's the best vineyard site.

When we talk about Chablis, we are talking about the white wines produced there. Aligote, a lesser white wine, is produced there, but the predominant grape is Chardonnay. There are seven Grand Cru vineyard sites located in Chablis. These are considered the finest wines produced from the greatest vineyards in all of Chablis. Oh, and by the way, not only do the Grand Crus produce the finest wines, they are also the most expensive.

**Jimmy:** So let me ask you, as a professional in this industry, do you think that people should be worried about drinking Chablis that aren't Grand Cru status?

**Tony:** No, no, no! It all depends on what you're eating. This was a pretty intense dish. It had a lot of flavors going on. And this [the Drouhin Chablis] is a great wine with just a simple oyster dish. An oyster stew, or pan-fried oysters. Certainly, to me anyway—and I know this might be a bit of a controversial opinion—you wouldn't have oysters and have a Premier Cru or a Grand Cru. It's too rich, it's too developed. It would overpower the oyster. Drouhin Chablis is probably the better wine with a plain oyster. The Grand Cru has too much going for it; even an oyster would change its flavor. It's too many levels of intensity and is too complex for a simple oyster dish.

**Amy:** The smoke in the chowder gives a backbone to this dish that can stand up to the mineral quality of the Grand Cru Chablis. People think of fish as being such a delicate thing, but really the most important thing you need to look at when pairing a wine with a fish is how it's prepared. Of course, that will completely change what you drink.

**Jimmy:** You have levels. Like you were saying before, Amy. Thyme adds a level, and cheese adds a level, or smokiness adds a level. So you have all these levels, so should you always be matching levels, or do you option out and say I'll have this one-dimensional wine with this 10-dimensional dish?

**Amy:** Well, I think that's what we're learning here. You can't ever really make up a hard and fast rule that completely sticks, although there are some basic rules you can use as general guidelines. Really, what it boils down to is what you like.

**Tony:** You can say the best wine with raw oysters is Chablis. Okay, that's a great wine with this pairing. But then you get into *what* Chablis. I would say a Sancerre like the one we had [Domaine Bailly Reverdy] is also an oyster wine, and the Vaudon Chablis is also an oyster wine. There was a lot of taste going on in the chowder dish, though, so in this case the Grand Cru stood up to it. But you also have to look at the difference of about $30 a bottle!

## Course V: Savor the Noir

Lobster is the pick, so what do you say? White? Ah, we would say think again. In this case the lobster is surrounded by rich, savory flavors: crispy pancetta, whipped, creamy parsnip, and a beef broth, of all things! So now what do you do? We say Noir's the word …

**Jimmy:** Pinot Noirs are known for their fruit.

**Tony:** These are three wines made from the same grapes.

**Amy:** The third one, the Meerlust Pinot Noir from South Africa, it's got this brownish color to it …

**Tony:** That's what happens with age. Remember, this is a 1993 Pinot Noir. You look at the edge and you see the brownness there. That's from the wine getting oxidized. Sometimes even the cork shrinks a little.

**Amy:** When I first smelled this it was very pleasing, all I could smell was caramel. But the more I smell it, the more I can detect other things going on that aren't so pleasing. It's almost taking on a burnt oil odor.

**Jimmy:** It tastes like tea, like wood.

**Amy:** Yes! It tastes like nasty old tea! The smell is almost pleasing, but when you taste it, there's no fruit, there's no complexity anymore.

**Tony:** Okay, let's rinse out and concentrate on the other two. With Pinots, not everyone understands when I say this because Pinots also tend to be very mushroomy, very earthy. But I always get a distinct smell of mustard. Dijon mustard.

**Amy:** I think I understand. It's mustard seed. Have you ever cooked Indian food at home? When you add mustard seed it completely changes the flavor of the curry and the other spices because it's sweet and savory at once.

**Jimmy:** You've also got cherry, but there's a distinction in red wines of red fruit, black fruit, and stone fruit. So you have in this wine, in Pinot Noir, red fruits. Cherries, raspberries, but occasionally you'll get a black fruit, like blackberries or plums. Or even stewed fruits, like prune. What's interesting here is we're getting to taste Old World Pinot [Drouhin Chambolle Musigny 1999 Premier Cru] versus New World [Miner Family Vineyards Pinot Noir, "Gary's Vineyard," 2000]. You get earth in the Old World.

**Amy:** When I smell them, they smell identical. But when you taste them, the California has this sharp, clean flavor, almost like a white. It's a little assaulting. The French feels fuller when I taste it. More elegant.

**Tony:** But for the dish, I like the Miner.

**Amy:** The sharp taste I was describing before in the Miner, I think because the beef broth is so rich, and the lobster is sweet, that sharp taste of the wine dissipated and complemented the sweetness of the fish and drew it out.

**Tony:** The Chambolle is young and is going to develop into a beautiful wine but for right now, by the nature of the beast, the Miner is the right pick. California almost always has perfect weather and it's always sunny, so wines tend to be picked at higher sugar levels than the French wines. Burgundy is a very troubled spot come late August and September when they start with the thunderstorms. It's a much cooler climate. That's why the Chambolle will age well because of the natural acidity that's there, whereas the American wines are a little more fruit-forward to start.

**Amy:** I love the French Pinot on its own. If I were just drinking it without a meal, that would be great, very satisfying. But when you add in this very rich dish, the air goes out of it. All of the nice, full qualities that it has on its own are overpowered by the food.

**Tony:** See how much more exciting wine becomes when you're eating?
**Daniel:** The difference between Burgundy and California is that the Burgundians put their dirty socks in it and the Californians put their clean socks in it! That Miner is very flattering for this dish with the parsnips and the pancetta.

## Course VI: Salt of the Earth

And how should you approach the conundrum of salty? After all, salt is a very, well … assaulting (forgive the pun!) flavor. It takes center stage before the rest of the flavors in a dish are allowed to make their debut. For this final course, Boulud challenged us with a braised pork belly surrounded by root vegetables and drizzled in a porcini and black truffle jus. What to drink? We made two very interesting choices: a hearty Italian Vietti Barbera "La Crena" from 1998, and a 1999 spicy, earthy Turnbull Syrah from groovy California.

*Amy and Daniel take a break before Course VI.*

**Tony:** Okay, we've got Old World, New World. You can't get older than Barbera. And then we've got a California Syrah from Turnbull in Napa Valley.

**Daniel:** So basically, this pork is cured, then it's poached, then it's braised. And so with the fat and the salt and curing, it's got a rustic flavor, but that's why you need a rustic wine as well in this case.

*The braised pork belly with lentils, seasonal root vegetables, porcini, and black truffle jus awaits the perfect wine pairing.*

Barbera is the workhorse grape of Piedmonte. This is the land of Barola, Barbaresco, and truffles—all-things-expensive. Barbera is what you would drink for lunch and dinner at home or in a trattoria. It is a fleshy wine with great natural acidity, which makes it a perfect wine for the table. Were Tony marooned on a desert island and had to choose which Italian grapes to have for the duration of his stay, they would be Sangiovese and Barbera, hands down. Bring on the pasta!

**Tony:** Barbera is really on the edge of a rustic wine, it's a bit wild in the glass, and is made better once you begin to eat some food with it. Some winemakers try to tame the grape with oak aging, but I don't agree that this is necessary.

**Daniel:** But it's a little like Rhône, it has those characteristics of a Rhône wine. I like both wines. For sure the California Syrah has much more concentration of fruit and oak. The Barbera is a lovely wine. I would drink more from the Barbera as it's a more friendly wine. I would enjoy drinking the Syrah in a small dose because it's too powerful. I don't know that I'd enjoy drinking a whole bottle. I would go for the Barbera for this reason.

**Amy:** I like the aroma of the Barbera.

**Tony:** The Barbera has a lot of acid, and that was cutting through all the salt and the fat. So for me, this was the one.

**Daniel:** I like them both, but again, as I was saying, I would enjoy a full bottle of Barbera and not a full bottle of Syrah. You know there's a balance. The California Syrah drinks well, but the Barbera with the food does better.

**Tony:** So again, we see that bringing them together changes the complexity, changes the makeup of the wine *and* the food. Usually for the better if it's a good match.

*Tony, Daniel, and Amy after a job well tasted.*

**Amy:** I felt like the food changed the Syrah more than it did the Barbera, but almost similar to what Daniel was saying, I feel like I would want to drink the Barbera throughout the meal. At first I was confused at which I liked more, but the Syrah has certain complexities in it that make me feel like I need to stop and think really hard about the flavors, to the point where I can't think about it anymore. The Barbera allows me to be lazy, which when you're eating comforting food like this dish, that's what you want. To be lazy and enjoy!

# Try It for Yourself

Being the very generous soul that he is, Daniel Boulud slipped us the recipe for delicious mussel soup he made for our food and wine pairing. Why not re-create a piece of our tasting by making it yourself and getting your hands on the wines we tried, or a few reasonable facsimiles? The soup is easier to prepare than you'd expect and can be made in stages if time doesn't permit you to make it in a one-shot deal. The biggest surprise is the mussels can be cooked a day ahead, as can the velouté (in fact, the latter can be simmered, puréed, sieved, and frozen up to a month in advance). It's even recommended that the gratin crust chill, so you can toss it in the fridge while you go out to your local wine store to pick up the necessary pairing beverages.

## Mussels

1 TB. unsalted butter

3 medium shallots, peeled and thinly sliced, rinsed and dried

2 lb. mussels, well scrubbed

1½ cups dry white wine

Freshly ground pepper

Melt butter in a Dutch oven or large casserole over medium heat. Add shallots and cook, stirring until they turn translucent, about 5 minutes. Turn heat to high and add mussels, wine, and pepper. Cover and cook, stirring a few times, until mussels open, about 3 or 4 minutes. While you're waiting for the mussels to cook, place a cheesecloth-lined sieve over a large bowl. When all mussels have opened, turn them and their liquid into the sieve. Set aside mussels and broth separately.

Remove meat from shells when mussels cool off; toss out shells. Cover mussels, or refrigerate them if you aren't making soup until later on. There should be about 8 cups liquid.

## Mussel Soup

2 TB. unsalted butter

2 TB. extra-virgin olive oil

2 medium onions, peeled and thinly sliced

1 fennel bulb, trimmed and thinly sliced

2 stalks celery, peeled, trimmed and thinly sliced

1 medium leek, white and light green parts only, thinly sliced, rinsed and dried (see Rick Moonen's recipe in Chapter Eleven for directions on cleaning leeks)

1 large carrot, peeled, trimmed and thinly sliced

1 large Idaho potato, peeled and cut into small pieces

Large pinch saffron

Sachet (1 tsp. each fennel seeds, coriander seeds, and white peppercorns, 1 bay leaf, 2 sprigs thyme, and 4 sprigs Italian parsley tied in cheesecloth)

1 cup heavy cream

8 cups mussel liquid (from above)

4 cups unsalted chicken stock or store-bought low-sodium chicken broth

Salt and freshly ground white pepper

Heat butter and olive oil in a large pot over medium-high heat. Stir in onions and cook just until they turn translucent, about 5 to 7 minutes. Add fennel, celery, leek, carrot, and potato, and cook until tender (15 to 20 minutes). Add saffron, sachet, heavy cream, mussel liquid, and chicken stock. Season with salt and pepper. Once this is boiling, reduce to a simmer, skimming regularly, for 20 minutes until vegetables are tender.

Working in batches, purée soup in a blender. Push purée through a fine-mesh sieve. Add salt and pepper to taste. Bring to a boil before serving. If you're preparing ahead of time, the soup can be kept covered and refrigerated for up to 4 days or frozen for 1 month.

## Parsley Garlic Crust

¾ cup fresh breadcrumbs

1 stick plus 2 TB. unsalted butter, softened

2 TB. finely chopped Italian parsley leaves

4 cloves garlic, peeled and finely chopped

1 TB. finely chopped toasted almonds

1 TB. finely chopped speck ham

Salt and freshly ground white pepper

Mix together breadcrumbs, butter, parsley, garlic, almonds, ham, salt, and pepper and roll out between 2 pieces of parchment paper until crust is 4 inches square and between ⅛ and ¼ inch thick. Freeze packet for at least 30 minutes, then cut the rest into 4 squares; chill until needed.

Preheat the broiler and butter 4 shallow gratin dishes. Using a 2-inch baking ring as a guide, construct each gratin by filling the ring with mussels. Remove the ring and top mussels with a square of crust. Broil gratins—keeping a close eye on them—until the tops are golden brown, about 2 to 4 minutes.

When you're ready to serve the soup, bring it to a boil. Lift each gratin out of its dish into the center of a warm soup bowl, ladle hot soup around mussels, and serve immediately.

Makes 4 servings.

# *part three*

# Pairing a Stellar Wine
# with a Great Meal

# chapter ten

# Pairing Wine with Fish

*Certain scholars, and they none too orthodox, have argued that the ocean was the cradle of everything that exists; that mankind itself was born in the sea ...*

*—Jean Anthelme Brillat-Savarin,* The Physiology of Taste

Fish is woefully misunderstood. To many, grappling with how to handle it on the dinner table is as difficult as grabbing a fish in a lake—it slips through your fingers entirely.

- ❖ **Myth number 1:** Fish is boring. If you've never sunk your choppers into a thick, pan-seared, rosemary and kosher salt-encrusted piece of Chilean sea bass or a luscious, sweet, jewel-like bay scallop, you have no idea what a delicious world you're missing.

- ❖ **Myth number 2:** Fish is austere stuff; i.e., it's for diets or religious observances. Having both grown up Catholic, Amy and Tony know all about the fish-on-Friday rule during Lent. And yes, fish is extremely good for you because it's generally low in fat, and it contains omega-3 polyunsaturated fatty acids, which have proven to be most excellent for your physical well-being. But healthy is not boring—far from it.

- ❖ **Myth number 3:** Fish and white wine are the only way to go—red is always a no-no. This is where things are going to get interesting.

The choices you have among the creatures that dwell in the swimmy seas are as vast and deep as the waters themselves. There are tough-shelled crustaceans whose meat is Mother Nature's sweet reward for the difficult task of extracting it. There's the briny taste of moderately fatty, dense-but-tender-textured tuna, of which there are numerous varieties. There's the flavorful, fragile flatfish sole, whose delicate grayish, brownish flesh is as refreshing and delicate as a sea spray.

Much of the fish labeled as sole in the United States is actually of the plaice family, to which flounder also belongs, and not sole at all (for example, lemon sole). True sole is not found in the former Motown offices of Barry Gordy (okay, bad joke), but in European waters. One of the most popular varieties, Dover, is found in the British Straits of Dover, as well as the waters off the coast of Denmark and the Mediterranean Sea.

There are freshwater fish, there are saltwater fish, there are fish that live in salt water and spawn in fresh water (salmon), and fish that live in fresh water but spawn in salt water (eel). There are fish that dwell at the bottom, crustaceans that cling to rocks, and larger swimmers who'll take your arm off if you get too close. So it stands to reason that with all of these varieties, there are a lot of choices as to how to cook them (baked with a little lemon, grilled on a smoky pit, stuffed, sauced, et al.), which of course can influence what you drink with your seafood of choice.

## Red or White?

True, it's absolutely a good idea to match the "weight" of your wine with the "weight" of your food. What does this mean? Be as logical in your pairing as you would with anything else. Would you wear a down parka in the middle of August? No. Assuming you're not a member of the Polar Bear Club, would you traipse through wintery snowdrifts in flip-flops and shorts? Absolutely not. Would you think it fitting to pair a delicate, crisp Italian Pinot Grigio with foie-gras laden beef Wellington? Not likely.

This is where the "white with fish" rule stems from. The bright, crisp, clean-on-the-palate taste of many unoaked whites has made them the pin-up wine for delicate, simply prepared, extremely fresh fish (and, in many cases, fowl as well—we'll talk about that in Chapter Twelve). But the red-or-white question actually depends on a couple of things:

1. What's the texture of the fish?
2. How is the fish prepared?

As we briefly outlined, not all fish is created alike. It is true that, in general, fish is incredibly low in fat. This is because, in comparison to meat, fish has a much higher ratio of muscle versus connective tissue (muscle, if you were unaware, being the meat of the matter). This abundance of muscle is also what makes the fish tender and the reason it cooks so much faster than beef, fowl, game, pork, or lamb. Some fish are heartier than others, as well. Think about a slab of salmon or tuna or sea bass in comparison to a filet of flounder or tilapia or halibut. What about the sweet, hearty nature of lobster meat in comparison to the delicacy of a scallop? When you start to think about seafood in these terms as opposed to lumping it all into the same category, selecting a wine becomes an easier if not more organic decision.

As for the second point above, how the fish is prepared can be the deciding factor in what you choose to drink. Let's take oysters as an example. Oysters are usually paired with Chablis. This classic duo works so well because the mineral qualities in the wine play upon the mineral qualities inherent in the taste of the mollusk. Now, take that same oyster and throw in some parmesan, spinach, bread crumbs, garlic, and maybe a little hot pepper, and your oysters Rockefeller might take more kindly to a wine that can stand up to the bitter nature of the spinach, the nutty, salty influence of the parmesan, and the slight kick of the hot pepper. Maybe what you really want in that case is a fruit-forward Pinot Noir or Italian Merlot. They have the tannins to hang tough with the spinach, but are lower in them than other reds so as to not leave you with a bitter taste from the spinach or from the hot pepper. The earthiness of a Pinot Noir also goes well with parmesan cheese, but both wines cut through the saltiness of the cheese and brine of the oyster so that all the flavors get a chance to mingle.

This example is also a great case for matching levels or weight of food. This concept shouldn't cause you great distress—in fact, it's one of the best guidelines for wine and food pairing across the board. Let's go back to our example of oysters: Oysters on the half-shell are just pure, light, naked seafood (okay, maybe there's some lemon or cocktail sauce involved, but you get the meaning); oysters Rockefeller are rich, layered, and multi-faceted in the flavor sensations you experience. In this case, the "weight" of the food changed with the ingredients, so it's the ingredients and manner in which the water-dwelling creature is cooked that can make all the difference. Now, if you take that same naked oyster and compare it to a plain, unadorned grilled New York strip steak, which food do you think has the greater weight? The steak, of course. By now you should understand that when we say "weight" we're not talking pounds—we're talking about richness, texture, and fat content. The food and wine pairing result is, obviously, a lighter-bodied wine with the oysters (like a Chablis) and heavier-bodied wine with the steak (a Cabernet Sauvignon, or even a buttery Chardonnay if that's more to your liking).

The richness of oysters Rockefeller is what gave them their name. The dish originated at Antoine's, the lovely New Orleans restaurant that's been packing 'em in for more than 160 years. In 1899, Jules Alciatore, son of the original Antoine, made up the recipe and decided that his creation was so rich it should be aptly named—hence, the borrowing of the surname of the richest man in America at the time, John D. Rockefeller. While there are numerous interpretations of this dish, the actual recipe remains a family secret of Antoine's.

Of course, it's impossible to cover each and every manner of cooking and adorning fish in this chapter. However, what we are going to do is give you a basic guide to general methods of preparation and steer you in the direction of the wines that will likely pair well.

## Sauced and Brothed

Sauces and broths with fish can be the deciding factor in determining what you choose to drink. Is the sauce or broth creamy? Clear? Influenced by other ingredients, like herbs, potato chunks, bacon, shallots? Each of these is a deciding factor in selecting a wine.

❖ When fish is served with a creamy sauce or broth, there are a couple different directions that we both like. You want something with high acidity that cuts through the cream. Riesling, rosé, or Sauvignon Blanc all have the acidic backbone to handle a creamy sauce, plus the fruit to bring out the sweetness of the cream and the seafood. On the other hand, Chardonnay works well also, but we recommend going with a French Chablis. The acidity, creaminess, and mineral qualities of the wine reflect these same qualities in a creamy seafood dish and really allow the flavors in both to sing. Also, Chablis is not oaked, which would overpower a dish like this.

❖ Clear. When we say clear, we don't mean transparent, of course—just not creamy. So let's say you've got a craving for Manhattan clam chowder. Tony had just that recently at the Manhattan's famous Oyster Bar in Grand Central Station, and he found that rosé was the way to go because the acidity of the rosé cut through the cream. The fruitiness of the wine paired well with the sweetness of the cream and the seafood.

## Grilled, Seared, and Otherwise Seasoned

Because these methods are generally left to more substantial fish that aren't going to flake off into a million little pieces when they hit the hot irons of the grill, you're likely to be dealing with heartier fish fare if you're using this cooking method. Now is the time for an oaky California Chardonnay. Grill that salmon, swordfish, or halibut and go directly to Napa. The acidity can handle the fat of the fish, and the creamy, buttery texture and flavor work really well with grilled, smoky flavors. If you want to go in a totally different direction, though, go for a low-tannin Merlot or Beaujolais. The tannins and acid can handle the fat, and the fruitiness is a great complement to the sweet nature of the fish.

# Fried

Health concerns aside, there's nothing like a nice basket of fish and chips, the guilty pleasure of fried shrimp, a golden basket of crispy calamari, or a po'boy sandwich of deep fried oysters smothered between tangy remoulade-laden French bread. But what do you drink?

When indulging in the fried side of life, think clean, crisp, light—you want something that will cut through the oil, clean your palate, and allow you to taste the fish as well as the fry. We recommend going with an Austrian or South African Sauvignon Blanc or a French Semillon to provide this sensation.

Talk about acid—ceviche is a great way to start a meal. The fish is marinated in lemon or lime juice and spices either overnight or a few minutes before serving. The overnight version basically cooks the fish in acid and is a delight on the palate. When this marinade is applied just prior to serving, you really taste the essence of the fish and it's a bomb of acid all at once. This is a Latin American dish and sometimes it can be hot ... so what to drink? We're sticking with a crisp Pinot Grigio from Italy or a Sauvignon Blanc without oak aging, preferably a dry steel-aged wine like a Sancerre or a Pouilly Fume.

David Pasternack, the chef at New York's Esca, does the southern Italian version of ceviche called *cruda*. He serves the raw fish with virgin olive oil, salt, and pepper. This makes the dish richer because no acid (i.e., no lemon or lime) is added. The fish or shellfish remains raw with the addition of only the olive oil and some spices. Tony really loves to drink Prosecco from the Veneto region of Italy with this. Nino Franco Rustico, from the village of Valdobbiadene, has a finer, more elegant texture and a great long finish on the palate which make a great match for the *cruda*.

# Au Natural

Raw to poached to steamed—whatever the method, what you're left with is the fish and only the fish, save for a squeeze of lemon and maybe a little light herbal accoutrement.

What follows is a chart of commonly eaten fish found in the United States, and some wine-pairing suggestions for raw, poached, or steamed preparation.

| Fish | Description | Best with ... | Suggestion |
|---|---|---|---|
| Bay Scallop | Saltwater shell-fish; they look a little like squat wine corks, but taste entirely sweet. | White | Pouilly-Fuisse |
| Bluefish | Saltwater fish; has an unctuous, slightly fatty, but lean texture. | White | Gewürztraminer |
| Catfish | Mostly a freshwater fish; the flesh is firm and flaky. | White | Pinot Gris |
| Caviar | The roe of sturgeon, these tiny orbs are like salty little grapes in your mouth. | White | Champagne (of course!), Chardonnay |
| Chilean Sea Bass | Saltwater fish; hearty, thick flesh. | White, Red | Pinot Noir, Chardonnay |
| Cod | Saltwater fish; solid, chunky texture with mild flavor; is also frequently dried. | White, Red | Riesling, Beaujolais |
| Clams | Saltwater mollusk; briny, somewhat chewy texture. Can be eaten raw or cooked. | White | Chablis, Pinot Grigio |
| Crab | Fresh- or saltwater crustacean (most often we see the latter variety); sweet, fine texture. | White | Chardonnay, Vernaccia |

| Fish | Description | Best with ... | Suggestion |
|------|-------------|---------------|------------|
| Dover Sole | Saltwater fish; lean, delicate flesh. | White | Sauvignon Blanc, Semillon |
| Flounder/ Plaice | Saltwater fish; mild in flavor, lean, fairly delicate texture. | White, Red | Chablis, Valpolicella |
| Grouper | Saltwater fish; of sea bass family, the flesh of this large fish is firm enough to be served as a steak. | White | Arneis |
| Halibut | Saltwater fish; despite its large size, the flesh is delicate and mild in flavor. | White | Roussane |
| Lobster | Saltwater shell-fish; firm, luscious, and sweet. | White, Red | Rosé, Chardonnay |
| Mahi-mahi (a.k.a. dol-phinfish) | Firm, meaty, almost sweet flesh. | White | Pinot Noir |
| Monkfish | Saltwater fish; only the tail on this odd-looking swimmer is edible, but it's similar in texture and sweet taste to lobster. | White, Red | Merlot, Dolcetto, Pinot Bianco |
| Mussels | Saltwater mollusk; velvety, tender texture and a mildly sweet flavor. | White | Soave, Riesling |
| Oysters | Saltwater mollusk; despite their gooey appearance, the flesh is briny, but tender and sweet. Can be eaten raw or cooked. | White | Chablis, Muscadet, sparkling white |

| Fish | Description | Best with ... | Suggestion |
|------|-------------|---------------|------------|
| Red Snapper | Saltwater fish; lean, firm, pinkish flesh. | White, Red | Lagrein, Gavi |
| Salmon | Saltwater fish; rich, slightly fatty, sweet pink flesh. | White | Pinot Noir, Burgundy, Chardonnay |
| Sea Scallop | Saltwater mollusk; larger than the bay scallop and not as sweet, this cylindrical shaped seafood is mild in flavor, solid but velvety in texture. | White, Red | Sparkling whites, Cru Beaujolais |
| Shrimp | Saltwater shellfish; when cooked, the flesh is sweet, firm and pink. | White, Red | Rosé, Viognier, Tempranillo |
| Skate | Fresh- and saltwater fish (the latter being the most commonly eaten); the fins are consumed, and they are solid and sweet, similar to a bay scallop. | White | Pouilly-Fumé, Riesling (Kabinette) |
| Striped Bass | Saltwater fish; solid, slightly fatty texture, mildly sweet flavor. | White | Merlot (aged), Côtes du Rhône |
| Swordfish | Saltwater fish; sold in steak form has a briny, mineral-like flavor. | White, Red | White Burgundy/ Chardonnay, Pinot Noir, Syrah |
| Tilapia | Saltwater fish; its delicate texture is sold in filet form and it has a mildly sweet flavor. | White | Red Burgundy, Chianti Classico, Roussane |

| Fish | Description | Best with ... | Suggestion |
|------|-------------|---------------|------------|
| Trout | Fresh- and salt-water fish (the former is most common); slightly fatty, solid texture. | White | Gewürztraminer, Chenin Blanc |
| Tuna | Saltwater fish; hearty, solid, fatty texture. | White, Red | Dolcetto, Albarino |

What we suggest in the pairings is that even with fish, weight plays a part. The weight of the dish can be naturally inherent in the amount or lack of fat contained in the fish, the sweetness of the meat, and the texture, but it can also change depending on how you serve it. What we hope you come away with from this particular chapter is that fish is *much* more versatile than it is generally billed, and the pairing possibilities here are as vast as the seven seas themselves.

# chapter eleven

# Vintage Words: Interview with Rick Moonen, RM Restaurant

*I've tasted a lot and I have a good memory for flavor. And I know when I'm most happy, and that's all about balance.*

—*Rick Moonen*

Even among those of us who know better, there is a tendency to put fish in the category of ho-hum dining. How many times have you been out to dinner with friends and heard someone say, "Oh, I'm *just* going to have fish—I'm watching my weight"? Yawn. And then there's the old "white with fish, red with meat" rule as far as wine goes. Ever-more ho-hum. And quite untrue.

Enter Rick Moonen, the man who has not only taken the fruits of the deep blue sea and made them as exciting and innovative as the *haute*-est meaty cuisine, but he also—gasp!—often drinks red with them.

Moonen, inarguably one of the best and most respected chefs of fish cookery in the country, made his mark in epicurean eateries like the legendary La Côte Basque, The Water Club, and the three-star Oceana in New York City. The fall of 2002, though, saw Moonen at the helm of his own ship, opening the much-anticipated RM restaurant to great and well-deserved accolades. But more than just a man who has a way with finned creatures, Moonen's innovation and enthusiasm (there's a clearly distinguishable twinkle in his eye when he refers to the ocean as "the last wild frontier") are the mark of a man who loves what he does for a living. Which must be why he does it so well.

We gathered in the intimate, subtly boatlike dining room of RM for an afternoon of pairing and discussion. Our conversation sprang from the following:

# Course I

Atlantic salmon with French lentils, parsnip, and red wine lobster jus
Daniel Gehrs Grenache/Syrah, 1999
Patz & Hall Russian River Pinot Noir, 1999
Verdad Grenache/Tempranillo Rosé, 2001

# Course II

Striped bass wrapped in pancetta with carrots and a clam and celery vinaigrette
Ratti Dolcetto, 2000
Alois Lageder Lagrein "Lindenburg," 1998
Acacia Pinot Noir, 2000

# Course III

Pistachio-crusted skate and parsley monté with baby spinach and pickled onion
J Pinot Gris, 2001
Hanzell Chardonnay, 1999
Rudd "Bacigalupi" Chardonnay, 1999
Knyphausen Kiedricher Sandgrub Riesling Spätlese, 1999

# Course IV

Potato leek soup with watercress and scallops
Brocard Fourchaumes Chablis, 2000
Hanzell Chardonnay, 1999
Rudd "Bacigalupi" Chardonnay, 1999
Knyphausen Kiedricher Sandgrub Riesling Spätlese, 1999
Alois Lageder Lagrein "Lindenburg," 1998

# Course I: The Riches of the Earth and Sea

For Moonen's rich Atlantic salmon with French lentils, parsnips, and a red-wine lobster jus, we began boldly with nary a white wine in sight if only to prove once and for all that some rules are meant to be broken. From right to left, our glasses were filled with a fruity yet spicy Daniel Gehrs 1999 Grenache/Syrah, the fruit-forward California stylings of Patz & Hall's 1999 Pinot Noir, and a palate-cleansing 2001 Verdad Grenache/Tempranillo Rosé.

**Tony DiDio:** Let's start this salmon with the Patz & Hall Pinot. To me, it's got that forward-fruit of California.

**Rick Moonen:** Yeah, it does. But then again it's got good terroir. It's earthy. And when I think of lentils I think of root vegetables, and that's what this salmon dish is all about. If you compare foods to music, this salmon dish would be a bass note. It's got a lower voice. It's bigger, it's richer; it can handle a red wine. This "white-wine-with-fish" thing— it's crazy! In this dish there's a red-wine reduction and lobster stock, so it's quite rich. It's all about autumn, colder weather.

**Amy Zavatto:** That's lobster stock? It's very beefy tasting. I can't believe how rich this is considering it's a fish stock.

**Rick:** When I first tasted the Patz & Hall Pinot, I could almost feel the alcohol and the tannins, but once you have the richness of this dish in your mouth it softens it. The fruit of the wine becomes more apparent in your palate.

**Tony:** See, with the second wine I'm tasting both the wine and the food as a finish, and that's really, really nice.

**Amy:** The Pinot, for me, is the only taste left in my mouth when I drink this with the dish, and that's really something considering how rich the salmon is. For this kind of pairing, I want more of a complement.

**Rick:** I think so, too. It takes a little bit of the fruit away.

**Tony:** I think the fruit gets pretty bright with the Pinot. But don't forget that Grenache/Syrah. Let's taste that; it's a real fruit bomb.

**Rick:** It can almost get bubble-gummy. The Syrah adds the bass note I was talking about. The perception of the Grenache in it, though— taste the sauce on the fish and then drink it, and you get that sweetness of the Grenache.

**Tony:** Let's experiment with the Verdad Rosé that has a 5 percent Tempranillo.

**Rick:** Bone dry, clean, delicious, refreshing. But you know, Tony, not one of these doesn't work. It depends on what you're in the mood for—and that, to me, is what pairing is all about. None of these is a loser. The Verdad Grenache/Tempranillo is the most refreshing, but if you came in here freezing cold, you wouldn't necessarily go with that. Because it's got a little contrast going on, it tends to rinse your palate, though, which might be what you're in the mood for. I think the fruitiness of the Grenache/Tempranillo holds up.

**Amy:** And you wouldn't expect it to with this dish.

**Tony:** I would say for me, I would go 1, 2, 3—Patz & Hall Pinot, Verdad Rosé, and Daniel Gehrs Grenache/Syrah.

**Rick:** Even the Pinot, as it sets in and your palate goes through this adjustment, the Pinot becomes even smoother.

**Amy:** I agree. My first impression of it was that it was too much, but now that it's had some time to aerate and settle, it's complementing the salmon. Rick, do you think that seafood in general needs a sweeter wine?

**Rick:** Not necessarily. But it can handle a sweeter wine on some levels.

**Amy:** Is it fun for you to show people how versatile fish is? Because even people who like to eat out and eat out often still have this thing in their head that it's something that's so delicate that you need to have an equally delicate wine to pair with it, which most often will take the form of a white.

**Rick:** It blows my mind how many big reds we sell here. My wine list has a lot of red, not out of design, out of request. We watch what direction people are going in. It's certainly damn the torpedoes! I'm going to order what I want, but you'll see somebody having cold oysters and cucumber and caviar and drinking a dark red, a big red …

**Amy:** Well, that's a big theme of ours in this book—drink what you like.

**Rick:** I completely agree. You know, there's too much pressure being placed on the perfect marriage. It's what you're in the mood for, and that's what I was talking about with these [wines]. I like the Pinot and then the rosé. I think all of them work, but it just may be the way I'm feeling today.

*Tony checks out the choices for the next course, while Rick and Amy continue tasting.*

**Amy:** But also, think about it—even the weather can affect what you choose. Today, it's cold outside so I'm gravitating toward the Pinot, despite my initial reaction to it. On another day, I could absolutely see preferring the Grenache.

**Tony:** We're going in a different direction with this next dish, this is going to be fun …

## Course II: Good Things Come in Savory Packages

Taking our fish and red wine experiment one savory step further, Moonen prepared a hearty striped bass wrapped in thick, salty pancetta with sweet carrots and a complementary yet contrasting clam and celery vinaigrette. And to drink? A 2000 Ratti Dolcetto, a 1998 Alois Lageder Lagrein "Lindenburg," and a deceivingly Burgundian-style 2000 Acacia Pinot Noir.

**Rick:** Look at the color of this Dolcetto. I can actually smell pancetta in the Dolcetto! The Acacia Pinot we have here is almost Burgundian in style, despite that it's from California. That first Pinot was very Californian.

**Tony:** Although his Lagrein is outstanding, Alois Lageder is considered the greatest white wine producer in Italy. Alois is a dear friend of mine.

**Rick:** Tony, who's not a dear friend of yours?!

*Rick examines a red.*

**Tony:** The Pope. I'm not close to the Pope anymore. After he beat me in bowling …

*[laughter]*

**Tony:** Okay, back to business—these are pretty interesting wines.

**Rick:** I could describe the flesh of striped bass as having an earthiness to it. Which is why I think it goes great with something like pancetta. Now, on your palate, could this not be veal?

**Amy:** Absolutely. The texture and the flavor of the fish with the pancetta give it that same kind of quality as really tender veal.

**Rick:** Forget the fact that it's a fish—there's nothing fishy about what you just tasted. Nothing. Zero.

**Tony:** Let's note that here we are at a three-star fish restaurant and we haven't poured one white wine yet.

**Rick:** Exactly. Now, to the business at hand—Dolcetto is big. It's got tannins. These are interesting wines you chose here. There's some distinct lineage that links them although they all have their own individual personality.

**Tony:** The Lagrein is interesting, eh? It's got a great acidity to it because it's a cool-weather grape.

**Amy:** The Lagrein to me really brings out the flavor of the pancetta.

**Rick:** I agree.

**Tony:** I like it! I like them together.

**Rick:** I might alter this dish slightly to marry the Lagrein to it even more. I would probably include some kind of a green vegetable that might carry a little bit of tannin, like Swiss chard.

**Tony:** You know what? I think the Pinot is too bright. It's a good Pinot, but the fruit is too bright for this dish.

**Rick:** I agree.

**Amy:** It takes away from the earthiness of the combined pancetta and striped bass.

**Rick:** If this had mushrooms, or even earthy lentils, then the Pinot would work better. But because this dish is sort of bright as well as earthy—you've got celery, you've got clam—these are a higher note. However, I think this meal really strips the fruit of the Dolcetto.

**Tony:** The Lagrein is really working.

**Rick:** It's an awesome choice.

**Amy:** The finish on the Dolcetto is really stripped when I'm tasting it with the food.

**Rick:** That's because with the Dolcetto, the acidity of the celery/clam vinaigrette takes this wine and strips it a little because it doesn't have crisp acidity—nor is it supposed to. The Lagrein, however, has a certain acidity that stands up to this.

**Tony:** I think the pancetta changes everything. So what do we think, boys and girls?

**Rick:** I think the Lagrein is number one. Number two, I'd go with the Dolcetto, and I agree with you that the Pinot, although a great quality of wine, almost screams for some more earth, more terroir.

Indigenous to the Alto Adige region of Italy, Lagrein is a little-known grape varietal that is a distant cousin to Syrah. With a pronounced cherry and prune aroma, this spicy wine is paired with mostly red meats and game in Italy. To us, the pancetta changed the whole dish and gave the fleshy striped bass another dimension. The "Lindenburg" vineyard is in Balzano, the capital city of Alto Adige. Grown in deep and rich alluvial soil along the banks of the Talvera River, this Lagrein is well balanced with a floral nose and powerful, well-structured body. Seek out this wine and try it with lamb, beef, cheeses—and don't forget pancetta-wrapped striped bass.

# Course III: The Chef Challenges the Authors

For our third course, Moonen raised the bar and challenged us to find a wine for a dish on his menu that had been eluding him thus far. It was a conundrum, as there were several sensations and flavors at work on the plate: the slightly sweet nature of skate, nuts, herbs, the bitter bite of spinach, and the sweet and sour subtlety of pickled onion. For this challenging course, we broke out the whites: a 2001 J Pinot Gris, two California Chardonnays—a 1999 Hanzell and a Rudd of the same year, and finally a refreshing 1999 German Riesling Spätlese from Knyphausen.

**Rick:** I don't always intellectualize everything, I go by gut. That's how you play around with food, and that's why this is so much fun. What does this dish need? What we have here is baby spinach, which is the epitome of tannin. Your teeth get squeaky when you eat it. Then you've got pickled onions, which is acidity. Then you've got skate, which has all the profile of a scallop. And then you've got parsley monté. So you've got cleansing herbacity in the parsley, you've got almost a shellfish scallop flavor, then you've got spinach, and then the pickled onion, which has a real high acidity. The dish itself is well balanced. What wine, which is my challenge because I don't have the answer, goes with this?

**Amy:** I feel like that's the best way to learn with food and with wine. Sometimes the more intuitive way to figure out why something works and why it doesn't is not by somebody telling you, but by learning it on your own. You tasted it yourself and came up with your own logical conclusion. Not that it's bad to be told, everyone needs some background to give them a basis for their food and wine decisions, but with eating and drinking it boils down to your own senses, not what you read or hear.

**Rick:** I agree with you 100 percent. I think that if you pay attention in your life, that's where you learn. I've tasted a lot and I have a good memory for flavor. And I know when I'm most happy, and that's all about balance. That's what our goal is here. And I think that's your goal with this book, as well. What does wine have? The first thing that you appreciate on your palate when you take a sip of wine is the acidity. It's the first thing you react to. With a lot of it, you're taken aback. But that's good, because the acidity kind of opens your palate up, like salt with food. Salt opens your palate and allows you to taste the natural flavors; acidity plays that role with wine. And then you've got fruit, you've got the way it's been vinified—wood, no wood—the degree of brix, does it have any degree of residual sugar. And then you've got how the wine is stored. Is it a wine that's fresh? Is it like Beaujolais Nouveau and you're tasting Gamay juice that just has alcohol, or are you tasting something that's been sitting around long enough to have time for the tannins to mellow, the flavors to evolve? A well-balanced dish has the same kind of profile. So with this dish, you've got skate with a little pistachio, which is fun. You've got pickled onions, that's acidity. Without that, this dish is kind of boring. You've got spinach, skate, and parsley. Yawn. But with the pickled onion, it really comes together.

**Tony:** Okay, the first wine is the J Pinot Gris; second wine is the Hanzell Chardonnay, that's Sonoma; the third wine is the Rudd 1999 Chardonnay Russian River, also Sonoma, Bacigalupe Vineyard; and then the last wine is Knyphausen Spätlese [Riesling].

**Rick:** Smell the fourth one, just for fun. Swirl it around. While you're doing it, think about that really inexpensive plastic that's used for beach balls? You can smell that in it.

**Amy:** I don't know if you guys are going to understand this at all, but it smells a little like new Barbie.

**Tony:** Right! It's got a petrol, bubble-gummy aroma. It's a 1999. It's from the Rheingau. Rheingau has a lot of those elements in it.

**Rick:** This first wine, the Pinot Gris, definitely has residual sugar.

**Tony:** But it also has a ton of acid.

**Rick:** The Rudd tastes like acid to me.

**Amy:** Like a Cortland apple!

**Rick:** The Hanzell is a more serious wine.

**Tony:** Well, when you think of Hanzell, you need to think of Burgundy. Always think Montrachet. The Rudd is definitely California; Hanzell, though …

**Rick:** When you taste it, you almost sit up a little straighter.

**Tony:** But, of course, we're talking about Pinot Grigio and Chardonnay. Chardonnay is a noble grape. Pinot Grigio is not really an aged grape; not a grape that's going to last for 20 years. The Hanzell will last for another 20 years and it'll be a delight to drink.

**Rick:** What do you think of the marriage of the Hanzell with this dish?

**Amy:** I'm having a hard time with the Hanzell because the wine, on its own, is so austere and gorgeous, it seems too serious for this dish. The power of the grape in it is overwhelming the whimsy of the sweet onion, the nuttiness of the pistachio, the astringent quality of the spinach …

**Tony:** I just tasted the Bacigalupi. On its own, I get a rush of eucalyptus at the end of it. It's all menthol. It's a great wine.

**Amy:** The Rudd Chardonnay really brings out the bitter taste in the spinach.

**Rick:** It does. But between the Rudd and Hanzell Chardonnays, I like the Rudd better than the Hanzell.

**Tony:** The Hanzell to me is bringing out the spinach more, but I'm losing the fruit and I'm losing the skate.

**Rick:** I like the Rudd better with it. I had the same sensation of getting more bitter spinach with that, and at this point in our tasting, I'm kind of in the mood to taste bitter.

**Tony:** See how that works? It's what Amy and I keep talking about in the book—what are you in the mood for? What do you like? Now go back to the first wine again—the J Pinot Gris.

**Rick:** The Pinot Gris almost tastes like a Riesling or a Kabinette. It feels like a Kabinette on my palate.

**Tony:** And right now, to me, the only wine that brings out the taste of the dish and brings it together is the Spätlese.

**Rick:** *[sipping the Spätlese]* Holy smokes!

**Amy:** Wow. It has a whole different taste at this point than when we first tried it on its own and it had that heavy petrol aroma. With the food, it completely changes the composition.

**Rick:** Taste all this together—the skate with the pickled onion and the spinach, and then taste the Spätlese. It creates a flavor reminiscent of smoked meat, a German food flavor.

**Tony:** That wine really changed the whole taste of this dish. I don't mean that it's made it bad or better, it's just utterly changed it.

**Rick:** It made it a different dish. It almost made it seem smoky to me. I tasted cabbage, and yet there's no cabbage in it!

**Amy:** Well, the first thing it does is remove all the saltiness you're tasting. It just goes away.

**Rick:** Right, it balances it.

**Amy:** And it seems to bring out any sweet flavors in the dish, like the pickled onion.

**Rick:** All right; well, what's the consensus?

**Amy:** The Spätlese for me.

**Tony:** I think you really need a fruity wine with this dish, with all the acid going on. To me, it was the Spätlese as well, and the J Pinot Gris.

**Rick:** Out of the Chardonnays, I thought the Rudd showed better. There's a whole different flavor in this wine that I didn't get when I initially tasted it before eating. The fruitiness was brief.

**Tony:** Before we even tasted, my first choice was the Spätlese when I looked at this dish and what was in it.

**Rick:** You know what? It's funny, because as a customer not asking anyone, reading the menu, you decide what you're going to order, and then you're empowered to make a purchase; open a bottle of wine. And that's the point of anxiety in a dining experience. Like, we all turn to you, Tony, because you do this for a living; *you* know about wine. Here's what I'm eating, here's what he's eating, here's what you're eating— what do we drink? And what do you do? Because that's what this book is all about—you're trying to tell people to chill out.

**Amy:** In one of the chapters we wrote about how when Tony goes out to dinner with certain people—family or friends—they all turn to him and say, okay, you pick the wine. But when either of us goes out to dinner with friends who are chefs, we don't turn to them, hand them the menu, and say, "Will you please pick out what I'm going to eat?"

**Tony and Rick:** Exactly!

**Rick:** It's one of the things I love about Italian wine with food. Most Italian wines—and this is generalizing, fair or unfair—aren't meant to be pontificated over; the layers or lusciousness or all that. Italian wines are meant to be drunk with food and friends. End of story. You drink it, you take a bite of food, and you continue. Where there are a lot of other wines that really stand on their own and are almost a course in themselves. They've got so many layers and the finish never ends. It's funny because today, the wines that we tasted, I can't think of one that's got this finish that went so far, interfered into the next taste. There was a good balance; they had specific components and personalities, and they go or they don't go. It's like any gathering of people. There's always one guy who's a jerk!

*[laughter]*

We could sit here and try to intellectualize the whole situation, but whatever wine works for you may or may not work for me.

## Course IV: A Spoonful, Then a Sip

For our final course, Moonen brought out a dish that he was considering for his menu, but was still in the stage of fine-tuning. Of course, the opportunity to preview a great chef's creation was one we were honored to be part of. Add to that the challenge of finding a wine that works with it, and we rolled up our sleeves. We went back to some of the wines we used in the last few courses, giving the 1999 Hanzell Chardonnay, 1999 Rudd Chardonnay, and 1999 Knyphausen Riesling Spätlese a new try. To make things even more interesting, we threw in the 1998 Alois Lageder Lagrein "Lindenburg," just in case the earthiness of the dish warranted red.

*Rick, Amy, and Tony rest up before the final course.*

**Rick:** This dish that we're about to taste is not on my menu, so I'm curious to see which wines are going to work. It has a certain earthiness that might work with the Lagrein.

**Tony:** Let's start with the Chablis. The first thing you generally get with this is a mineral quality.

**Rick:** The first thing I always, always get out of Chablis is that you're hit in the face with slate.

**Tony:** You've got to remember that the predominant soil composition is chalk there.

**Rick:** Which is great, generally speaking, with oysters.

**Tony:** The Brocard family, in their cellar, they exposed a wall about 50 feet high of chalk and you can actually go into the wall and pull out shells that are thousands of years old. That's what Chablis is about. It's not wood; it's clean; it's all about the Chardonnay grape, it's all about the fruit.

**Amy:** So far, for me, the Chablis is fine initially, but then its finish seems to take away the sweetness of the soup.

**Rick:** Okay, now the Hanzell almost tastes caramelized to me.

**Tony:** It has a hot finish.

**Rick:** This Chardonnay [the Hanzell] is almost like you've taken it and reduced it to the point where it caramelized. It's got that richer, smokier, deeper flavor.

**Amy:** The Rudd Chardonnay with the soup, it really brings out the vanilla flavors in the wine.

**Rick:** That's *diacetyle*.

> *D*iacetyle is produced in wines that go through malolactic or secondary fermentation. With the best results, diacetyle adds a buttery, sometimes vanillin flavor in a wine, as well as greater complexity of flavor.

**Tony:** Hey, let's try this. Try the Pinot Gris with this. I would say the Chards don't work. The Spätlese definitely doesn't work.

**Rick:** It's hard to dislike Chablis Premier Cru of this quality with any kind of shellfish. Be it a lobster, be it a clam, or a scallop.

**Tony:** The Pinot Gris brings it in another direction; though they're both [the Chablis and Pinot Gris] working very well.

**Rick:** For a very brief forward moment you have a little issue with the alcohol, and then the potato in the soup takes care of that. Try this: Stop and inhale through your mouth and exhale through your nose, and just taste what's there. What's left on your palate is very enjoyable.

*Red, white, and cork all over.*

**Amy:** Absolutely! You can taste the greens, you can taste the sweetness of the scallops ...

**Rick:** I do this whenever I'm trying to think the flavor combinations through and I can't quite put my finger on it. So what did we learn from this dish?

**Tony:** I think what the dish needs is a very clean acid-driven wine that's uncomplicated by oak and uncomplicated by over-ripeness, like the Chardonnays. I think the J Pinot Gris works really well; my second choice is the Spätlese.

**Amy:** The Pinot Gris is my favorite of all of them. It's so clean that it really carries the creaminess of the soup.

**Rick:** I agree. Absolutely. No question. The Pinot Gris goes great with this dish.

**Tony:** You need a little bit more of a leaner wine with a creamy soup like this, and Chablis to me has always been the leanest of all the Chardonnay grape styles.

**Rick:** It's very simple. Nothing in that wine gets in the way. It complements the soup.

*Rick pops open a Pinot.*

## Try It for Yourself

To re-create some of the tasting experience we had, Rick supplied us with a coveted recipe for his potato leek soup with watercress and scallops. Pick up a few or all the wines we used, and see if you agree (or disagree—remember, it's all about what you like) with our results.

## Potato Leek Soup with Watercress and Scallops

4 Idaho potatoes, peeled and sliced

4 TB. unsalted butter

1 large Spanish onion, peeled and diced

2 medium leeks, cleaned well

1 *bouquet garni* (available prepared at specialty food markets)

Salt and white pepper to taste

4 cups chicken stock (or canned low-sodium chicken broth)

1 cup heavy cream

1½ bunches watercress, cleaned, stems removed and rough-chopped

1½ fresh bay scallops, such as Nantucket or Peconic Bay (if you can't get them, sea scallops will do—you also may substitute rock shrimp or crabmeat if you prefer)

Chopped chives for garnish

In a medium saucepan, cover half the potatoes with cold water and a pinch salt. Bring to a boil and blanch until tender (about 5 minutes). Remove from heat, drain, and reserve.

In a large pot over medium heat, melt butter. Add onion and leeks and stir. Cover the pot and sauté onions and leeks until they are translucent, stirring occasionally, for 5 minutes. Uncover and add remaining potatoes, bouquet garni, salt, pepper, chicken stock, and cream, and stir. Bring the soup to a simmer, uncovered, over medium heat. Simmer until potatoes are soft, cooking for about 15 minutes. Remove from heat.

Using a food processor or blender, purée soup in batches. Taste for seasoning and adjust with salt and pepper. Return soup to the pot, add blanched potatoes, and place over medium heat. When soup begins to simmer, add watercress and scallops and cook for 30 seconds, stirring once. Ladle soup into bowls and sprinkle with chives. Serve immediately.

Leeks are known for being dirt-clingers, so if you haven't worked with them before, here are some instructions to make sure you clean them well:

Trim the leeks, cutting away the root from the bottom and one to two inches of green from the top. Holding each leek one at a time on the cutting board, insert a sharp knife into the middle of the solid white portion of the vegetable and slice up through it lengthwise to separate its layers. Give this leek a one-quarter turn and repeat the slicing process. Place the cut leek under cold running water, green portion down, and thoroughly remove any dirt that may be lodged between the layers. Dry with paper towels and repeat the process until all leeks are cleaned.

# chapter twelve

# Pairing Wine with Fowl

*What is sauce for the goose may be sauce for the gander,*
*but is not necessarily sauce for the chicken, the duck,*
*the turkey, or the guinea hen.*

*—Alice B. Toklas*

Just like fish, fowl is oft misunderstood in pairing. It's "chicken with white wine," and call it a dinner. But that's being pretty unfair to fowl. It's got so much more potential than that.

True, the white-meat portions of a chicken or a turkey are low in fat and, therefore, don't necessarily have the natural makeup to tango with a Rioja or tarantella with a Barolo. Ah, but what about finger-licking fricassees? A savory stuffed turkey? Vivacious coq au vins? What about the dark meat—those rich, fattier sections that are packed with savory flavor? And then there's duck, goose, quail, pheasant, squab (that's *poissin* to all you Francophiles), and partridge. How could all of these be paired with a single wine?

The obvious answer is they can't. They won't!

## Chicken

Let's begin with the fowl that most often appears on tables, domestic and otherwise, across the country: chicken. White meat, with its low fat content, does complement a lighter style of wine. Of course, this does not necessarily mean white and white only, although many whites do pair well. As we've seen and will continue to see throughout these pages, the weight of a wine is not necessarily dictated by its color. There are lighter- to fuller-bodied reds just as there lighter- to fuller-bodied whites, and they should be matched accordingly to the food you eat.

As far as chicken goes, it's impossible to list every possible method of preparation, but what follows is a list of basic preparations and what they match best with. Again, we encourage you to go beyond our guidelines and try other things based on what you've learned. But every good explorer can use a guide, and so ...

- ❖ **Grilled.** Grilling meat, any kind of meat, adds a smoky, earthy flavor to the dish that's so good, it requires minimal seasoning. If this is the way you'll be eating your chicken, go for a full-bodied Chardonnay like Long Vineyard's version. The smoky flavor of the meat and the rich, buttery taste of the Chardonnay are a great match. However, a case for red can be made here because of all the previously mentioned influences added to the meat from grilling. Try an Oregon Pinot Noir like Benton Lane. The lower tannic nature of this red can be paired with chicken without overwhelming it, and the charcoal-grilled taste of the meat works really well with a red of this ilk.

- ❖ **Baked and roasted.** If you're doing a simple baked or roasted chicken, try a Côtes du Rhône if you want to go red. If white's on your mind, Pinot Gris adds a clean, lovely flavor to a juicy, perfectly cooked bird.

- ❖ **Stewed and simmered.** Think about what else is in the pot. Are we talking acidic (tomatoes, capers, olives) or earthy (mushrooms, garlic, onions)? What are the influences? If we're talking cacciatore, you can absolutely play it safe and go right for a Chianti Classico like Badia a Coltibuono or a Barbera. The stewed, hearty nature of the dish complements the earthiness of these wines, as both of them mimic their origins (that's right—back to *terroir* again). They also bring great fruit and acidity to rich dishes like this that take on a sweetness the longer they stew.

- ❖ **Sauced.** For citrus-based sauces, a floral, citrusy influenced Muscadet will bring out the best of all flavors. For cream-based sauces, you need a wine with enough acidity to cut through the cream as opposed to swimming around and making both taste too fat and too rich. Go for a bright, dry Riesling from Burklin Wolf. If the sauce has a vinegar influence to it, this pairs acid on acid. Try a fino sherry. If the sauce has a heavy herbal influence, a good pick would be Sauvignon Blanc.

We'd like to make a case for cooking with the same wine you drink, and we can't find a better reason than coq au vin (literally, chicken with wine). As you can make this dish with red or white, you can choose whichever type tickles your fancy. If you're going red, try a simple Bourgogne Rouge (French Pinot Noir) with its fruity, low-tannic nature. If the vin in your coq is white (i.e., coq au vin blanc), try Bourgogne Blanc, a simple country Chardonnay, the rich nature of which is excellent in the stew and your glass.

❖ **In the pan.** When sautéing or browning for dishes like chicken Marsala, picatta, or those of this ilk you have a couple of things to consider. For one, these dishes (and many that require the browning and sautéing of meat) require the addition of wine during cooking. Second, these dishes tend to come with earthy accompaniments like mushrooms, onions, or root vegetables. For these dishes, try a ground-worshipping wine like Rioja to complement the earthy influences in the dish.

You may think of Marsala wine as an inexpensive item that you pick up off the shelf of your local grocery store and use for cooking. But to drink? No way. Marsala wine may be Sicily's best-kept secret (that and its stunning beaches—but that's another story). It is fortified, which means that brandy has been added to increase the alcohol content, and is made from Grillo and Catarratto Bianco grapes, which you'll only find in western Sicilia. It ranges in color from amber to gold to ruby (the most rare—and most expensive) and can range in flavor from dry and semisweet to lusciously thick and sugary. Generally, they are consumed the way you would have sherry or port—i.e., on their own. Although you might use them to cook with, you wouldn't be likely to consume fortified wines such as these with your meal.

❖ **Fried.** Wine with fried chicken? Why not? There's no reason not to drink what you like because of what others may or may not think is acceptable. If you like it, drink it. As far as wine and fried chicken go, follow the same rules for fried seafood in Chapter Ten. You're going to want a wine that cuts through the oil and any residual greasiness. For this, go for the herbaceous aroma and crisp, clean flavor of a South African Thelema Sauvignon Blanc or a French LaBoure Roi Vouvray.

What's the difference between free-range chicken and regular ol' chicken? The way they're raised. The school of thought is that chickens that aren't mass-produced and that are allowed to live a normal little chicken life free of added hormones to enhance their growth, antibiotics, and various by-products pumped into their dinners, make for better, healthier birds (and, thus, tastier, healthier eating). They also make for more expensive birds, but then again the great irony of foodstuffs is that anything that is organically produced costs more. You pay *less* for additives—go figure.

# Turkey

Turkey has become a commonplace dinner item throughout the year instead of just Thanksgiving Day. Turkey burgers appear on most informal restaurant menus, and you can buy turkey breast in your supermarket meat section. For nonholiday cooking, it falls into a similar category as chicken. If you're looking for pairing suggestions, use the suggestions above for chicken as your guide. But it's that annual conundrum that brings wine to the forefront of the conversation: What do you serve with Thanksgiving dinner?

The fact is you have more choices than you might believe. It's just a matter of taking a different perspective. Instead of thinking of this as a difficult decision, view it as an opportunity full of options. In fact, you may want to view Thanksgiving as the ultimate wine-tasting party. With the bird, the stuffing, and all the side dishes—not to mention all the company and diverse tastes likely to be at the table—this is a wonderful chance to diversify as far as wine choices go.

With reds, we have several favorites that we like. Amy is a big fan of Zinfandel on her Thanksgiving table. It has the fruit and the spice to really bring out the various flavor influences generally present on this holiday's table. Along those same lines, Côtes du Rhônes are also excellent foils for a flavorful, stuffed bird. The fruit in a Pinot Noir complements not only the turkey, but also many of the usual suspects (cranberry, squash, yams, etc.), and its other earthy qualities match nicely with mushrooms, onions, and herbs.

Thanksgiving Day is perhaps the most palate-challenging holiday. So many different flavors, so many wine choices, too much football.

Because there is no definite wine match for every dish on the table, follow this precise, scientific method: Just go for it. Crack open what you like to drink, but bear in mind that someone will show up with some Beaujolais Nouveau to further fluster the host who has carefully selected the wines for the evening. Beaujolais Nouveau is that grapey beverage that the French have very successfully marketed to the world as wine. Barely aged three months, it arrives with great fanfare on our shores, and every shop displays case after case with great pride. Is it wine? Well, yes it is. Is it good wine? Now, that's a matter of opinion. The fruitiness works well with most of the Thanksgiving meal, but a serious wine drinker may prefer to crack open a bottle of something a bit more interesting.

When Turkey Day rolls around, Tony has a few suggestions: (1) drink American; (2) drink older Zinfandels and older Cabernets; (3) drink young Rieslings from California or New York State. Because it's an American holiday, it makes sense to go regional. Tony likes older Zins and Cabs that have shed their tannic side, and have opened up and developed in the bottle. And those great Finger Lakes Rieslings, as well as the Napa versions such as Trefether White Riesling, are a great way to start the meal.

As far as whites go, the spicy qualities of a Gewürztraminer are an excellent accompaniment to herbaceous side dishes, as well as some of the commonly found herbs used on the bird itself (rosemary and thyme, for instance). If full and rich is more to your liking, a buttery Chardonnay matches well with the dark meat and the crispy outside of the bird. The fruity qualities of a Viognier work well with cinnamon-spiced sides like yams, or an orange-influenced cranberry dressing. And of course, Tony's favorite, Riesling—with its fruity apple aroma—is an obvious choice for the holiday.

Rosé can work with a turkey as well, but it probably should be a medium-bodied dry one. Those sweet white Zins don't have the acid or structure to stand up to all the tastes on the table. We just love Miner Family's Rosato and Verdad's rosé. These are two suggestions if you want to keep it American, or you wouldn't be doing too badly with a Spanish Rosado on your table either.

## Fowl Game

If a forkful of roasted duck has ever passed your lips, then you know the rich, decadent sensation of consuming this fantastic fowl. Goose, pheasant, and quail also have that same dark-meat texture that makes you want to stand up at the dinner table and sing, "If loving you is wrong, I don't want to be right!" (Forgive us, Luther Ingram.)

Because of the fatty essence of dark meat, reds tend to be favorable matches. If fowl like duck or squab is your bird of a feather, the gamey, earthy flavor of a Côte-Rôtie is a lovely parallel. The bold flavor of a Châteauneuf-du-Pape is able to stand up to the wildness of the flavor inherent in game, and the tannins cut through the fat and allow you to really taste the meat in all its luscious glory.

However, birds like wild turkey, wild goose, and squab have delicately flavored dark meat and tend to be very lean, and thus lower in fat. As Côte-Rôtie tends to have an earthy, gamy flavor to it, it reflects the nature of the dish beautifully. You could also try a rosé, as the acid can handle the fatty nature of the meat and the fruit tames the gamy quality.

The flesh of quail and partridge is white, but still has a bit of a gamy flavor. The sweetness of a Spätlese Riesling sooths the gamy quality and allows the luscious flavor of the meat to come to the forefront.

Just like with fish in Chapter Ten, you can forget all about white wine being the end-all for fowl. There is as much diversity within winged creatures as there is with cooking methods. Keep this in mind when pairing and you'll open yourself up to a whole new world of eating and drinking combinations.

# chapter thirteen

# Pairing Wine with Beef, Veal, Lamb, Pork, and Game

*It makes us proud and happy to see our customers sucking the marrow out of veal bones, munching on pig's feet, picking over oxtails or beef cheeks. It gives us purpose in life, as if we've done something truly good and laudable that day, brought beauty, hope, enlightenment to our dining rooms and a quiet sort of honor to ourselves and our profession.*

—*Anthony Bourdain, from* A Cook's Tour

We have a bit of love-hate relationship with meat in America. We worry about fitness and health and fat content and calorie intake. We have our cholesterol checked regularly and avoid the menu items that can make it shoot up into the uh-oh zone. We exercise, we drink lots of water, we avoid meat.

Now, with the exception of that last item, this is all well and good. But red meat has gotten some undeserving bad press (of course, one of the authors of this book might be ever-so-slightly biased—Amy's father Mike Zavatto is a butcher). But when it comes down to it, we're quite a meat-and-potatoes kind of place. We like our pork chops thick and tender, our stews chock full of sigh-inducing savory chunks of beef, and our steaks big and juicy. In fact, once Amy and her husband, Dan, were entertaining some visiting relatives from Milan and took them to the famous Peter Luger's steakhouse just for the fun of watching them gape at the gigantic T-bone for four that was placed on the table. "We don't have this in Italy," they exclaimed. Indeed, like it or not, Americans love their meat.

But, seeing as you're reading this chapter, we're assuming you do like meat and you'd like to know how to enjoy it even more. A glass of wine, perhaps?

> Meat is muscle. Whether some cuts are more tender than others largely depends on how much that muscle is used. High-use muscles in the forequarter of an animal (front legs and neck, for instance) tend to be tougher and do well when braised or stewed, as the long cooking makes them more supple. Low-use muscles in the hindquarter (loin being the best example, but also the rear legs and the ribcage) are incredibly tender. Cuts like filet, sirloin, round, etc., come from the hindquarter and don't need a lot of fussing. Simple grilling or roasting shows off the best attributes of these cuts.

# Beef

Red wine with red meat is actually not such a bad hard-and-fast rule. This isn't to say that white must be avoided at all costs. Absolutely not. As you probably know by now, we're not fans of limitations. But there is a reason for the red-with-meat rule and it has to with the matching the weight of your wine to the weight of your dish, something we mentioned on several occasions in this book. It's the tannins and the acid that play the important role with red meat. You need those tannins and that acid to balance the heaviness inherent in meat, which contains fat. But, within that realm of red, there's an abundance of choices. Here are some pairing ideas for your next carnivorous endeavor:

❖ A plain, lightly seasoned, juicy strip, T-bone, or sirloin steak begs to be paired with Cabernet Sauvignon. The heftiness of this wine and the hearty nature of these excellent cuts of beef are the perfect match. We love the 2000 Cab from Jordan for meaty pairings. What about filet mignon? Filet mignon is as tender as the previously mentioned cuts, but what many people don't realize is that it's less flavorful. Go for a wine that won't overwhelm this particular (expensive) cut, like a Merlot. It gives you the flavor you crave, but its lighter tannic nature makes it less overpowering than a Cab. Chalk Hill's 1999 Merlot has a gentle but full-bodied nature that goes great with filet. If you're going au poivre, adding steak sauce, or sinking into a glazed prime rib, we suggest a fruity yet peppery Zinfandel like Ravenswood Lodi 2000 or a Syrah such as Qupé's 2000 version.

❖ Braised beef. Braising can take a flavorful but tough cut of meat and turn it into a savory, juicy, tender treat. Braising adds more complexity to the pot. For stewy delights that have the influence of broth, you need a red that can cut through the saltiness and bring out the other flavors you've added, whatever they may be. Try a Jade Mountain Mourvedre 2001 with your next pot roast or beef stew. Some other methods of braising include the addition of wine to the sauce; frequently Cabernet is used for this. In this case, the smoky influences of a Château Faugères 2000 from Bordeaux, with its black currant and cherry notes, will do the trick in and out of your dish.

❖ Are burgers and meatloaf too ordinary for wine? We don't think so. In this case, think earthy, basic, round. Try a Barbera or a Chianti. We like G. Conterno Barbera D'Alba 2000 and Renzo Masi Chianti Rufina 2001.

What about veal, though? Veal, of course, is very young beef. With its youth comes incredible, unrivaled tenderness and a delicate nature that makes big, bold reds a big, bold error in pairing. Here are some more complementary suggestions:

❖ For a dish like osso buco, you can go either red or white, depending on what you've braised the meat with. If you're using red, the deep, dark fruit of a Tuscan Brunello di Montalcino is a savory delight. (We like Aleramici's 1996 version.) Grown in volcanic soil that has limestone and clay, this grape's complex flavor of earth and fruit complement the myriad melded flavors in the osso buco. If you're braising the meat in white wine, the complexity of a dry Riesling complements the depth of flavor inherent in a dish like this with so many ingredients stewing together for hours on end. Also, as osso buco recipes frequently call for lemon or orange rind, parsley, and carrots, the acidity in the Riesling accentuates flavors like these.

❖ For simple grilled veal chops or a basic roast with the addition of some light seasoning (salt, pepper, fresh rosemary, or thyme), try the earthiness in the 1999 Cune Rioja "Viña Real Crianza."

❖ Veal stews frequently require the addition of Sherry into the mix, and they also frequently have earthy accoutrements like mushrooms and root veggies. With that in mind, try a Pinot Noir like the 2000 Omaka Springs.

❖ If you like your veal Italian style (parmigiana, saltimbocca), you're going to need something that can stand up to the creaminess and saltiness of the cheese. For this, we suggest a rustic Primitivo from Apulia like the 2000 Apollonio Primitivo, which will cut through the salt and bring out the other flavors in the dish as only a regional pairing can. If scallopini—thin, incredibly delicate medallions of veal—are more to your taste, a Valpolicella like Boscaini's 2000 "San Ciriaco" is a lovely foil.

## Lamb

For such a young meat, lamb has an awful lot of flavor personality. It's a little gamy, a little earthy. Sometimes the meat can even seem tangy or almost smoky (and depending on how it's cooked, it can actually be all those things!). To be called lamb, the animal must have been slaughtered before it is a year old. After that, the meat is referred to as mutton (if it's being used for eating purposes). Lamb is found in abundance in Middle Eastern cooking and often looked to as a "special occasion" meat. We love it any time, any way, and as far as wine goes …

❖ For basic lamb chops or roasts, a Rioja like the 2000 Pequera Tinto brings out the earthiness in the meat. Lamb also is an excellent accompaniment to a well-aged Cabernet Sauvignon like the Miner Family 1999 version, or a Zinfandel like Howell Mountain's 1999.

❖ When lamb is included in a dish like shepherd's pie, try a Rioja like Lorinon's 1999 Rioja or even a peppery Petite Syrah like the Ridge 1999 Petite Syrah.

When we did our spicy-food pairing with Michael Lomonaco (see Chapter Twenty-One), he threw in an extra dish that wasn't part of the theme, but that was a bonus in its own right: a savory shepherd's pie made with both beef and lamb. We loved it so much, we've made it ourselves. Now you can, too. Pair it with an earthy Rioja like the 1996 Contino Rioja Reserva, invite some friends or the in-laws over, and enjoy:

**New Shepherd's Pie a la Michael Lomonaco**

   2 TB. olive oil

   2 lb. combined beef top round and lamb shoulder, cubed or sliced

   1 cup diced onion

   2 cloves garlic, finely chopped

   Several fresh sprigs of rosemary, thyme, and savory, chopped

   Salt and pepper to taste

   2 TB. flour

   ½ cup dry red wine

   ½ cup hot beef broth

   2 lb. hot mashed Yukon gold potatoes

   ¼ cup melted butter

   2 egg yolks

Heat olive oil in a large sauté pan over medium heat. Add beef and lamb in batches, searing until crisp and brown on the outside (avoid crowding meat in the pan because it will steam). When done, in the same pan, increase heat to high and add onion, garlic, and herbs. Season with salt and pepper. Sprinkle mixture with flour to thicken. Add wine and simmer for 3 minutes. Add beef broth and simmer for 5 minutes more.

Meanwhile, combine hot, cooked potatoes with butter and egg yolks. Place meat mixture into a round, deep casserole dish (a deep-dish pie plate works well), top with mashed potatoes, and brown under the broiler for 5 minutes. Serves 4 to 6.

# Pork

Pork has made quite a showing on menus in the last few years. Where once folks seemed to shy away from this supposedly fatty meat, now it's the darling of the meat-eating food world. You find it everywhere and in every way—pulled, smoked, roasted, barbequed, stuffed. You name it. But, despite its inclusion in the red-meat category, it is probably the most versatile meat as far as wine goes (although, in the last chapter, we saw that turkey was a similar ringer in the land of fowl).

❖ For basic loin chops or roasts, the light-bodied supple, plummy nature of Pinot Noir doesn't overpower the meat with flavors that are too big for simple cooking methods. We suggest the 2000 Rex Hill Pinot for pork.

❖ The salty nature of pork and the sweetness of fruit are excellent foils. That's why you'll often see pork served with some kind of apple, pear, fig, prune, date, pineapple, or other fruit accompaniment. If this is the way you'll be dining, Riesling will cut through the salt and bring out the fruit in your dish. Go for a Schloss Saarstein 2001 Riesling Kabinett.

There's nothing like a backyard barbeque in warm weather—the aroma of grilled meat alone is enough to cause traffic accidents. So what do you do when barbeque sauce is added into the mix? Think about the flavors involved—barbeque sauce is tangy, acidic, honey-sweet, slightly spicy. The lower tannins in a Pinot Noir or a Merlot will withstand the tang and acid, but accentuate the earthy, smoky quality of the meat.

# Game

The most common animal game that you'll find is venison (deer) or rabbit. There are others—buffalo, boar, reindeer, etc.—but they are usually imported and not readily available in most states. Because of this, we're going to deal with the game animals that you're most likely to find on a menu. Game's slightly unctuous nature makes it a shoo-in for a high-acid wine.

❖ **Venison.** When we talk about venison we mean deer (which is what it means in most butcher shops), but technically venison includes any number of larger-size game animals, like elk or moose. Although deer is a popular hunting animal, the venison you find in your local butcher shop is usually from deer confined to a large stretch of private land to ensure that they live in a natural environment, but don't suffer the fate of many deer (starvation due to overpopulation, for instance) in the wild. Venison can be served in similar ways to beef—as steak, ground, braised, etc. A Domaine Drouhin 2000 Pinot Noir undercuts some of the gaminess of the meat with its full fruit, yet its earthy qualities allow the nature of the meat to remain in the forefront.

❖ **Rabbit.** Although rabbit can be roasted, you will more often than not see it braised (for a great example, check out our pairing with Don Pintabona and the rabbit cacciatore he makes for us in Chapter Fourteen). For this method of cooking, again, you've got to get down to basics. A simple Chianti like the 1998 Deivole "Novecento" Chianti Classico Riserva we had with Don, or a Barbera, has that earthy quality that pairs so lusciously well with braised rabbit.

Because meat (even the leaner cuts) contains fat, it is richer and heavier in texture and taste. Therefore, you need to find a wine that can stand up to its bold nature. A delicate, low-acid wine will lose all its charm when sipped with steak au poivre—it's like putting a ballerina in the ring with a heavyweight boxer, not something you want to do. This doesn't necessarily always mean red, but just make sure what you drink has the acid to stand up to the meal. Again, match the weight of the food to the weight of the wine, and don't forget to think about what's influencing the meat (Barbecue sauce? Braising? Pepper?). Experiment with different styles of wine, and when you find yourself confidently extolling upon your personal preference for Rioja with lamb while your dining companion claims that California Cabernet is the only way to go, you'll know you've gained the kind of confidence and experience that has put you on a whole new and exciting level of food and wine pairing.

Not so familiar with your meat cuts? This short primer on the finer points of meat ought to help you navigate the anatomy of your carnivorous craving in question:

**Chops:** A cut from the rib section. Chops are a commonly found cut for lamb, pork, and veal.

**Chuck:** From the neck and shoulder blade areas. Good for ground meat, but also is excellent for slow cooking and braising, as this makes the meat much, much more tender.

**Crown roast:** Rib bones of a lamb or pork loin tied into a circle with the ribs pointing up.

**Porterhouse:** A steak that has portions of both the tenderloin and the top loin muscles and contains a bone. Generally good for feeding larger groups (more than two).

**Shank:** Front leg area of a cow, pig, or lamb.

**Short loin:** Area located in the center of the back between the rib cage and the sirloin with two main muscles running through it—the tenderloin and the top loin.

**Sirloin:** Tender cut of meat located next to the short loin, usually made into steaks or roasts.

**Skirt:** A cut of meat from the diaphragm muscle. Can be tough, but is very flavorful.

**Strip:** From the tenderloin with the bone removed. Also called a New York steak, New York strip steak, or shell steak, Delmonico steak, or Kansas City steak.

**Tenderloin:** This is the muscle where you get your filet mignon from. It's the least-used muscle and, thus, the most tender.

**Top loin:** The muscle where Delmonico, Kansas City, and New York strips come from.

# chapter fourteen

# Vintage Words: Interview with Don Pintabona, Tribeca Grill

*I'm sick of hearing sommeliers saying, Well, you can't use asparagus and you can't use artichokes. Guess what? We're going to use it!*

—Don Pintabona

The life surrounding a great chef can be extremely glamorous and exciting, what with all the famous clients, the accolades, the acclaim, the eponymously named cookbooks, and interviews in glossy national magazines. In fact, in the last decade chefs have experienced the kind of fame more akin to the latest hot rock 'n' roll star than that of someone who toils behind a hot stove.

There's an interesting thing that many of these revered epicureans have in common, though. It seems that as their fame grows, their hearts do as well. Truly, it makes sense—anyone who loves to cook or simply loves to eat knows that wonderful feeling of wanting to share it, talk about it, and experience it collectively. Food brings people together. It fulfills us, makes us smile, even teaches us about each other.

Don Pintabona, the star chef of Tribeca Grill (better known around downtown Manhattan as "De Niro's place"), is someone who knows a little about big hearts. Although his culinary talents have been lauded by *Wine Spectator, GQ, Food & Wine, Gourmet,* and *Bon Appétit,* to name just a few, it was the difficult and tragic events of September 2001 that made this lifelong New Yorker stop to answer the calling of his community at large. Pintabona dreamed up and spearheaded Chefs with Spirit—the campaign he led to feed the tireless relief workers who toiled at Ground Zero for months on end. Serving up to 25,000 meals a day around the clock, he used every resource he had to bring some sustenance and comfort at a time when it was needed most.

About a year later, Pintabona stepped down as Tribeca's executive chef to gather his family 'round their own hearth fires, as well as pen a tome close to his heart, a cookbook drawing on his Sicilian grandmother's recipes. It seemed fitting, then, that we gathered at his Brooklyn home for a real family-style hearty tasting.

*Don prepares dinner.*

As we sat in the warm, French-country style kitchen, the meaty, hearty aromas wafting from the stove became the focal point of the evening—as well as which wines would come out the pairing champions.

## Course I

Roasted venison loin with a lemon-herb crust, root vegetables, and the Pintabona (secret) cardoon casserole
Livingston-Moffett Cabernet Sauvignon, "Stanley's Selection," 1999
Honing Cabernet Sauvignon, "Stagecoach Vineyard," 1999
Elyse Syrah, 1999
Qupé Syrah, 2000

## Course II

Veal tenderloin with porcini gnocchi and creamed leeks
Di Gresy Barbaresco "Martinenga," 1996
San Filippo Brunello di Montalcino, 1995
Domaine Confueron Contetidot "Vosne Romane," 1997

## Course III

Hunter's-style rabbit cacciatore
San Filippo Brunello di Montalcino, 1995
Deivole "Novecento" Chianti Classico Riserva, 1998

## Course I: Into the Woods

Don gave us a tough challenge to start off the evening. To find a match for the venison on its own wasn't too difficult a task, but to it Don added a monkey-wrench of a side dish—his version of his grandmother's cardoon casserole. With meat, this is a conundrum you may well come across. Meat itself can be a fairly easy match (most of the time). But with meat usually is a side dish or two, and as far as this goes the sky's the limit. What do you do when the side becomes a formidable challenger?
**Don Pintabona:** Okay, this is the roasted venison.
**Tony DiDio:** And to go with it we've got two Cabs and two Syrahs—a Livingston Cab and a Honing Cab; and an Elyse Syrah and a Qupé Syrah.
**Don:** That's a great selection.

**Amy Zavatto:** What's the seasoning on the venison?

**Don:** It's got a lemon-herb crust on it with a strict Cabernet reduction. There's also parsley, rosemary, thyme, and I put a little bit of oregano in there.

**Amy:** Of course, I'm thinking it's a shoo-in that the Cabernet is going to do really well with the venison, but maybe the pepper of the Syrah will do well with the herbs. I'm really curious ...

**Don:** We've also got the cardoons, baby turnip, and chipolini on the side.

**Tony:** Chipolini is like the lost onion these days.

**Amy:** What's in cardoon casserole?

**Don:** Parsley, garlic, Parmesan cheese ...

**Tony:** Cardoons to me are like a cross between celery and artichoke. Actually, it's a cousin of the artichoke. It's a tough wine match.

**Don:** It *is* actually a tough thing to match. But this dish was a little selfish. I was testing the recipe for my new cookbook.

**TD** and **Amy:** So selfish!

*[laughter]*

**Don:** But I'm sick of hearing sommeliers saying, well, you can't use asparagus and you can't use artichokes. Guess what? We're going to use it! How do we fix the problem?

**Tony:** I would say to anyone who has a problem with asparagus, etc., I think you have to use a wine that has more of a grassy nature to it. I would use a Sauvignon Blanc from New Zealand. I would also consider going to a Sancerre; something from the Loire that has a high grass taste to it. However, this—the cardoons—is a little different.

**Amy:** What about Châteauneuf-du-Pape? That's a blend of both red and white, right?

**Tony:** Yes, but you don't necessarily use all of the white grapes in that. Really, it has nothing to do with being white or red, it has to do with what the nature of the grape is.

**Amy:** What about a Viognier with this?

**Tony:** Viognier is too aromatic for the meat, but it might be good for the cardoon. It has a peachy essence to it, which would also temper the salt and herbs. What we've got here is cheese in the cardoon. Normally, the cardoon would do well with an un-oaked esoteric white, but the addition of cheese changes that. The fat in it can stand up against the tannins in the red wine.

**Don:** I really like the Honing Cabernet.

**Amy:** I like that with the meat. This is really great venison, but even so, it's going to be gamy. The earthiness of the wine works well with that. The other Cabernet, though, seems a little harsh.

**Don:** To me too.

**Tony:** I think the Honing is the one for venison. The Livingston Cabernet is a big, big wine; it's unforgiving at this point. It's still tightly wound. The Honing has a lot of nice fruit to it.

**Don:** Definitely, of these two Cabernets, I prefer the Honing.

**Tony:** I think the Honing across the board—it's working with the cardoon, too.

**Amy:** Well, I'm still trying to get my brain around the whole dish— the meat and the cardoon side. I think there is such a thing as the perfect wine/perfect dish combination. If you look at this dish, you have an aromatic root vegetable—the cardoon—you have the cheese, you have seasonings. You have the Cabernet reduction to temper and to complement the venison, so you already have Cabernet in the dish. Now what you need is a wine that won't be so light that you lose the flavor and all you have left is alcohol and heat. And you don't want a wine that's complicating things further because this dish is already complicated. What we learned at Daniel was if you have a complicated dish, you need a one-dimensional wine; you can go just so far. A three-level wine matches a three-level dish but once you get past that, the more levels you have on one side, the less levels you want to have on the other so it doesn't get muddy.

**Don:** So, do you think there's one compatible mate for every person in the world?

*[laughter]*

**Tony:** Well, I don't know about that—there's billions of people, but there aren't billions of wines!

**Amy:** I don't know, Tony, if there's anything I'm starting to see it's that there's a lot of wines …

*[more laughter]*

**Tony:** But you know, if the cardoons were presented a different way, it would have changed the whole complexity of the meal. The way you prepared the cardoons really made them very intense. I think we're going back to the notion of what do you do when you have such a complex dish that you need to match a wine to, but you don't have any wine that's really going to do it except something one-dimensional. But in this case, the Honing is more than that because it's fruity.

**Amy:** Hey, here's a crazy idea—what about a Chardonnay at room temperature?

**Tony:** That might work, you're right. I think another wine that could work would be a Nebbiolo rosé because you have the red, you still have some of the qualities of the fruit [of the Honing], but it's still considered a white, so the cardoons would go with a Nebbiolo rose.

**Don:** This dish definitely has some of the qualities of a full, heavy meal and some of a light one. Which is this wine?

**Tony:** That's the Qupé Syrah. Actually, now, how is everyone feeling about the Syrahs?

**Amy:** I'm finding the fruitiness of the Elyse Syrah tempers the salt in the cardoons.

**Don:** It's definitely got a lot of fruit to it.

**Tony:** That's the nature of it—big and fruity.

**Amy:** I think that's what counteracts the saltiness. To me, that fruitiness is working with both the venison and cardoon. I don't like the Qupé with the venison, though.

**Don:** Me neither, but the Honing is the one that I keep going back to.

**Amy:** Yeah, I can see that. But both of these, the Elyse Syrah and the Honing Cab, have that similar fruitiness which is, I think, why either can work.

**Tony:** Exactly. To me, the Honing is the way to go. But the Elyse Syrah isn't bad. Fruit-forward was the key.

## Course II: Tender Is the Dish

Veal tenderloin, soft porcini gnocchi, creamed leeks—our second course was one luscious wonder complementing the next. And so, of course, only a big, elegant wine would pair. We brought along three selections to compete in round two: a Di Gresy Barbaresco, a San

Filippo Brunello di Montalcino, and Domaine Confueron Contetidot
from Burgundy.

**Don:** This is earthy, man.

**Tony:** This is Eartha Kitt!

**Amy:** No kidding. I love the way the textures of this dish are so incredibly comforting. The color of this Barbaresco—it's so rich, so earthy itself.

**Tony:** The tannins in it go beautifully with the richness and the creaminess of the leeks.

**Don:** It's really working with the porcini.

**Amy:** Yeah, that's what I'm really loving. The Montalcino, I don't know …

**Tony:** It's packed with fruit. It's got some earthy undertones, but there's a chocolaty essence to it that I don't think is working well with the delicate nature of the veal.

**Amy:** It also seems to be mowing over the 'shrooms.

**Tony:** Well, you have to remember, these are two wines that can be unpredictable in some ways. They're both elegant, old wines—Brunello de Montalcino is made from Sangiovese Grosso in Tuscany and Barbaresco from the Nebbiolo grape in Piedmonte. We're talking royalty here, but …

**Amy:** The royals can get riled.

**Tony:** These are elegant wines, but there's a lot going on.

**Don:** The last one …

**Tony:** The Contetidot.

**Don:** Yes. That isn't working for me with this.

**Amy:** I took a sip of that before trying the dish, and then went back to it and it really seemed to have changed. But I'm not sure it's just from the food.

**Tony:** Well, that's possible with that.

**Don:** Although the Montalcino is a beautiful wine, really stunning, I think the earthiness of the Barbaresco is the one that's working best here.

**Tony:** I agree.

**Amy:** I do, too. It doesn't overpower the veal but picks up on all the other great influences in the dish. Plus, the tannins are hanging in there with the creamed leeks.

## Course III: Rabbit Is Rich

Our finale was Don's gamy twist on an Italian classic—cacciatore. The result was a tender, aromatic braised delight that was ever more rich because of the substitution of hearty rabbit for the usual chicken of this dish. It cried out for a regional accompaniment ... but which one?

**Tony:** I have a feeling the Chianti is going to be the winner here, but I'm trying to withhold judgment ...

**Amy:** Well, again, in the last dish we saw that this Montalcino had some great depth to it, and it could do well with a dish like this.

**Don:** The Chianti is what I would choose off the bat. It's really working well here. It's a rustic wine and this is a rustic dish.

**Tony:** The interesting thing is both of these wines are made from Sangiovese grapes, so we're really going regional here, which is always the way to go as far as I'm concerned.

*Tony and dinner guest Jimmy Rose talk cacciatore, while Amy and Don keep tasting.*

**Amy:** Don, this is really delicious. The meat is falling off the bone. I could eat the entire pot!

**Don:** Thank you.

**Tony:** It's true. This is great. Now this is cold-weather food.

**Amy:** Exactly.

**Don:** This Chianti—it's hands down the right wine for this dish. The acid is great with the tomato.

**Amy:** I think it has a spiciness to it, too, that enhances the flavors of the vegetables. It's also got a plummy flavor to it that really works well with the meat. I think fruit-forward wines with that acidity you were talking about—they really work with game.

**Tony:** What about the Montalcino with this dish? How does everyone feel about that?

**Don:** Again, it's a really nice wine, but I can't get away from the Chianti. The Montalcino is a little too elegant.

**Amy:** I think so, too. I don't dislike it at all—if this were the only choice I had, I would be perfectly happy. It's certainly got the acidity. But in comparing the two, the Chianti just seems to have that spice and that fruit that do the trick.

*Amy, Tony, and Don discuss pairing particulars.*

**Tony:** Exactly. So we're all in agreement?

**Don:** Chianti for me.

**Amy:** Me too.

**Tony:** *Perfetto.* If only we were in Tuscany …

You would be hard pressed to mention Tuscany and not think of Chianti. Dating back to the Middle Ages, this once small region is now the biggest wine-producing region in all of Italy. The Chianti region is subdivided into seven smaller regions, and all grow the same noble grape, Sangiovese. Chianti Classico is the subzone in central Tuscany, and deserves the highest praise for its reputation for fine wines. Any Chiantis with the prestigious label of Chianti Classico Riserva means that the wine sees more aging, both in barrel and bottle, before release.

As you move away from the Classico region in central Tuscany and head farther south, you reach the town of Montalcino, home of the great wine Brunello di Montalcino (*Brunello* literally translates as "nice dark one"). These dark, almost purple wines are made from a strain of the Sangiovese called Brunello di Montalcino. With minimum aging of three to five years, this incredible cousin of the Sangiovese thrives in the soil surrounding the village of Montalcino. It yields a very dark and concentrated wine. These are perhaps the finest wines to come out of Tuscany today. With its patient, long-aging process, a Brunello may change your notions that Italian wines come in little straw-encased bottles and are served on the requisite red-and-white checkered table cloth, as this is the stuff of grace and elegance.

## Try It for Yourself

Forget the supermarket—head for your favorite butcher shop and get some rabbit to make the luscious, tender cacciatore that Don made for us. Pair it with a Montalcino or a Chianti Riserva as we did, and let the tasting (and savoring) begin.

## Cacciatore

1 (2½- to 3-lb.) young rabbit, cut into pieces

The zest and juice from 1 large lemon

1 tsp. fresh rosemary

6 whole white peppercorns

2 cloves garlic, chopped

6 TB. olive oil (divided use)

½ tsp. salt

¼ cup flour for dusting

Pepper to taste

1 cup chicken broth

1 medium onion, chopped

1 carrot, diced

2 stalks celery, diced

1 (12-oz.) pkg. button mushrooms, sliced

1 cup red wine

1 (28-oz.) can whole peeled plum tomatoes, crushed (i.e., you crush them—don't buy them crushed already!)

1 bay leaf

Salt, pepper, red pepper flakes to taste

¼ cup chopped parsley

Thoroughly wash rabbit under running water and pat dry. Trim any remaining connective tissue. Using a spice grinder or a mortar and pestle, grind together lemon zest, rosemary, peppercorns, garlic, 2 tablespoons olive oil, and ½ teaspoon salt into a coarse paste. Rub this onto rabbit and let sit for 30 minutes. (Of course, you can let it sit longer if you want to prepare earlier in the day.)

Dust rabbit pieces with the flour, shaking off any excess. Heat remaining 4 tablespoons olive oil in a large saucepot (a Dutch oven would be best, if you have it) over medium-high heat. Season rabbit with salt and pepper, and brown well on all sides (about 10 minutes).

Add onion, carrot, celery, and mushrooms, and sauté with rabbit on low flame until soft, but not brown—about 5 minutes.

Pour in red wine and reduce by half. Add stock, tomatoes, and bay leaf. Season with salt, pepper, and red pepper flakes, and bring to a boil. Lower heat to a simmer, cover and let simmer about 2 hours, until rabbit is tender and sauce has thickened. Add parsley and serve with spaghetti or rice.

Serves 4.

If you have neither a spice grinder nor a mortar and pestle, don't panic. A good wooden spoon and a small but deep bowl ought to do the trick. Combine the ingredients as instructed, find a good, solid chair and table, and mash away with the wooden spoon until you get what appears to be a coarse paste.

*chapter fifteen*

# Pairing Wine with Vegetables

*After all, I can compare bliss with near bliss, for I have often, blessèd me, eaten superlative green peas.*

—*M.F.K. Fisher,* The Art of Eating

Think about this: (1) There are around 2,000 native varietals of *Vitis vinifera* in Italy alone; (2) there are around 2,000 different edible plants growing today on Earth. Whether or not you remember how to find the probability of all possible pairings in this scenario (don't even attempt to add to this the grape varietals of France, Spain, the United States, South America, New Zealand, South Africa …), it neatly adds up to one conclusion: There are a whole lot of wine and herbivorous combinations out there.

To pair wine with vegetarian food is to experience the boon of biodiversity. But whether you only consume plants in your diet or you're a carnivore who just loves what nature has to offer in the way of veggies, overlooking the influence of wine on vegetables, and vice versa, is like visiting Rome and passing on the Pantheon.

When we think about a vegetarian dish, we consider the ingredients to be a cast of characters in a show. The star, the sidekick, the chorus, the charming villain—and we are its willing (possibly salivating) audience. Some, like a stuffed artichoke or eggplant prepared any old way, can really take center stage; and some, like root vegetables, sautéed onions, or neatly chopped pieces of pepper, quietly support the main character by adding texture, color, and flavor to the dish.

What is a vegetarian exactly? We all know (or some of us are) different versions of this umbrella term. Some people call themselves vegetarians but eat fish; others won't touch any animal product, including dairy. So who's who?

- **Vegetarian.** Someone who consumes no red meat or flesh. However, as noted earlier, some vegetarians will consume fish, but no other meat.
- **Ovo-lacto vegetarian.** No flesh is consumed at all, but animal products are A-Okay.
- **Lacto vegetarian.** All vegetables, no eggs, but dairy is okay.
- **Vegan.** The vegetable and nothing but the vegetable. Vegans won't consume any animal or fish flesh, nor the byproducts of animals (dairy, eggs, and sometimes even honey).

Whatever title they take, there are a lot more vegetarians in the world these days than ever before (just for fun, check out www.famousveggie.com/peoplenew.cfm for a list of famous veggie lovers, past and present). As more and more restaurants are offering vegetarian options on their menus, learning how to pair wine with vegetarian main and side dishes is on the cutting edge of pairing.

When it comes to wine pairing with vegetables, much of what works and what doesn't boils (or steams or sautés) down to one thing: the presence of dairy product or eggs in the mix. The reason is that without these items in the mix, any wine with a highly tannic nature is likely to overpower the poor little green bean. It's like putting Mike Tyson in the ring with Art Garfunkel. There's just no contest.

But take away the brute force of fat, and you still have a world of options. Actually, you have a world of options with either scenario.

## Nude as a Pea

Without the fat of meat and dairy, what wine will complement the dish? This question can make vegetables almost seem like a difficult dilemma—the tempestuous tomato or fungi of the night.

The answer is a curious experimentation with esoteric wines. In fact, there is an entire group of wines known as the esoteric white wines of the world. The term "Esoteric Wines" is used in circles when discussing wines, mostly white, that are not in the mainstream (i.e., the main varietals we talked about in Chapter Two). An esoteric wine is usually a single varietal or a unique blend, native to the region where it grows, and the wine drunk mostly by the locals.

An excellent example is *Arneis* from Italy, a native vinifera grape found growing in the wild. Someone took cuttings, planted a vineyard, and produced a wine that was new and locally appreciated. Then the world's wine community discovered the Arneis and a small village's dwindling economy was revived … by a humble little tart white grape.

Esoteric wines are notable for vegetarian cuisine because they are usually simple wines with unique flavor and aroma profiles. They are gentle, humble wines that play well with the many fragile flavors of plants and fungi. Also, one of the core principles of vegetarian cuisine is the story behind the food. If the food is locally grown it will be fresher and more vibrant. If the food is organic it will have a deeper flavor. If the produce is of heirloom origin (that is, of an ancient, untampered-with seed variety), the flavors will be unique. Who grew the food? What is the region's history? Is the recipe traditional or new? All these factors add to the story of the meal.

So what do you do with sweet and bitter greens, dark-skinned eggplants, and hearty root veggies? Here are a few suggestions for main dish or side pairings that would please even Mother Nature:

| Vegetable | Flavor Profile | Wine Suggestion |
|---|---|---|
| Mushrooms | Dark, earthy flavors, meaty texture when grilled | Well-aged Amarone, Pinot Noir, Champagne (with truffles) |
| Root vegetables (carrots, potatoes, onions, turnips, beets, parsnips) | When raw, crispy, sweet, starchy flavors; when cooked, earthy, hearty, sweet, smoky | Riesling (raw), Chardonnay (when cooked) |
| Leafy bitter greens (spinach, arugula, escarole) | Biting, herbaceous, austere | Semillon |

| Vegetable | Flavor Profile | Wine Suggestion |
|---|---|---|
| Dark-skinned vegetables (squash, peppers) | Earthy, starchy, acidic, sometimes sweet | Pinot Grigio, Dolcetto, Beaujolais |
| Leafy, sweet greens and stems (lettuce, celery, green beans) | Crisp, sweet, refreshing | Riesling |

# The Problem Children: Salad, Asparagus, and Artichoke

A few veggie items make for difficult—if not impossible—pairing. Forewarned is forearmed, so before you pour a glass of your favorite Chardonnay or Sauvignon Blanc, heed the following warnings.

## Salad

That last item on our chart, leafy, sweet greens and stems, has been known to make for some pairing conundrums when they come in salad form. The problem arises from the vinegar that they are usually dressed with. Vinegar, as you well know, is most often the result of good wine gone bad (and then turned into something downright delicious). However, the super sour, tangy nature of vinegar—be it red, white, or balsamic—is extremely acidic, to the point of throwing off just about any wine you might try to match. When vinegar is coating your veggies, you'd do well to steer clear of wine until the next course.

## Asparagus

Asparagus, with its intense racy, grassy flavor, makes wine pairing surprisingly difficult, even for the most sophisticated sommelier. When dealing with straight asparagus (lightly steamed with maybe a little lemon and salt), we like Cailbourdin Pouilly-Fumé "Les Cris" from 2001. We also found that a Giesen Sauvignon Blanc from 2002 did the trick as well.

If you want to manipulate asparagus by adding a little fat, this eases the dilemma slightly. Also, white asparagus has a much milder and thus easier pairing nature. Tony has a tradition every April when he visits

Alois and Veronica Lageder in Bolzano, Italy. Tony and his boss, Ed Lauber, go to the Lageder's home for dinner and they pray for one dish: white asparagus. Usually grown in Spain or Sicily, white asparagus appears in the food markets in northern Italy during the first two weeks of April, and they are fat, stubby, and meaty. Veronica steams the asparagus until fork-tender, makes a béchamel sauce for them, and crumbles hard-boiled eggs on top. Between fighting for the last spear, Tony and Ed usually wash them down with Lageder Pinot Bianco "Haberlehof," which they find to be the perfect accompaniment.

## Artichokes

On their own, artichokes present another strong-flavored vegetable dilemma. But just like asparagus, if you add a little fat into the mix, the pairing becomes much more amenable. There are lots of ways to doctor an artichoke: marinated hearts in olive oil, leaves dipped in Hollandaise, or stuffed Italian style. The addition of a dairy product like cheese or cream gives you many more pleasing options.

Rose DiDio, Tony's mom and a great Sicilian cook, stuffs her artichokes with bread crumbs, garlic, parsley, and grated parmigiana. This method takes away from the vegetal taste of the artichoke and adds another layer of flavor without masking the artichoke's appeal. We tried two wines that worked and didn't overpower: Vietti Arneis 2001 and Villadoria Lavi 2001. Both wines tamed the aggressive taste of the artichoke and worked well with the stuffing.

# Fat Farm

Of course, certain vegetables and fruits do contain some kind of fat. It exists in nuts, seeds, avocado, olive and vegetable oils, soybeans, and other plants as well. This is not the same fat that's marbleized through a steak, or that coats your mouth when you nibble on cheese. It is, instead, of the polyunsaturated nature. Polyunsaturated fat is rich in omega-3 fatty acids (also found in fish), which have been proven to lower blood cholesterol levels. However, it is lighter than the type of fat found in animal products and can only go so far with tannins. For example, hummus (a mix of chickpeas, tahini paste, and lemon) has fat to match the tannins of white Burgundy or buttery California

Chardonnay; it even has enough fat to handle a Pinot Noir, or a soft, well-aged Amarone—but it'll lose against a young, feisty Cabernet or a big Barolo.

While you shouldn't ignore reds, the esoteric whites are where to explore. When pairing an esoteric white with, say, a nut-based dish, consider the following: varietal, which is a good clue to flavor and aroma profiles; climate or region, which can tell you a good deal about acidity levels, residual sugar, and alcohol levels; what nut or nuts are used in the dish; and what other ingredients are in the dish. Are the ingredients organic? Heirloom? Asking yourself these questions can help you to make a great, informed wine selection. Most important, consider what the star player is in the dish, as this is going to give you a starting point is your selection.

Let's go simple, like Sauvignon Blanc with almonds and Brussels sprouts. When deciding which Sauvignon Blanc is the best option, go for one from New Zealand that will complement the milky qualities of the nut. You could also pair this with a citrusy Pouilly-Fuisse, because the clean, brisk citrusy flavor of the wine deconstructs any overwhelming qualities of the sprouts with fresh lemon influences while sweetening the bitter qualities of the dish—yet keeps the flavors interesting. Or you can head to the Loire for a wine soaked with Boxwood and perfumed with refreshing, floral aromas.

When buying vegetables, going seasonal and, even better, organic is the way to go. You may have noticed this back-to-basics approach among restaurants, as many chefs love using local produce in season as opposed to hard-to-find items that don't showcase the freshness and earthy qualities inherent in great cooking. Organic foods are more in tune with the ecology of the area in which they are grown. Their depth of flavor can't be matched by preservative-filled, pesticide-dusted, bioplastic shipped items from thousands of miles away.

Not to be overlooked as a possible match for vegetables are rosé wines. They offer more body, slightly more tannin, but their fruit-forward nature never upstages that green diva on the plate. French rosés from Provence are floral and light and go well with raw vegetables as well as dishes that contain cooked onions. Spanish and Italian rosés are more fruity and exhibit some herbal qualities, and do very well with spicy dishes. New World rosés are packed with fruit and minerals, and pair beautifully with roasted tomatoes, eggplant, stuffed peppers, and the like.

And as tannins soften with age, one could drink wine of red varietals respective to their age. Pinot Noirs first, then Spain and Italy, then Bordeaux, then New World Cabernets, Merlots, and Syrahs. As we like our fruits and vegetables to be ripe, we also like our wine to be ripe and ready to drink.

The avocado may have fat, but as any fruit or veggie that does, it's the good kind—polyunsaturated. Avocados are also chock full of vitamin E, vitamin C, and thiamin. You also might find it interesting to know that in Central and South America, avocados are considered to be an aphrodisiac. Their name comes from the Aztec word *ahuacatl*, meaning testicle (shocking, we know!), and its powers were considered so great that young Aztec women were confined to quarters during the harvest time for the fruit. Next time you're planning a romantic evening, forget about the chocolate-dipped strawberries. Slice up some avocado, pop open a bottle of Verdad, and let the sparks fly. Verdad has great fruitiness that emerges when it bonds with the mouth-coating vegetable fat in the avocado.

Whether you've given up the dairy and meat or just like your greens, you've opened yourself up to the experience of ever-more challenging and imaginative food and wine pairing that encourages you to explore the bounty of nature's cornucopia.

# chapter sixteen

# Pairing Wine with Pasta

*Life is a combination of magic and pasta.*
—*Federico Fellini*

We haven't really focused on particular ethnic foods in this book yet. When you start talking about pasta, though, it's hard not to get a vision of that boot-shape country in your head.

Noodles exist in many cultures, and prominently so. But in Italy, pasta is to dining tables what sunshine is to flora; absolutely necessary for existence. The stuff is taken very, very seriously (in the laid-back manner that only Italians are capable of purporting, of course).

Amy witnessed this firsthand when she and her husband, Dan, were visiting family in the tiny town of Maenza outside of Rome. They happened to arrive during a particular saint's festival in August. The morning after their arrival they awoke to a flurry of activity outside their window. They opened the shutters and peeked out onto the piazza to find groups of aproned women making gnocchi. For days, that's all that happened: Strong-handed women rolled and cut pounds and pounds of gnocchi morning, noon, and night, boiled in gigantic vats of water, and then topped from equally large vats of sauce. And it was given away without charge to anyone who wanted it as part of the celebration. This was serious stuff!

Having both grown up in Italian families, Tony and Amy know that it's nearly impossible to get away from the family dinner table without consuming some kind of noodle. But pasta dishes aren't all about heavy sauces. Real Italian cooking relishes simplicity: simple, fresh ingredients combined to create one gorgeous dish (see Chapter Seventeen for chef Mauro Mafrici's take on the topic).

As far as pairing goes, it's easy enough to navigate a wine list and a dinner menu following basic rules of weight, acid, and balance. We have confidence that, at this point, you could certainly do that just fine on your own. But when it comes to Italian cooking, there are few greater arguments for going regional with your wine, as nearly every area of Italy's verdant land has its own specialty cuisine and grape. With this in mind, we'd like to take you on an abbreviated culinary tour of sorts. To go through each region isn't quite necessary for our purposes here—plenty of grape-growing areas produce small amounts of vino that's consumed only in that area and never (or rarely) leaves its borders. But others are well worth the discussion here because you will not only learn about important varietals from one of the motherlands of wine production, but also the food that is intrinsic to them. Pull up a chair, grab a fork for twirling and your favorite glass, and get ready to match bottles to noodles.

> The food of Italy is often referred to as one of the Mother Cuisines of the food world. And its wine? The Ancient Greeks dubbed southern Italy *Oinotria,* meaning "land of wine." The Romans, not being fond of border barriers, extended the title to all of Italy, calling it *Enotria.* The origins of pasta are a little less decisive. Most of us learned in our history classes that it was Marco Polo's expedition to China that bestowed noodles upon the boot. However, there are other theories. Sicilians believe that they learned of pasta from Ancient Greeks or Medieval Arabs. Romans claim that pasta was being consumed by its emperors long before Marco Polo was even born. Wherever it came from, one fact is undeniable: Italians make a darned good noodle.

## Abruzzi

Bordered by the clear, blue waters of the Adriatic on the east and the Apennines mountains in the west, Abruzzi is known for the soft, rustic nature and vibrant fruit of its Montepulciano d'Abruzzo (from the Montepulciano grape).

Culinary traditions mark those of an area bound by sea and mountain. Pasta—particularly maccheroni alla chitarra, a fine, long noodle—is flavored with diavolino, a red chili pepper notable to the area, saffron, lamb sauce, and the great cheese culled from the milk of goats that roam the mountainsides.

It's fitting, then, that Montepulciano d'Abruzzo is low in tannins to pair well with the spicy side of Abruzzian cuisine. Its rustic nature, however, lends itself beautifully to earthy, meaty sauces made with lamb. Next time you're topping your pasta in either of these delectable manners, try a Montepulciano by Zaccanini or a Trebbiano from Villa Cieri for the proper terroir-inspired coupling.

There are more than 300 varieties of pasta in Italy, all of which fall into two categories: pasta secca and pasta fresca. The former is made from durum semolina flour and water, and sold dried (i.e., what we get on the shelves of our local grocery stores). The latter is generally what you consume when you have fresh pasta, and it is made from eggs, wheat flour, and water. Of course, from here there are countless variations in which different influences are added to the dough—spinach, squid ink, sun-dried tomato, potato, and, of course, stuffings like ricotta, gorgonzola, seafood, meat, and anything else you can mash or dice and put inside.

# Apulia

The food of the Apulia (or for mental picture purposes, the heel of the boot) is influenced by four important staples that are widely produced, highly prized essentials of the region: vegetables, olive oil, *frutta di mare,* and pasta secca (specifically, several versions of *orecchiette, troccoli, fenescecchi,* and *mignuicchie*). Amy's mother-in-law, Aurora Marotta, comes from the seaside town of Lecce in the southernmost part of this region. Having eaten her cooking and visited her town, Amy can tell you that the freshness and simplicity of the dishes is rivaled only by the incredible hospitality of the people.

In Apulia, where long, hot summers are cooled by breezes off the crystal-clear Adriatic Sea, there are two grape varietals of note when you are dining southern Italian style. From negroamaro the rustic red wine Salice Salentino is made. Primitivo (made from Primitivo grapes) produces a spicy, dark-berry-influenced red similar to a California Zinfandel.

For hearty vegetable and pasta dishes, Salice Salentino is an excellent accompaniment. When dealing with meat-based sauces atop your orecchiette (which, by the way, means little ears after the shape of the pasta), a medium-bodied Primitivo, like the 2001 version from Villa Fanelli, complements the meat and acid of the tomato incredibly well.

For Apulian-inspired seafood and pasta fare, borrow a bottle of Soave from the Veneto or Nosiolo from Trentino (they won't mind!).

## Emilia-Romagna

With a capital like Bologna, which literally means "fat one," one might imagine that Emilia-Romagna is especially known for its cuisine. And one would be right. This is the land of Parmigiano-Reggiano, balsamic vinegar, prosciutto di Parma, not to mention pastas too innumerable to list. But you do start to notice something among this region's popular items: salt and tang.

Sangiovese di Romagna cuts through the salt of a prosciutto-topped pasta dish. If you're looking for something on the lighter side, a fizzy, refreshing sparkling red like Lambru or a mellow, fruity white Albana allow you to pair a light body with a starchy meal.

## Piedmonte

The food and wine of the northern Piedmonte region are among the most noteworthy in all of Italy (and that's saying a lot!). Home to the noble Nebbiolo grape, as well as Barbera and Dolcetto varietals in reds and Moscato d'Asti in white, the vino that comes from this area ranges from earthy and rustic like a Barbera to complex and exquisite, like the fine Barbaresco and Barbera, to floral and honeyed like a Moscato, providing a range of beverage to complement any dish.

And speaking of dishes, what do you say to white truffles shaved atop your buttery-tinged *tagliatelle* (an egg-based pasta particular to the region) with a glass of Dolcetto to cut through the dairy and egg and bring out the earthy flavor of the truffle? Or how about some *agnolotti* (half-moon-shape ravioli) stuffed with veal and sage with some Barbera? Perhaps instead you would prefer some pan-fried polenta sprinkled with gorgonzola cheese sipped with an elegant Barbaresco, or a Ghemme to drink with a risotto that has absorbed the rich flavor of beef broth used to cook it.

If you're following all of this by savoring some hunks of local gorgonzola, a sparkling, floral Moscato d'Asti counteracts the strong flavor of the cheese with its sweet, honeylike taste.

## Sardinia and Sicily

The wines produced here are less the dinner variety than the specialty quaffing ilk, but this doesn't mean pairing is a problem. Italians are a generous people—borrowing the food or drink from another region is perfectly acceptable. As far as Sardinia and Sicily go, the flavors and influences of the wines from sister regions take the incredible pasta specialties renowned here and create a dining experience to be reckoned with.

Maloreddus is the pasta of note in Sardinia, and also renowned are—that's right—the sardines. Myrtle and mint are also great influences on the food here. When you've got salty and starchy and herbaceous together like this, a wine like Nuragus is a great match, because it's a crisp, clean-tasting wine that cuts through the salt and cleanses the palate. (Most southerners believe this grape was first brought to the island and planted by the Phoenicians a few short years ago.)

In Sicily, each of the island's nine provinces has its own specialty pasta dish, further proving to Amy that the tenacious pride exhibited by her father-in-law, Felice, is no accident of personality. For each, we have a match made in Italy (that's heaven, if you didn't know):

- ❖ **Palermo.** *Pasta con le sarde* (also known as the dish that made Amy like sardines)—sardines, pine nuts, fennel, and raisins with a refreshing white Corvo.
- ❖ **Trapani.** *Spaghetti alla trapanese*—pasta with sheep's cheese, ripe tomatoes, and fresh basil with a Nero D'Avola from Cusmano.

- **Agrigento and Catania.** *Maccaruneddi con salsa rossa e melanzane* and *pasta alla Norma*—Each of these provinces do their own version of a sauce made from tomato and eggplant. Try it with a Rosso from Donna Fugat.
- **Caltanessetta.** *Gnocchetti di semola al sugo di maiale*—pork ragout with gnocchi with a Rosso del Conte from Regaleali.
- **Siracusa.** *Pasta fritta alla Siracusana*—fried vermicelli is the one dish here where we recommend going really local with a Sicilian-made Marsala Superiore Riserva.
- **Ragusa.** *Rigatoncini con maccu di fave*—rigatoncini with bean paste with a Vigna di Gabri from Donna Fugato.
- **Messina.** *Pasta ai quadrucci di pesce spada*—pasta with swordfish goes beautifully with a Faro from Bagni.
- **Enna.** *Frascatula di polenta di grano e verdure*—vegetable polenta matches perfectly with a Nozze d'Oro from Regaleali.

It is true that American Italian food and real Italian food tend to differ at times. Many of the items—like heavy, thick sauces and cheese-laden casseroles—you won't find in Italy. It was a lack of fresh ingredients in America that led to the creation of many American Italian standards. With that said, that doesn't mean you should shun your local favorite red-and-white checked cloth spot. Quite the contrary—just find the best wine for the job. Let's take lasagna, for instance. A traditional Italian American version tends to be loaded with noodles, meats, and cheese. That's a lot of flavor in one pan, so this is when Tony must evoke the mantra of Ravenswood Vineyards: "No wimpy wines!" Try a gutsy red with enough body to handle the beef and enough acid to cut through the trio of ricotta, mozzarella, and parmigiana. Any takers? Well, Tony says go south (in Italy, of course) until you come to Campania, and look for the great producer Mastroberardino. Ask for a Taurasi, and you've got the perfect pairing of Old World and New.

# The Tre Venezie

The northernmost area of Italy, known as the Tre Venezie, is composed of three well-respected wine regions: Friuli, Trentino–Alto Adige, and Veneto. Because the climate is more akin to bordering Austria as opposed to the hotter south, the white grape varietals produced here are particularly good. This is not to shun the reds of this area, though—some excellent, high-acid wines are made from red varietals as well.

From Friuli come racy whites like Tocai, Pinot Grigio (the two are often blended), Pinot Bianco, Sauvignon Blanc, and Chardonnays, which are very different than those of California. These are fresh, honest, aromatic, with lots of fruit. Native whites such as Verduzzo, Ribolla Gialla, and Tocai Friuliano all possess some, if not all, of these qualities. These are truly wines made in the vineyard, not tampered with in a winery. The Friulian Chardonnay, by the nature of its delicacy and aromatics, would not benefit from wood aging, like most California wines. That delicate and perfumed nose would be lost and replaced by a nose of oak and vanilla. Wood aging has its place in the wine world, but Friulian producers, for the most part, have resisted and we the consumers have benefited. Friulian reds like Cabernet Franc, Cabernet Sauvignon, and Merlot have great acid and are also worthy of note on your dinner table.

Trentino–Alto Adige, although also known for great Pinot Biancos, Pinot Grigios, Sauvignon Blancs, and Chardonnays, is the birthplace of Traminer—also known by its German name, Gewürztraminer. The Traminer version is a dry yet fruity white with notes of honey and allspice.

High-acid Alto Adige reds have great aging potential. You'll find Cabernet Sauvignon, Lagrein (you'll remember that from our tasting with Rick Moonen in Chapter Eleven), Merlot, and the smoky, spicy, dried-cherry and dark chocolate influences of Teroldego.

Veneto is home to the reds Amarone and Valpolicella. Valpolicella is a light red wine with a bouquet of black cherries, a wine to be drunk young. When the Valpolicella grapes from the hills north of the city of Verona are harvested and partially dried, they are made into rich and intense wine called Amarone, a wine made for aging. The Veneto is also the place of Tony's all-time favorite starter white, Prosecco, as well as Soave.

In the northern area of Friuli, fish is a popular choice, and fish with pasta is an even better choice. A popular dish of the Tre Venezia is the creamy, sweet, slightly briny seafood risotto (or *risotto alla maranese*). For a dish like this, go right for the 2001 Puatti Tocai.

The cooks of Trentino–Alto Adige are pretty crazy about potatoes—so much so that they even put it in their pasta. Particularly, gnocchi (a potato/pasta dumpling) and polenta made with spuds as well. For starchy dishes like these, a wine with good acidity will balance out the heavy feeling of the food. Try a 2001 Lageder Moscato Giallo.

As Veneto is the largest corn-producing region of Italy, polenta is obviously well loved here as well, but they like their version straight with no potatoes. *Pasta fagioli* is a traditional manner of eating noodles here, too, as is pasta with anchovies and tomatoes. In the latter, the salt and acid need a proper foil, which can be found in a Valpolicella like the 2000 Boscaini. Straight polenta with maybe the addition of some sage and pepper is refreshed by a glass of sparkling wine like Ferrari rosé.

# Tuscany

The Italian Renaissance, which was given life among the rolling hills and fertile lands of Tuscany, was about more than an outpouring of great art, architecture, philosophy, and literature. It was a movement based on particular ideals—balance, harmony, order, proportion—that permeated all of life, including food and wine.

Tuscany is home to one of the most important varietals in the country: Sangiovese. The Sangiovese grape is a bit of a chameleon, due to various clonings of the vine. The three most well-known wines that result are Chianti, Brunello di Montalcino, and Nobile de Montepulciano. When blended with cabernet grapes, Sangiovese is also the root of the complex, esteemed, and much-celebrated Super Tuscans. Tuscany is also home to *Vin Santo,* the sweet, biscotti-dipping white dessert wine that no self-respecting Southern Italian table is without following the main meal.

The hedonistic Italian dish fettuccini Alfredo—ribbonlike egg noodles bathed in a combination of heavy cream, parmesan, butter, and fresh pepper—has become a favorite beyond the shores of the boot. Invented in the decadent 1920s by Roman restaurateur Alfredo di Lello, this filling, creamy delight is well suited to a wine that refreshes rather than coats. Go for a 2000 Avignonesi Chardonnay "il Marzocco."

For our purposes here, though, Sangiovese is what we need to be concerned with. Along with that gorgeous grape, the Tuscans have great adoration for the fruit of the land. Fresh herbs, cauliflower, cardoons and artichokes, escarole, porcini mushrooms, spinach (you've undoubtedly noted this on menus billing items as Florentine style), briny capers and olives, and beans, beans, beans.

For spinach pastas or those accompanied by this bitter green veggie or escarole, we suggest that you try a Tuscan quaff like the 2001 Badia a Coltibuono "Trappolina." For a rustic, hearty *pasta fagiole* (pasta with beans) a Chianti Riserva like the 1999 Renzo Masi "Basciano" Riserva will stay within the theme of the dish. Porcini mushrooms take kindly to a 1999 Villa Puccini Vino Nobile.

## Umbria

The delicate nature of the food in Umbria is redolent of its austere Franciscan past. Birthplace of St. Francis of Assisi, Umbrian cuisine is best known for its delicate, simple nature. Herbs, extra virgin olive oil, anchovies, and the famous black truffles of Norcia permeate the pasta dishes of this fairytalelike region.

The wines, too, reflect the ideal of simple ingredients allowing for big results. The lush, big flavor of Sagrantino de Montefalco belongs beside a dish of anchovy and black truffle–topped pasta. The pale color and crisp, clean flavor of Orvieto has hints of honey and peach, yet remains dry. We like to sip a Barberani Vallesanta Orvieto before a meal—it's a lovely way to savor the anticipation of good things to come.

Didn't think there was so much to pair with just noodles, did you? What you probably can see by now is that what you drink depends on how the pasta is prepared. Is it a plain noodle covered in pungent olives and herbs? Cheese-filled dumplings with a light olive oil and sage coating? Or the heavy-handed but comforting plumpness of potato-filled gnocchi? However you'll be taking your pasta tonight, you'll do well—as always—to match the weight of your food to the weight of your wine and, of course, to pay attention to the balance of flavors between the glass and pasta bowl. *Buon appetito!*

*chapter seventeen*

# Vintage Words: Interview with I Trulli Chef Mauro Mafrici and Sommelier Charles Scicolone

*Some people think simplicity is boring—I don't think it's boring. I think simplicity is something that can really make a dish different. It's much more difficult than you'd think.*

—*Mauro Mafrici*

*People don't understand that this is work! People look at you like you're crazy, but it is work. Thinking about it and discussing it, having a philosophy of food and wine ...*

—*Charles Scicolone*

The city of New York overflows with celebrity chefs and the highly touted restaurants in which they create epicurean enchantment. This is not to say, of course, that fine dining is lost on the rest of the country. Quite the contrary—there are exciting regional innovations going on in food from shore to shore. But there is a slightly competitive spirit in NYC that has made dining out feel a little more like a sport than a purely pleasurable activity. In fact, you can't even get a reservation at many all-the-rage spots without having an in with the staff, or the tenacity to hang on for a two-month-long waiting list. Some deserve the hype; others don't. Warranted or not, visitors and natives alike take to restaurant exploration like Lewis and Clark on a mission to discover all that is new and wonderful.

There are some eateries, however, that quietly shirk the spotlight and, instead of creating an atmosphere of frenzied trendiness among their clientele, find themselves with throngs of steady, loyal diners who know a good thing when they eat it. Such is I Trulli.

When you meet chef Mauro Mafrici, a native of Friuli who comes from a long line of restaurateurs, you begin to understand. He is a quiet, unassuming, humble man. So much so that when you see him chatting away as a frequent guest on the Food Network discussing the delicacies of southern Italy, it comes as a bit of a shock. But this is Mafrici's style. To him, it's all about love of the food.

The ideal foil for Mafrici is the self-possessed, straight-backed sommelier of I Trulli, Charles Scicolone. He has the kind of assured presence that lets you relax a little, knowing that whatever he recommends is going to be the perfect complement, and you'd best follow suit. With more than 20 years in the business concentrating on the wines of Italy, Scicolone's all-Italian list at I Trulli is the fruit (pardon the pun) of years of study and work. He's also married to Michele Scicolone, the famous Italian cookbook author whose most recent tome, *The Sopranos Family Cookbook,* was in its eighth week on *The New York Times* best-seller list at the time this book was being written.

Mauro, Charles, and Michele joined us for an Italian-style tasting at I Trulli restaurant to glean the best circumstance for the mingling of wine and pasta. This was how the noodle boiled.

# Course I

Tagliolini with Fresh Tomato and Langoustines
Nino Franco Prosecco
Tocai Pinot Grigio, 2000, Volpe Pasini
Mulderbosch Sauvignon Blanc, 2001
Puatti Pinot Grigio

*The calm before the tasting.*

## Course II

Risotto with black truffles and porcini mushrooms
La Montecchia Cabernet Franc, 1999
Fattoria Chianti, 1999, Le Sorgenti
Pojer & Sandri Rosso Faye, 1998
Terre di Trinci Sagrantino di Montefalco, 1999

## Course III

Maloreddus (saffron-flavored gnocchi) with sausage, black truffles,
extra virgin olive oil, little garlic, and anchovies

Leone de Castris Salice Salentino, 1999 Riserva
Aleramici Rosso di Montalcino, 1999
Nadaria Nero D'avola, 2001
Terre de Rinci Sagrantino Montepulciano, 2000
Rivera Il Falcone, 1998
Le Sorgente Chianti, 1999

## Course IV

Timballo—Half Rigatoni Wrapped in Eggplant with Tomato,
Mozzarella, and Basil
Le Sorgente Chianti, 1999
Aleramici Rosso di Montalcino, 1999
Colle Carpito San Luciano, 1999
Deivole Chianti Classico, 1999
Lacryma Christi Iovormanni, 2001

## Course I: By Land or Sea

When it comes to pairing wine with pasta, it's most often the sauce
that creates the conundrum. For our first pairing course, Mauro presented us with taglioni—long, paper-thin noodles that resemble linguini
in width—coupled with fresh tomatoes (read: acid!) and langoustines,
the sweet, succulent lobsterlike prawns. The tomato in the dish might
make one go right for red, but we went instead with a few different
high-acid whites that could stand up to the tomato and enhance the
sweetness of the shellfish.

**Mauro Mafrici**: This is *tagliolini* with langoustine.

**Michele Scicolone:** It's beautiful, Mauro. There's so much shrimp in
there!

**Tony DiDio:** So we've got Nino Franco Prosecco, which I highly recommend with this dish. It's a great way to start with shellfish. The
second glass is the Tocai Pinot Grigio. The third wine is the Mulderbosch Sauvignon Blanc from South Africa, and the last one is Puatti
Pinot Grigio, also from Friuli, just like Mauro. Boy, there are a lot of
great flavors in this dish. Mauro, are you using butter?

**Mauro:** A little bit, yes. Extra virgin oil and butter.

*(Right to left)* The Sopranos Family Cookbook *author Michele Scicolone,*
*Tony, Mauro, Charles, and Amy toast before digging in.*

There is a great fruitiness that plays well with the sweetness that you find in shellfish. Scallops, lobsters, and langoustines all have that briny-sweetness to them, and the
Prosecco fruit and great acid on the finish makes it a great
marriage. Primo Franco, the owner and winemaker of Nino
Franco Prosecco, grows his grapes in a cool part of the
Veneto that adds to the crispness and good acids in it.

**Tony:** The oil's nice and rich. It's beautiful olive oil. Actually, I think
that's playing a part in why I'm enjoying the first two wines so far,
the Prosecco and the Tocai Pinot. Charles, have you tried the Mulderbosch yet? The acid in it just cleans your whole palate. I think it took
away the taste of everything.

This was a case of too much acid and obviously, the wrong wine for this dish. Mulderbosch is one of Tony's favorite Sauvignon Blancs, but the fruit and acid were out of balance for the dish. Where the Prosecco had an undercurrent of acid at the finish, the Mulderbosch was too aggressive and cleansed the palate of any taste of food. This great Sauvignon Blanc would go much nicer with raw shellfish, especially oysters or clams.

**Charles Scicolone:** I find it much too aggressive.

**Tony:** It really wiped the finish of the pasta, so that I had no idea what I was tasting.

**Charles:** Have I given you my theory on tasting? With wine and food, there are three things that can happen in your mouth. First, there are two things that don't go—in other words, you have the food and the wine and the combination makes both of them feel terrible. Like if you, let's say, have some kind of white fish with a red wine. You get a metallic taste, and that's not good. And a lot of times that combination of both isn't good at all. Then there's the second combination in which each thing you taste doesn't taste bad, but you taste them separately, which is something like what's happening here with the Mulderbosch Sauvignon Blanc. You get the taste of the pasta and the tomato and the langoustine; you get the cleansing of the wine, and it's not a bad combination yet, but the two things are too separate, really, to be any good. Yet with the Tocai Pinot Grigio, I get a much more preferable combination. The food and the wine actually come together and complement each other, making both the better.

**Amy Zavatto:** I'm finding that the clear, crisp flavor of the Tocai really brings out the sweetness of the shellfish, but stands up to the acid in the tomato.

**Tony:** Mauro, sit down and eat!

**Mauro:** I can't eat.

**Tony:** You can't eat?!

**Mauro:** I have to look over the food.

**Michele:** Oh, have a shrimp!

**Tony:** You want to know something? The Puatti Pinot Grigio is singing with this dish.

**Charles:** The Tocai is good, too.

**Tony:** But I think, to me, it's the Pinot Grigio.

**Michele:** I liked the Sauvignon at first, but then I didn't like the finish because it was too aggressive.

**Tony:** Charles, did it make sense to you when I said that the finish on the Mulderbosch wiped clean the memory of the dish?

**Charles:** Yes, it was exactly what I was talking about. It's not a bad combination; it doesn't taste bad in your mouth. It's just that wine was overpowering. It wasn't a proper match for the food.

**Amy:** I found the [Mulderbosch] Sauvignon Blanc way too fruity. It just overpowered all the flavors of the dish for me.

**Tony:** What do you think of the Nino Franco with this?

**Amy:** It was nice for a toast in this case, but ...

**Charles:** I don't think it does anything for it.

**Tony:** If anything, it's maybe too heavy for the pasta.

**Charles:** It's too yeasty.

**Tony:** Charles and I are both leaning toward the Tocai Pinot Grigio as the best match here. The Sauvignon Blanc I liked as a wine, but I don't like it with this dish. It's a struggle between the two flavor sensations. It's just too heavy.

**Michele:** Which one was this?

**Tony:** That's a very dry La Gazella Moscato D'Asti.

**Michele:** The food tames some of the floral quality of the Moscato. It's a very nice marriage; I wasn't expecting that.

**Tony:** So many people think that it's the food reacting to the wine, but it's often the wine reacting to the food as well. It's the food that plays a major part in how that wine tastes. And sometimes it's bringing out things in the wine that it would not get with a bad match.

**Charles:** The finish on this dish is very unusual.

**Tony:** I think you're right. I think that most of us would probably agree that the Pinot Grigio is the proper match.

**Charles:** Yes, I agree with that.

**Amy:** Me, too.

# Course II: The Good Earth

When Mauro presented us with his luscious, earthy risotto, it was nearly a no-brainer as far as wine choice went. The black truffles he used were from Umbria—as was the Sagrantino di Montefalco.

**Mauro:** Here's the risotto with black truffles and porcini mushrooms.

**Tony:** Okay, we've got Tuscany, Trentino, we've got the Veneto. I love the nose on the Cabernet Franc.

**Michele:** You don't even have to eat it, just smell it!

**Amy:** I know, God, that aroma. It's so earthy. It's perfect for the truffles and porcini mushrooms.

**Michele:** When I go to Rome, you find black truffle with the *strangozzi*.

**Tony:** This dish is gorgeous. We've got the truffle oil, black truffles, you've got porcini mushrooms. You've got three earth flavors.

**Charles:** Mauro wants us to try the Sagrantino with this.

**Mauro:** The Sagrantino with the truffle, I think will match the best.

**Tony:** *[examining the bottle]* Ah, well, this wine is from Umbria! This is exactly right. This is what we've been talking about, that it's hard to place wine outside of a region. I mean, it's difficult in this country because even our ingredients, as close as they get, they'll never be the same as if you walked into a market in Italy. It's drinking regional, and eating regional.

**Mauro:** I think this Sagrantino is a very interesting wine. It's very easy to drink.

**Charles:** To me, there are four great grapes in Italy. Nebbiolo, Sangiovese, Aglianico, and Sagrantino. I think the Sagrantino works very well here.

**Amy:** The Rosso Faye doesn't work at all for me. It's too pungent.

**Tony:** See, I like the third. But the fourth, the Sagrantino, works much better.

**Charles:** There's a lot of flavor.

**Amy:** It almost tastes like it has a licorice flavor to me.

**Michele:** The other three are just not interesting with the risotto.

**Charles:** I thought the Rosso Faye was.

**Tony:** But the earthiness in the Sagrantino. Yes, that was definitely the wine. Mauro, your instincts were spot on.

**Mauro:** Honestly, for me it's the Sagrantino with the risotto. It's one of my favorite wines.

# Course III: Duking It Out on the Dish

Aside from pastas that are flavored (with spinach, pumpkin, squid ink, or any other number of add-ons) or stuffed, likely the most challenging pasta as far as pairing a wine goes could arguably be gnocchi. It's fat, it's hearty, it has a personality all its own that won't be out-wowed by sauces or other epicurean accoutrements. Add in a little saffron, ricotta selato, sausage, anchovy, and truffles, and you need a wine with serious backbone. Here's what we tried ...

**Mauro:** When I worked in Rome, I always went to Umbria and Abruzzo on my time off. Always when you go in the trattoria you find the black truffle. It's a very strange combination because they use garlic and anchovies with the black truffle, which is very unusual. Here, it's *maloreddus* with the black truffle. What's inside is extra virgin olive oil, a little garlic, anchovies, sausage, and truffle. Really, it's a simple dish, but it's very much a dish of Umbria and Abruzzo.

**Tony:** Anchovies are always a challenge for pairing.

**Michele:** I just coined a new phrase! Instead of saying that someone threw a monkey wrench into the works, you could say someone threw an anchovy into the pot. Because, I mean, a dish that you would expect to work really well with a wine, if you put anchovy in it, the whole spectrum is different.

**Charles:** Hey, it's a hard job, but someone's got to do this!

*[laughter]*

This wine is Uova de Troia and Montepulciano d'Abruzzi. These are the grapes in "Il Falcone."

**Tony:** This is delicious.

**Charles:** You know with this one, it's fruit. Michele wanted fruit, I give you fruit.

**Tony:** This is a very aggressive dish, so this Le Sorgenti Chianti is a little light for me.

**Michele:** I think I like the Falconi better.

**Tony:** Let's try the Rosso.

**Michele:** This wine clobbers it.

*Charles pours while Tony swirls.*

**Amy:** Wow, yeah. The Rosso is way too big for this dish. Which is funny to me because I'd think that the wine would need to be big for this dish, but in this case there's a world of difference between a wine with backbone and a wine that has too much brawn.

**Tony:** The Falconi goes very well.

**Mauro:** Again, to me, the Sagrantino works the best.

**Charles:** Sagrantino is a great wine. But the Falconi stands up to this.

**Mauro:** This is with the ground sausage and the ricotta selato. It's one of my favorite dishes to make.

**Charles:** The Cabernet Franc does not work with this. Ooo!

**Amy:** That's my least favorite, too. It's just too, too big.

**Tony:** The Rosso is really nice with this.

**Amy:** It softens the flavor of the cheese a little bit.

**Tony:** It's got a good acidity. Charles, the Sicilian wine [Nadaria, Nero D'Avola] is really good.

**Charles:** This is the wine for this course. It's Tuscan. It's a combination of Sangiovese and Montepulciano. It's an earthy wine, and this is an earthy dish.

**Michele:** *Como si chiama?*

**Charles:** Colle Carpito. This is not a wine for oak, and it wasn't done that way.

**Michele:** What happens with the oaked wines is that the pepper, the cheese, the sausage clobber the fruit and all you get is oak, so you wind up with a mouth full of coconut.

**Charles:** This is done in big barrels [as opposed to small ones]. So you don't get the vanilla, you get the wine with its honest flavor to it, the terroir. That's why I think this is the perfect wine for this dish.

**Tony:** It seems the Sangiovese-based wines with the good acidity, no barriques, no oak, really work for this dish.

**Michele:** I would say, as far as red wines go, those are the most amenable to the widest range of foods. High-acid reds with no oak to interfere.

**Tony:** I wasn't a big fan of this wine, the Nero. I thought it was overpowering. The Salice tastes great, a beautiful balance of fruit. Another good bottle from Apulia. Nicola would be proud!

**Charles:** I have a big problem with oak with small *barriques* barrels because they end up not being food-friendly wine. Especially not with Italian food. A dish like this, if you get a vanilla *barriques* flavor in the wine it's like putting ice cream on your pasta. It's terrible!

The modern technique of aging wine in small, 225 liter, new oak barrels, known as *barriques* (pronounced *bah-reek*), has become a point of controversy among winemakers, sommeliers, and wine enthusiasts around the world. It is argued that wine aged in this manner takes on flavors from the wood, primarily a strong influence of vanilla. This vanilla and wood flavor is said to trample the natural fruit flavors and influence of the terroir, making the wine overwhelming to almost all foods.

# Course IV: The Big Finish

If you saw the film *Big Night,* you will well remember the fuss and flurry over the final course in the dinner—the *timballo. Timballo* is taken very seriously by Italians. Directly translated it means "drum," which isn't a bad name for it, as its ingredients are molded into a high-sided drumlike shape. At its best, it is the perfect melding of pasta, cheese, vegetables, and sometimes meat or fish, into one (sometimes) gigantic presentation. It's practically a centerpiece!

Mauro, who has prepared his own version of *timballo* for the Food Network's *Sara's Secrets,* made it for us as the grand finale to our tasting. These individual-size *timballi* were a mouthwatering combination of rigatoni, tomato, mozzarella, and basil wrapped in rigatoni. Mauro claimed it to be typical. We claimed it to be glorious, and took to the task of finding a wine that was worthy.

**Mauro:** Next is the timballo. It's a very typical dish from the south. It has the Pecorino, the mozzarella, rigatoni, and eggplant.

**Michele:** That is beautiful, Mauro.

*Mauro with his delectable eggplant timballo.*

**Charles:** I'm going to go to sleep after this!

*[laughter]*

**Michele:** Oh, he's so tired from working so hard.

**Charles:** People don't understand that this is work! People look at you like you're crazy, but it *is* work. Thinking about it and discussing it, having a philosophy of food and wine …

**Amy:** It's a career, it's a wonderful career, but with that said, I think what happens is that it becomes hard to enjoy a meal or a glass of wine and not think about it! Just to simply enjoy something becomes hard. Although, most of my friends and family roll their eyes at me when I say things like this. There are a thousand violins out there playing just for poor ol' me.

*[laughter]*

**Michele:** Sometimes you just want to eat pizza or a sandwich or a salad, but you've got to eat it all!

**Tony:** Speaking of, let's get down to business, shall we? The first wine is the Sorgente Chianti, the second wine is the Rosso di Montalcino from San Filippo, the third wine is the Colle Carpito, and the fourth is the Chianti Classico.

Charles, what do you think of the Le Sorgente Chianti with this dish?

**Charles:** I think the same thing I did for the last dish—the Chianti and the Colle Carpito "San Luciano." The others are too perfumy and too gummy. They don't go at all.

**Tony:** Oh my God, this is a great dish.

**Mauro:** It's very rich.

**Tony:** That's why I thought a Sangiovese or a Barbera would go well, but the Sangiovese has that beautiful acidity to it to cut through the acid in the dish. You've got eggplant, which is acid. You've got tomatoes, which is acid, but the dish is rich at the same time because of the cheese. You need something that can stand up to all of that.

**Amy:** That's why the Rosso absolutely didn't do it for me. My tongue was completely tingling, the acid was entirely too much.

**Mauro:** It's a very earthy dish, I think.

**Tony:** I Like the first two wines a lot, and then Colle Carpito.

**Charles:** For me, again, it's the Colle Carpito and the Chiantis, both of them.

**Mauro:** Did you try the Nero?

**Charles:** It was much too rich.

**Mauro:** Too much?

**Michele:** Yes, I agree. Too rich.

**Charles:** Barriques does not work with this.

**Michele:** You might get away with a steak or a meat dish with it, but not this.

**Tony:** Mauro, when you thought of this dish, what wine were you thinking of?

**Mauro:** Honestly, more south.

**Tony:** Well, everything in this dish points to that. You're right. Regional tasting with regional foods. These are wines that people have been drinking for hundreds of years.

**Michele:** We talked about that in the class that we taught: When in doubt, find a wine from the region the food comes from if possible.

**Tony:** It's true, getting to drink the wine with the food of a particular region, that's the way to pair.

**Mauro:** You know the first dish that we had, the langoustine with the tagliano, I think Lacryma Christi would be wine that would match really well. Because, honestly, when you think about langoustine, you think about the south.

**Charles:** Yes, a Lacryma Christi would go really good with langoustine.

**Tony:** Charles, will you explain to Amy what Lacryma Christi means?

**Charles:** Tears of Christ! The Neapolitan legend is that when …

**Michele:** You'll find this in *The Sopranos Family Cookbook!*

**Charles:** … when the archangel Lucifer was thrown out of heaven he took a piece of paradise with him. And as he was fleeing across the heavens, he dropped a piece of that paradise and that became Vesuvius and the Bay of Naples. When Christ saw this paradise lost, he cried, and when his tears fell, the vine for these grapes grew.

**Amy:** Wow. That's quite a name for a wine. Leave it to Italians … Mauro, growing up you were exposed to a lot of good food and good wine. Do you think about wine when you create a dish, or are you leaving it up to Charles or Nicola?

**Mauro:** It's up to the owner. My job now is more to create the concept for the owner. I think about region, originality, and simplicity.

Something the people easily understand. Like the timballo. It's not too fancy, it's not a thousand things, but when you say the pasta wrapped with eggplant, mozzarella, and tomato, the people say, Ooo! I want that! It's not too difficult to think about. It's easy food. Simplicity is what the southern Italian food is.

**Tony:** Simple, and yet when you taste this you think, "Genius!"

**Mauro:** I think you can make something simple that's great. That looks great and tastes great. When someone tries to create something that's too difficult, or just too complicated, for, say four people, maybe one person likes it because it's difficult to understand. When you do something great and simple, the plate looks clean. Some people think simplicity is boring—I don't think it's boring. I think simplicity is something that can really make a dish different. It's much more difficult than you'd think.

**Amy:** It's like the difference between watching a circus and a monologue—there's so much going on in a circus that maybe it's easy to fool the patron if it's not really very good; with a monologue, you'd better be saying something really interesting!

**Mauro:** Exactly. In a simple dish, a chef can't hide behind three or four ingredients. It better be good. But you know, last spring I asked Tony to make a reservation for me at The French Laundry [in California]. I went with my wife for her birthday. We had many courses. We have with every dish, one wine. We had French, Californian, everything. The check was very big—but we say, you know what? It's like we went to the opera. It was a performance.

**Tony:** So lunch is more of a concerto, and dinner is an opera?

## Try It for Yourself

This glorious dish is so popular at I Trulli, that even the Food Network had Mauro come on and make it on *Sara's Secrets*. If you make this dish, be sure to get into the true spirit of the Italian way and invite friends to join you. A meal shared always tastes better than when you eat it alone. Grab a bottle of Chianti Classico, and you'll have your own *Big Night* to remember.

*Try to make it yourself—the recipe for Mauro's timballo follows.*

## Eggplant Timballo with Cavatelli

6 eggplants

Olive oil

Salt and pepper

6 (5-inch wide, 2-inch tall) ceramic soufflé cups (a.k.a. ramekins)

¼ cup olive oil

1 bunch basil, chopped

4 cups tomato sauce

1 lb. fresh cavatelli (if you can't find fresh, frozen is fine)

1 ball fresh mozzarella, chopped

1 cup grated Pecorino cheese, plus extra for sprinkling

Cut eggplant into ¼-inch slices and place atop a cookie sheet layered with parchment paper. Drizzle with olive oil and add salt and pepper. Roast in a 350 degree oven until golden brown (about 30 minutes). Remove from oven. When cool, layer 6 or 7 eggplant pieces in a circular pattern in each of the soufflé dishes allowing the excess to hang outside the edge. In a 12-inch sauté pan, add oil, basil, and tomato sauce with salt and pepper. Bring to a boil and cook for 3 to 4 minutes, then remove from heat. Cook cavatelli in a pot of boiling water for less time than directed on package (you want the pasta to be slightly underdone). Over medium heat, add cavatelli, mozzarella, and Pecorino to sauce and blend. Spoon out the mixture into the eggplant-lined soufflé dishes and fold the overhanging eggplant over the top. Bake in oven at 350 degrees for 5 minutes.

To serve, spoon a little tomato sauce onto a dish or pasta bowl and turn the soufflé upside down onto it. Sprinkle with Pecorino and garnish with basil leaf. And as Amy's mother-in-law, Aurora Marotta, says before every meal: *Buon appetito!*

# *part four*

## Pairing Wine with Difficult Flavors

*Pairing Wine with Cheese*

*Vintage Words: Interview with Cheese Steward*
*Pascal Vittu, Restaurant Daniel*

*Pairing Wine with Spicy Foods*

*Vintage Words: Interview with Michael Lomonaco*

*Dessert and Dessert Wines*

# chapter eighteen

# Pairing Wine with Cheese

*Cheese—milk's leap toward immortality.*

*—Clifton Fadiman*

Once upon a time—about 5,000 years ago, give or take—a herdsman in Mesopotamia (what is now modern-day Iraq) packed up his lunch and beverage for the day, and went off to work shepherding his flock. The beverage he chose was milk, and, as thermal, cold-keeping materials weren't available way back then, he carried it in a pouch made from the dried stomach of a calf. At the end of the long, hot day toiling in the Tigris Valley, this herdsman went to take a final swig of milk from the pouch. When he opened it, though, he didn't find any more milk— he found a strange, solid substance he'd never seen before. It seemed the bacteria left in the calf's stomach curdled what was left of the dairy product. He tasted it, thought it was pretty good, and there you have it—cheese was born.

Since that clever (or desperate—curdled milk in the bottom of a dried calf's stomach couldn't have been all that appetizing) herdsman's discovery, the world hasn't been able to get enough of the creamy stuff.

With more than 1,500 known varieties around the world, there's an awful lot from which to choose.

The cheese department of your favorite supermarket or gourmet store might seem a little overwhelming, especially when it comes to pairing it with wine. However, wine and cheese pairing is one of the easiest, most fun, and economically savvy ways to learn how flavors work together.

The very first cheese factory in the United States opened its doors in Oneida, New York, in 1851. Wisconsin, though, became known as the cheese state because of Swiss immigrants who settled in Green County in 1845 and began churning the stuff out like crazy to keep up with the nation-wide demand. A plant devoted entirely to Limburger cheese opened there in 1868. Today, more than one third of the dairy products produced in the United States is cheese.

## How Cheese Is Made

With all apologies to artisanal cheese makers and stewards (like the venerable Pascal Vittu, whom we interview in Chapter 19), we're going to give you an abridged version of how cheese is made so you can better understand what you're eating and why it tastes the way it does.

Of course, all cheese begins as some kind of milk product, usually from a cow, sheep, or goat, but it can also be made from buffalo, camel, or mare milk. Bacteria produces acid and sours the milk, allowing it to ripen (because of laws of pasteurization, many cheeses must be made from pasteurized milk, and therefore bacteria cultures are added as opposed to being allowed to naturally occur). Next, the solid product (i.e., the curd) left over from this acid-producing bacteria is extracted. Sometimes this is the final product and is simply drained off of liquid (soft cheese), but often the curd is drained and broken down, sometimes salted, heated, and then formed into its final shape. The cheese is then aged for anywhere from a few months to years and years.

The older a cheese is, the more sharpened its flavors become. Younger cheeses tend to be mild, soft, and subtle. As with people and wine, though, age can add some serious personality to cheese.

## Pairing Tips

As a rule of thumb, try fruitier reds like Beaujolais or Pinot Noir or crisp whites like Pinot Grigio or Sauvignon Blanc with mild cheeses. Save the full-bodied reds like Cabernet Sauvignon or Zinfandel and heavy-hitting Chardonnays of the California ilk for stronger, older cheese. Also, crisp whites are lovely with goat cheeses; with young, extremely creamy cheeses (as opposed to very aged, harder cheeses), champagne can be delightful.

One thing we insist upon: *Buy good cheese.* This doesn't mean you have to run off to Spain for Manchego—good cheese can be found in your supermarket. But with certain more well-known, higher supermarket sale varieties, such as Muenster, Monterey Jack, or (especially!) Parmesan, avoid the pre-packaged, garden-variety generic versions. They won't give you the authentic taste of the cheese, nor will they provide you with the pairing experience you're looking for.

For a product always made from the same thing (that is, milk in some form), there's quite a lot of cheese out there and cheese "personalities," too. If you've ever stood in a cheese store or at the gourmet cheese case of your supermarket, you know there are way more cheeses than you can shake a bread stick at. What follows is a handy-dandy cheese chart that we created for you to use as a reference. In it, you'll find an array of cheeses that are easily found in the United States, what they generally taste like, and a good pairing suggestion to get you started.

| Cheese | Description | Best with ... | Suggestion |
|---|---|---|---|
| Boursin | A mix of three cheeses, frequently used as a spread because of its buttery texture; often flavored with herbs | White | Gewürztraminer, Champagne |
| Brie | Soft, rich, creamy, with a slightly tangy flavor | Red | Big Chardonnay, Riesling, Champagne |
| Buffalo Mozzarella | Extremely creamy, firm, yet delicate in flavor | White, Red | Fiano de Avellino, Greco di Tufo Orvieto |
| Camembert | Pungent, creamy with an oozing center and a pungent flavor | Red | Chenin Blanc, Champagne, Rully (Chardonnay) |

| Cheese | Description | Best with ... | Suggestion |
|--------|-------------|---------------|------------|
| Cantal | Smooth textured with a fruity aroma and nutty taste | White | Pouilly-Fuisse, Manzanilla, sherry |
| Cheddar | Tangy; when young, it's mild, sharper tasting when aged | White, Red | Chardonnay, Oregon Pinot Noir, Beaujolais |
| Cheshire | Similar to cheddar in taste | White | Chardonnay |
| Chèvre | Straight-up goat's milk cheese; you might see it also called Banon, Montrachet, Bucheron, or Crottin Chavignol | White | Sancerre, Sauvignon Blanc |
| Colby | A version of cheddar, it's a little sweet, a little tangy; generally mild | White | Chardonnay (preferably California) |
| Danish Blue | A milder version of blue cheese; rich and on the soft side | Red | Cabernet Sauvignon |
| Edam | Mild and nutty, with a slight saltiness and all-around savory nature | White | Riesling |
| Epoisses | Tongue-clicking tanginess combined with a silky smooth texture, woody aroma, and brandy-washed rind | White, Red | White Burgundy if cheese is young; red Burgundy if cheese is aged |
| Feta | Crumbly, tangy-tasting cheese made from goat's milk | White, Red | Riesling, Pinot Noir, Beaujolais |

| Cheese | Description | Best with ... | Suggestion |
|--------|-------------|---------------|------------|
| Fontina | Creamy but solid, with a mildly nutty easy-going flavor | White, Red | Pinot Grigio Dolcetto |
| Gorgonzola | Strong, pungent flavor; creamy, soft texture | Red | Barolo, Barbaresco, Zinfandel |
| Gouda, regular | Sort of a flavor cross between Edam and Fontina, it is generally higher in fat, which shows in its texture | White | Riesling (Spätlese) |
| Gouda, smoked | Same makeup as regular Gouda, but with (obviously) a smoky, earthy taste | Red | Pinot Noir, Merlot, Cabernet Sauvignon |
| Gruyere | Sharp and salty, but rich and solid; some-what similar to aged white cheddar | White | Chardonnay (French or Italian), Pinot Noir |
| Havarti | Gentle, mild, but with a tangy backbone that keeps it from being wimpy or non-descript; often found herbed with dill | White | Sauvignon Blanc Muscadet, Chenin Blanc |
| Ibirico | Creamy texture, tangy flavor | Red | Rioja, Syrah, Albariño |
| Limburger | Extremely strong, pungent aroma | White | Trockenbeeren-auslese, Icewine |
| Mahon | Soft, creamy texture, with a little tang, a little nuttiness | White, Red | Rioja Reserva (red or white) |

| Cheese | Description | Best with ... | Suggestion |
|---|---|---|---|
| Manchego | Nutty and creamy to Amy, it's Spain's softer answer to Parmesan; very versatile cheese | White, Red | It's hard to fail in pairing, but try going regional with a Cava or a fino sherry; Rioja Tempranillo is also lovely |
| Monterey Jack | A laid-back cheese reminiscent of the attitude whence it comes—California!; like an extremely mild cheddar, it's soft in texture and unassaulting in flavor | White | Big, oaky California Chardonnay |
| Muenster | Yellow, creamy interior with a semi-strong almost astringent taste; believe it or not it actually originated in Alsace | White | Pinot Gris, Gewürztraminer |
| Parmesan | Nutty, salty, at times almost crunchy | White, Red | Barolo, Barbaresco, Prosecco, Taurasi |
| Pecorino Romano | Very sharp, very salty | Red | Tawny port, Amarone, Marsala Vergine |
| Provolone | Real Provolone (not the generic super-market stuff) is firm but creamy, with a sharp bite to the flavor | White, Red | Montefalco Sagrantino, Vin Santo Primitivo |

| Cheese | Description | Best with ... | Suggestion |
|--------|-------------|---------------|------------|
| Neufchâtel | Cow's milk, velvety, smooth; salty flavor when young that grows stronger with age | Red | Beaujolais |
| Raclete | Smoky, earthy, almost mushroom flavor with a tangy after-taste | Red | Syrah, Sangiovese, Côtes du Rhône |
| Roquefort | The best of the blue—rich, pungent, and salty | White, Red | Vintage port, Sauternes |
| Stilton | Similar to Roquefort, but a little less assaulting | White, Red | Vintage port, Icewine, Sauternes |

Although it's not uncommon to find Americans eating cheese before their meal, technically it should be an after-dinner event. Why? It's heavy and the dairy coats your tongue and dulls the taste buds. Do as the French do, and save the dairy for last.

## Low-Cost Learning

A great advantage to cheese and wine pairing is the increased ability to pack a lot of learning into a single tasting at a relatively low cost. Not to mention that it's a great excuse to pop open a few bottles of wine, sample some cheese styles with which you're familiar or maybe some you've been curious about, and invite some friends over for a full-on tasting.

Purchase (or ask your guests to bring) four to six different cheeses. Make sure you vary them in milk type and age and use our guidelines to select wines or come up with different matches that you feel will work. Because so many cheeses are particular to a country or region, we suggest that you try going entirely regional on a few of these pairing exercises (i.e., wine from France paired with cheese from France, etc.). Provide each of your guests with paper and pen and make sure you all record your pairing discoveries.

*chapter nineteen*

# Vintage Words: Interview with Cheese Steward Pascal Vittu, Restaurant Daniel

*The more the cheese is aged, the more there is a certain complexity, so the association with the wine changes totally.*

*—Pascal Vittu*

Did you know in France alone there are more than 500 varieties of cheese? Some are aged, some are not, some are soft, some runny, some hard, some creamy. Some have a washed rind or rind brushed with brandy, others go through a brining process. Some are aged for years, others are eaten in their raw, fresh state. And all can come from different kinds of milk: goat, cow, or sheep.

With so many varieties and ways of making cheese, it's not a bad idea to put some thought into the kind of wine you plan on pairing with it. And who better to discuss this with but one of the country's most renowned cheese stewards? Pascal Vittu is cheese steward extraordinaire of Restaurant Daniel. Here's what he had to say on the topic of pairing this dairy delight with the fruit of the vine.

**Tony DiDio:** What I wanted to talk about was the aging in a cheese and how it changes the wine you would pair with it.

**Pascal Vittu:** Yes, definitely, the more the cheese is aged, the more there is a certain complexity, so the association with the wine changes totally. I can give you an example from an epoisses, a wash rind, calmion cheese from Burgundy.

**Tony:** One of my favorite cheeses.

**Pascal:** If it's really a running epoisses, white wine goes very well. If you take a young epoisses, with a kind of clay texture in the middle, a red Burgundy would be more appropriate.

**Tony:** So would it necessarily be a white Burgundy?

**Pascal:** If the epoisses is ripe and running, yes. Then a white Chardonnay from Burgundy.

**Tony:** One theme that recurs in this book a lot is eating and drinking regionally, and I can never imagine, and this is very parochial of me even though I'm not from Burgundy, but I can never think of drinking anything but a red or a white Burgundy with epoisses. Now, how about the changes of the milk? Let's say if it's a goat cheese, a sheep's milk, or a cow's milk, how does that change the ultimate pairing of a wine?

**Pascal:** Well, that's very difficult to establish a rule, a certain rule to apply to a certain wine. I will talk more in terms of fermentation. Any lactic product develops a natural acidity, and, for example, goat milk cheese acidity goes much better with white wine. On the other hand, even if the acidity of cow milk cheese is there, it's less pronounced, so most of the time we [pair that] with a red wine.

**Tony:** So you're saying that like every food product, it's basically the same. So if you're thinking about cheese, you also have to think about the acidity in the cheese. If a cheese has more acidity to it, then am I pairing it with a wine that has more acidity?

**Pascal:** A white wine [with good acidity], most of the time this will be better.

---

*Affineur* is the term given to one who ages cheeses, this being a job and art unto itself. Essentially, the aging of cheeses occurs in an aging cellar. Not all aging cellars are used for all cheeses. The type of cheese stored there depends on the type of temperature the cheese requires for proper aging (high humidity, lower humidity, cold, more temperate, etc.). Even though he is not an affineur himself, Vittu is a devoted pupil of the noted affineur Bernard Antony.

**Tony:** Now, that question had to do with if there's no wine on the table and you're at the point of choosing. Let's say it's the end of a meal and invariably people want to have cheese, and you're brought over and you're asked to pick out some cheese. Let's say there's a bottle of Cabernet on the table. Do you necessarily look to see what they're drinking or do you ask them what they would like?

**Pascal:** There are very different approaches in that case. The first is if there's no wine on the table. Unless the people are willing to choose a glass of wine or another bottle of wine and we are going to talk together of this choice. What they are going to choose, I am going to match with some cheese. On the other hand, if they would prefer to choose the cheese they like without regarding what they're drinking— that happens sometimes. Also the port is coming very often [at the end of the meal], or sweet wine, because they can keep it and have their dessert afterward.

**Tony:** When we were here and did our pairing with Daniel, we had some sweet wine. I have a question about port. Is there any rule about port when it comes to matching it with a good cheese? I know Stilton is the great match with port, but are we looking at aged port? A young 10-year tawny port? A ruby port? There are so many different types, what would you suggest if I wanted a Stilton cheese with something like that?

**Pascal:** It will depend on the producer of the Stilton and the way the cheese is seasoned [i.e., aged]. I like the complexity of a 20-year-old tawny port because you can move around on different categories. Blue cheese would be an evident association with the port, but also earthy cheeses.

**Tony:** So the earthy cheeses such as …

**Pascal:** I'm thinking about Cantal or an aged Salers from Auvergnes, which are both pressed and cooked cow milk cheese and offer a very nice complexity.

**Tony:** Are you talking with the sommelier during the cheese course, or are you suggesting "this would be very nice with …"

**Pascal:** Well, since we don't have a lot of time during the service, this talking most of the time is before the service. We talk a lot, though, yes. At least five times a day.

**Tony:** So if you're at a table and Jean Luc, or Janet or Philippe, are somewhere out in the ozone layer, you'll take it and say, "May I make a recommendation?" That's great, that's great. I think this is one of the advantages of people talking in a restaurant who work together and this is why you guys are four stars and why everyone else envies that. But it's a matter of having those discussions I think between the people serving the wine and the people serving the food that makes the difference in the service.

**Pascal:** I am very lucky in that case because I had the opportunity to live for three years in the wine country in Pouillac and at that time I had the opportunity to taste a lot and compare.

**Tony:** So you've been immersed into wine by choice and by profession. Let's go back to that question—if they do have some wines in their glasses and do want a cheese course, then …

**Pascal:** We go along. I am very lucky to be able to propose about 20 to 25 different cheeses that represent all the different wonderful families of cheeses, from the triple cream; wash rind; goat, cow, and sheep milk; hard cheeses; pressed and cooked; creamy and soft. So I'm able to play around a lot and all the time be able to match with any wine. I try to offer the same complexity that Jean Luc is offering in his wine list.

**Tony:** Now cheese has really come back into the consciousness of Americans in the past five years or so, in terms of service at the top restaurants. I've noticed a great absence of cheese because of the health factors that have been attributed to it. Not that it's unhealthy, but in terms of fat content people feel they can do without the cheese course. In terms of cholesterol. This is a phenomenon particular to Americans. In traveling in France last year I had the great opportunity of being 10 days in Burgundy and Champagne and you just couldn't avoid cheese. So now that it's back in somewhat fashion and vogue in this country, how has that helped your program? Maybe three years ago, four years ago you were offering less than you are now on your list of 20 to 25.

**Pascal:** I remember at the old place, the original Daniel on 76th Street, we were proposing a selection of five to eight cheeses. We had only the rare occasion that people were asking about it. I think the health was a problem also, during a long time it was so difficult to have a very good dairy product at one point the people put it on the side.

It was impossible. So because dairy products are very fragile, for example, if you have a temperature problem during transportation this natural acidity would begin to develop very fast and become really unpleasant.

**Tony:** It's amazing how it's changed and how so many restaurants are offering cheese.

**Pascal:** Now also there is a very separate difference made between the people with health problems about fat, for instance, so now we make a difference between the saturated fat, which is negative for your body, and the natural fat which is good. On the other hand, for example, if you have any, how do you say this? Square cheese? Totally industrial …

**Tony:** Oh, Velveeta!

**Pascal:** Yeah, for example. It could be very bad for your body because you keep this fat with you. But the natural fat from a two-year-old Gruyère, this fat is good.

**Tony:** So you're saying fat is good?

**Pascal:** Yes, some of it.

**Tony:** And we'll note to our readers that you weigh about 18 pounds. *[laughter]*

**Tony:** Are there any wines that really work well with cheese? Let's say our readers would really like to do some pairing at home and want to pair it with wine, are there any wines that you could think of in the general sense that maybe work better than other wines? Are there those very high alcoholic wines from California, let's say Zinfandels or really young Cabernets with a lot of tannin in them, can they be matched with cheese as a rule?

**Pascal:** They could be. It will be more with the port because of the alcohol content.

**Tony:** Is there a general rule?

**Pascal:** No. But I'm a big fan of Tocai Pinot Gris or Riesling from Alsace, or anywhere in the world.

**Tony:** It's funny because Riesling keeps coming up. To me, I find it's one of the most versatile food wines out there. We've done some dishes already with German wines and we've paired very well with them. Talk to me about a, let's say, a Spätlese-style wine and a little more fruitiness, and …

**Pascal:** I just found them very appealing, and you can go along from a hard to a creamy cheese without any problem. They're just food-friendly, those two grapes.

**Tony:** What about Italian Pinot Grigios?

**Pascal:** They are totally different, but on the subject of cheese I put them on the same plane as Sauvignon Blanc; they match very well, goes along with the acidity in the goat milk cheese. They are also very fruity, they have a freshness.

**Tony:** It's funny how Pinot Gris changes from country to country to country. I mean, every grape does when the terroir is different. I actually have in my bag today a great wine—a Leon Beyer Gewürztraminer from Alsace, and we're trying that with spicy chicken today with Michael Lomonaco at Noche. He had suggested a Pinot Gris as well, but I really thought that the dish sounded like it would lend itself a little bit more to a Gewürztraminer, so I wanted to try that. But those are great wines, Alsatian wines. I can see how they fit very, very well with cheese and how they do change from … Sometimes, unfortunately in this country, this being the number-one wine market in the world, everything good and bad comes here, so some people are really used to a very watery, one-dimensional Pinot Grigio and they don't realize how rich the grape can be until they start tasting wines like Alois Lageder, who makes a single-vineyard Pinot Grigio called Benefizium. In fact, it's been on the wine list here at Daniel. But it's a great, great wine and it has no relation whatsoever to any of that watered-down Pinot Grigio.

**Pascal:** Three weeks ago I had a crottin, a three-year-old crottin, a hard [goat's milk] cheese, and I had it with a Riesling from New Hope, Pennsylvania. There's a little vineyard there, and it was just great.

**Tony:** Well, this country is, everyone except maybe six or seven states that are *not* making wine. New York State, upstate region, is doing very well for Rieslings also. The Finger Lakes in particular. So it's, again, you can't discount where the origin is, because if it tastes good, then you can't discount it. One thing we were interested in asking you was, even though there's no best wine/worst wine rules, but is there a wine to maybe avoid that's difficult to match with cheese? For instance, are those Zinfandels with high alcohol—not to pick on Zinfandels—but are those high-alcoholic wines, like a young Zinfandel with a high 14.5 percent alcohol, is that possibly a difficult match?

**Pascal:** I don't want to say it's difficult, but it changes the rules. Having a high alcohol content, you need something to balance that. So for example, blue cheese could go along with a young Zinfandel. It just changes the rules.

**Tony:** You've had the gorgonzola, the Torta di gorgonzola, a lot of people match that with Barolo or Barbaresco. Are those good matches?

**Pascal:** Yes, yes.

> Just like with French wine, many French cheeses bear the stamp "Appellation d'Origine Contrôlée," or AOC. This stamp ensures that the produce originates from the region that is known to specialize in that particular cheese in order to preserve tradition, as well as adheres to the strict regulations of the AOC. At present, there are 35 cow, sheep, and goat milk cheeses out of 500 in France that bear the AOC stamp.

**Tony:** I was curious also, is there a general rule that you can tell the readers in terms of "these wines would work well with these cheeses"?

**Pascal:** Yes, I can apply as a rule that Pinot Grigio and Sauvignon Blanc will match a goat milk cheese. If we stay on the family of what we call lactic fermentation, it's a very fast aging, it goes from about three weeks to two months maximum. Also, the grape as a Gewürztraminer, the Tocai Pinot Gris and the creamy and wash rind cheeses, the Brescianella is a great example from Normandy. But also the epoisses could go along in that range.

**Tony:** That's interesting. The epoisses, as we said before, if it's a runny cheese, creamy, you like the white burgundy. And the red burgundy would go well if …

**Pascal:** It's younger, so a clay-texture cheese.

**Tony:** Right, right. So then from there maybe we can go to an American Pinot Noir.

**Pascal:** Yes, definitely.

**Tony:** And then veer off and do a little Pinot Nero [same grape as a Pinot Noir] from Italy, so it kind of opens up. I like the idea of goat cheese with wines like Sauvignon Blanc or Pinot Grigio, something with that racy acidity to it, I think that makes a lot of sense. We had talked before about the wine and cheese parties of the 1970s. I remember in college there were wine and cheese parties all over the place. And so cheese obviously came into the consciousness of Americans in the 1970s. My question is where should the cheese be served in the meal, forget a restaurant but at somebody's house—and you're just picking on things. I always say I'd rather have it at the end of the meal—that's my thing. But when they do come in the beginning as an appetizer, as many hors d'oeuvres do.

**Pascal:** Definitely, they go along as an aperitif. One of the most popular canapés we have here is Parmesan cheese baskets with fresh goat cheese flavored with herbs and decorated with pine nuts on top. That's been at Daniel for years and that's I would say once or twice every night, very frequently, people ask for extra. They just love it. The Parmesan cheese aged, I'm talking about two or three years old. The hard cheese. The crottin, the Gruyère, manchego for example, are excellent just like this—you have a glass of Champagne, you have a glass of wine, you take a bite of cheese.

**Tony:** I always like Prosecco with Parmesan cheese. So really, most appetizers here, first course, it's not a cheese course, but there is cheese intermingled with the appetizer. I always feel that a cheese sometimes changes the palate and it's always better to have it at the end.

**Pascal:** We've had some requests for an appetizer of a cheese plate, but it's very difficult to go from there.

**Tony:** What do you do if the customer wants that?

**Pascal:** Well, I say fine, but I try to stay on very mild and acidic cheeses.

**Tony:** The theme of this book is balance. We say it throughout the whole book; if this is what you like, go for it. If you want a delicate piece of Dover sole and you want a 1982 Chateau Latour, go with it, baby! But the running theme is maybe we can suggest a better match to make you even happier. Not the definitive match, but maybe a better one because it's all subjective.

**Pascal:** I would recommend more of a cheese as a canapé with an aperitif.

**Tony:** In the beginning of the meal.

**Pascal:** Like the Parmesan cheese I was talking about before, or we can also propose the cheese course before or after the dessert. It's the British way after the dessert.

**Tony:** What I usually do when I'm with my friends, is we have the cheese course in lieu of dessert and then maybe a sorbet. That's why I think there's a problem in this country of eating in restaurants where there are cheese courses: How much food can you possibly consume number one, and how much can you really enjoy?

**Pascal:** Because I'm tasting a lot of cheese every day, I try to avoid dairy products during my meal, or during the morning.

**Tony:** It's the same thing with me with wine. How are the laws changing now, are they more flexible or less flexible, in terms of pasteurized milks and cheeses that are coming in, and raw cheeses? I was curious about the law and I was curious how that changes the food and wine pairings.

**Pascal:** It changes a lot. We were talking earlier about the cheese epoisses. This epoisses, the epoisses we are having here for example, is a cheese that is aged less than 60 days, which is required by law. If you have one which is made with raw milk and one, which we have here, that is pasteurized, they're two totally different cheeses. There is less complexity, less flavor, of the pasteurized cheese.

**Tony:** Are you allowed to get unpasteurized?

**Pascal:** Aged less than 60 days, no we are not.

**Tony:** So you can get an aged epoisses from raw milk?

**Pascal:** No. If less than 60 days, it has to be pasteurized.

**Tony:** If they're older than 60 days then they can come in.

**Pascal:** But unfortunately over 60 days the epoisses is no good. What we call older cheeses, what we call lactic fermentation cheeses, the goat milk cheese for example, they are all pasteurized.

**Tony:** Is there any flexibility now with the law?

**Pascal:** No. I think what happens is that there is more and more demand [for unpasteurized products], that's for sure. Especially in New York. But there is also more and more control and traceability with dairy products, which is very good. For example, if you want a raw-milk product to come in, it has to be aged for at least 60 days. But what most people don't know is at the same time it has to come with a sanitary certificate with a stamp from the French and United States to guarantee that this product is really good.

**Tony:** So maybe that question about raw milk and pasteurized milk doesn't really play in with wine because there's so little raw milk coming in. So when you do get the epoisses, for example, or any other cheese that comes in the raw stage, or unpasteurized stage, that has to change the match with the wine. But if you have two cheeses, almost the same cheeses, and one is from pasteurized and one is from unpasteurized milk, they are two totally different cheeses.

**Pascal:** Absolutely. Totally different. You can think of it with wine, too. Let's say you have Cabernet Sauvignon. One is aged in new barrels and one is aged in used barrels.

**Tony:** Exactly!

Tony is a big fan of Barolo, the "king of wines," from Piedmonte. A well-made Barolo has power, elegance, and depth. At a recent tasting of 1997 Barolos, Tony served parmesano Reggio and Toma, a regional Piedmonte cheese. The perfect match? A 1997 Brezza "Sarmassa" or a 1997 Vietti Castiglione—two massive wines exhibiting deep and rich flavors. Both cheeses help tame the tannins in these young wines. The Vietti had a nose of rose petals, and the Brezza a deep nose of truffles. Both bottles and cheeses were finished within an hour—obviously, the right match.

# chapter twenty

# Pairing Wine with Spicy Foods

*Tell me what you eat, and I'll tell you what you are.*

—*Jean Anthelme Brillat-Savarin, author and gastronome*

We have heard ad nauseam that wine and spicy foods are two consumables that should never be at the same table. "Drink beer with spicy food!" is the sweeping rule of thumb proclaimed over and over when anything with a chili pepper or curry paste is placed in front of you. That's fine, but maybe you don't like beer, or maybe you're simply not in the mood for beer. Certainly, there's got to be a better alternative than plain water or cola.

It's true, pairing wine with cuisines that lean toward the "Wow!" end of the spice spectrum provide a challenge that's not for the bland of taste buds. Chances are, though, if you tend to relish spicy foods, you're not the play-it-safe type to begin with. It's easy to be dismissive and go for the easiest alternative, but if you do, you'll never know how a Trockenbeerenauslese with the aroma of pineapple can beautifully accentuate the taste of cardamom, or how a rosé can make all the ingredients in salsa spring to life.

This is not to say that in order to throw together any wine and any spiced-up food and have it be great, you simply need to open your mind. As with any pairing, you need to take into account what's in the dish or what the primary qualities of the wine are before proclaiming the winner, and there are a few principles that you can use as a guide:

1. Because spicy food enhances the tannins and thus the bitterness of wine, matching big reds can be a difficult task, especially with Eastern foods. That lovely Zinfandel you have will become a bitter, peppery mess and you'll lose all the gorgeous blackberry and plum notes in it if you decide to pair it with that beef in red-curry and coconut milk (and you'll also lose all the sweetness in the dish itself and only taste the hot, hot, hot). In the realm of spicy, you'll have an easier time matching reds with the kind of spice found in the Americas (see our interview with Michael Lomonaco in Chapter Twenty-One).

2. Think sweet. Wines that have a slightly higher sugar content, and thus are of a sweeter nature, ease the fire of spicy foods and allow you to better savor the rest of the flavors in the dish. This is a case of opposites complementing each other in the perfect way. The sugar in a sweeter wine cuts through the spice and cleanses the palate, allowing you to enjoy the kick that comes with hot food, as well as the rest of the flavors on your plate.

3. High alcohol content stokes the flames. Following on the second tip, the sweetest wines that are in the late-harvest style tend to have the highest alcohol levels possible in a wine, and thus will increase the spice-heat level in the dish. With that said, as wine in general has a lower alcohol content than hard alcohol, you're still more ahead of the game than if you consumed, say, a margarita with your chicken in mole sauce.

4. Acid is your friend. Spicy food tends to also be incredibly flavorful, enriched with various kinds of seasoning and tastes. It's possible for a dish to not only be spicy, but to have hints of sweetness, saltiness, bitterness, and sourness all at once. Acid prevents dishes with a multitude of flavors from being strangled into submission.

5. When in doubt, think German. If you are in a situation where you are absolutely unsure of where to go with a spicy dish, think Riesling or Gewürztraminer. Their fruity, slightly sweeter, solidly acidic nature makes them an all-around safety net.

What each of those tips has in common, though, is the ideal we've been hammering home throughout this book: balance. Spicy food isn't just about the spice. No matter what area of the world your favorite spicy dish comes from, it is likely an amalgam of many flavors: spices, herbs, acids, starch, and any number of other things thrown into the pot. Finding a wine that can take all the components of a spicy dish and keep them from being overwhelmed by the heat is the key to this kind of pairing.

With all of this mind, we'd like to take you through some specific epicurean areas of the world—from North America to South America to East Asia—and dive a little deeper into the heat of the topic.

# The Americas

From fiery Texas chili, to New Mexican tamales, to Louisiana gumbo, to Mexican salsa, the spice of chilies has long been the love affair of the Americas. Why? Chilies are indigenous to the area. It's in our blood, our *terroir*, our history. Despite the tendency to tame spiciness in this country (how many times have you been advised by a waiter that a dish is "very spicy!" only to find out that it has much less kick than you were expecting?), it's deeper in our culture than many people realize.

How deep do chilies go into our history? The first "outsider" we know of to take note of them was New World explorer Christopher Columbus, who brought them back to the Old World. Of the 200 varieties, more than half hail from Mexican soil. With so many choices of chili that come in such an array of primary colors, how do you know which is the hottest? The bigger the pod, the hotter the scorch (much of which comes from the seeds and veins inside).

Whether it be étouffée or fajitas, finding a wine that works with American chilies isn't as hard as you might imagine. For one, unlike certain highly spiced Asian foods, North and South American chilies are easier to pair with red wine (and, as many of the dishes that come from these areas use tomato, the acid-cutting nature of red wine is a preferable complement). Second, as you'll see elsewhere in this chapter, sweet trumps spicy. Wine with a fruitier nature and higher sugar level tames the fire in a chili better than any bottle of beer (which, actually, makes things worse!) or even soda, in our opinion.

To get you started on your American chili-and-wine pairing, we've given you some suggestions to guide you everywhere from Louisiana Cajun country to Southwestern spice to Mexican salsa:

- **Sauvignon Blanc.** The European version of this grape tends to produce a tart, grassy, herbaceous wine. However, the blending of Sauvignon Blanc with Semillon grapes in Bordeaux produces a more tame version with honey influences. On the other hand, New World Sauvignon Blanc tends to be more fruit-forward, cutting the overpowering kick of the chilies and allowing the other flavors in dishes like posole or shrimp étouffée to be tasted.
- **Riesling.** The Alsatian versions tend to be a little too straight-backed for chili-infused foods, but the fruity nature of German Rieslings pairs well, for example, with chicken mole or spicy shrimp fajitas.
- **Côte-Rôtie.** Although this much-hailed northern Rhône red is actually a combination of Viognier and (mostly) Syrah grapes, it is officially considered a red. The addition of the honeyed nature of the Viognier combined with the earthy, peppery nature of the Syrah make this a mellow red alternative for spiced-up meaty dishes.
- **Rosé.** We love that rosé is making such an across-the-board comeback on tables across the country. They're low in tannins and high on fruit, thus making them a much better partner for heat. Try a Rhône valley Grenache, which goes great with a salsa starter or a main-event carne *adovada*.
- **Zinfandel.** Although this berry-packed wine is actually of European decent, it is so firmly rooted in American soil that it's pretty much become part of the family. Because of that, the regional theme plays well here. If you're going for meaty South American fare (think Brazil), an aged Zinfandel is a good bet (the

young ones can have a little too much pow to handle the spice—see our poblano buffalo steak pairing with Michael Lomonaco in Chapter Twenty-One).

Amy loves anything that's got a kick to it and frequently has to have the chimayo chili powder she brought back from New Mexico or the ever-present cayenne wrestled from her hands in the kitchen. Tony, on the other hand, is not a fan of hot or spicy—but he *is* a trouper. After experimenting with some fiery dishes, we went south of the border—really south—to Argentina and Chile for some relief. If you're eating with chilies, especially from South America, go regional and do what the natives do. Both Argentina and Chile produce some great wines at reasonable prices. We loved the 2000 Malbec from Graffigna, the 2001 Cabernet/Carmenere from Montes, and the 2000 Carmenere from Montgras. These wines had a backbone of acid, without an overpowering taste of oak. Tony was looking for balance and found it in these great value wines from South America. They stood up to the heat and were a delight to match with the spicy chilies.

# Asia

The love affair that the United States has with Asian cuisine has gone far beyond Chinese takeout. We love the cuisines of Japan, Thailand, India, and a host of other Asian countries offering an incredible array of flavors to the culinary melting pot, from green curry to green wasabi. Here, we focus on wines that best complement the food of China, Japan, Vietnam, Thailand, and India. Of course, we realize that this is excluding a chunk of Asia, but these are the cuisines—whether offered by restaurants or as ingredients for the shelves of your supermarket—that are most often found in cities across the United States.

We feel that when you turn up the heat in the food, counter it with sweetness. But sweet wine alone won't do it—it needs acid, and that's why all eyes and glasses turn to Germany. If you go to Chapter Four on reading a wine label, you'll see that Germany lists the degree of ripeness, or sweetness, right on the label. The quality of the wine is based on the accumulated sugar in the grapes when they are picked. We feel that only three of these wines do well with spicy foods: Kabinett, Spätlese, and Auslese.

## Chinese, Japanese, and Vietnamese

The concept of balance is prevalent throughout Asian culture. The revered system of yin and yang can be applied to all areas of life, including that of eating. Yin represents foods that are subtle, cooling, moist, and soft. Yang, as you would expect, is the opposite side of the spectrum, and includes the spicy, the crunchy, the meaty, and the herbaceous. All dishes are made with this in mind. So when you hear someone proclaim that matching wine to Asian food is impossible, just remember that an entire culinary history based on balance can't be complemented by a mere glass of water. We can do better than that:

- ❖ **Spätlese.** High acidity combined with a light, late-harvest sweetness to cut the heat of super spicy foods.
- ❖ **Kabinett.** A light, delicate refreshing wine with an off-dry finish.
- ❖ **Auslese.** A step-up in ripeness, these are usually specially selected grapes that produce a full-flavored wine.
- ❖ **Sauvignon Blanc.** Fruitier, New World Sauvignon Blancs allow you to taste the bite of wasabi without taking it to such a blinding level that you lose the rest of your meal (in this case, likely sushi). The herbaceous undertone of the wine also allows the accompaniments like the snappy bite of ginger to be a player without taking over the whole show. It's also an excellent complement to the mild spices and fresh herbs and vegetables in Vietnamese cuisine.

❖ **Chenin Blanc.** Sparkling, refreshing, cleansing. Go for the slightly sweeter versions from the Loire.

When the French first settled in Vietnam, we're sure it didn't take long before someone realized that Bordeaux and Burgundy wines just didn't cut it with the local food. However, they just needed a little time to find the right blend of East and West.

We like Champagne with fusion food, especially a good nonvintage, full-bodied wine like Bollinger, Montaudon, Nicolas Feuillate, and especially the Rose Paradis by Alfred Gratien. An N.V. (nonvintage) Champagne can be found for around $25 to $30 a bottle in a good wine shop, and works great with spice (and is terribly romantic to boot).

Chenin Blanc, which has a slight effervescence to it, is also an excellent choice for Vietnamese food. Tony loves the Chenin Blancs from the appellation of Savennières. Wine production goes back there since before the Middle Ages, and they produce an off-dry white wine, floral nose, and high acidity. With a great mineral and crisp green apple taste, it takes the confusion out of the fusion.

## Indian and Thai

India and Thailand are, of course, very different places (one is a gigantic country with terrain as diverse as the dialects spoken within it, the other a smallish, Southeast Asian country twice the size of Wyoming). But one thing they have in common is the broad use of curry in their cuisines. Curry is actually an amalgam of many spices, and there are different kinds from different places—the spicy red and green curry of Thailand; the golden-hued curry of India that ranges in heat level. But to many a wine drinker, both pose a similar problem: What do you drink with it?

For those who like red, it *is* true that it can be much more limiting than white. Because we're proponents of never saying never, here's a trick for those of you loyal to red wine. As we said earlier, spicy food takes the natural tannins in wine and makes a bitter brew of something that, on its own or paired with something else, might be highly enjoyable. However, a salt shaker or a wedge of lemon or lime can turn this situation around. Salty and sour flavors tame the tannic nature of a wine's bitterness and make the wine taste milder. If salt is not on your table, think sauces: soy sauce or fish sauce, for example, are highly salty and can give you the flavor addition you seek. Also, as the skin of Merlot grapes is thinner, they just naturally have a lower level of tannin than other reds. This makes them milder in flavor and, therefore, a good fall-back red for spicy foods. And despite what normal circumstances dictate, if you chill the Merlot *ever so slightly* (we're not talking arctic freeze here, just a quick stint in the fridge or cooler) it also helps take the edge off a spicy dish. Break with tradition and try your *slightly* chilled Merlot while dining on curry- and cumin-infused Indian delight or a spicy, peanuty Thai beef saté.

As to other good options for spicy dishes, consider the following:

* **Gewürztraminer.** Whether it be Thai green curry or chicken vindaloo, the fruity nature of Gewürz is a siren song that tames the hot and lures the rest of the flavors into the forefront.
* **Pinot Gris/Pinot Grigio.** Its ripe fruit and great acidity gives balance to spicy curries and other seasonings.
* **Viognier.** The rich, honeysuckle, fruity nature of this French Rhône valley varietal makes it an excellent foil for the hot/sweet nature of many Thai and Indian dishes.
* **Sauvignon Blanc.** The sweeter New Zealand style or the milder Chilean versions of this crisp, herbaceous varietal are great for Eastern-spiced dishes. However, an unoaked Fumé Blanc (just another name for the same) from California brings out the sweetness and cuts the saltiness in dishes with spicy accoutrements, like a Thai peanut sauce.
* **German Riesling.** The low alcohol content (around 8 percent) of Riesling keeps the heat of a fiery curry turned down, while the fruity nature of the wine allows other flavors to make their appearance. Taking a Riesling to a sweeter level and going for a sweet, amber-hued Trockenbeerenauslese (which can have

up to 30 percent residual sugar) whips super-spicy dishes into submission while allowing you to experience the sweet, herbaceous, and/or citrusy qualities of the dish.

❖ **Moscato d'Asti.** Refreshing, honeyed, and floral. Like Rieslings, Moscatos are a good catch-all for spicy Asian food.

Pinot Grigio from Italy has been around a long time. With great producers such as Alois Lageder and Peter Zemmer in Alto Adige, and Giovanni Puiatti in Friulia, these wines have been taken to a higher plane. Alsace has also contributed, with a slightly different interpretation (remember—terroir can change everything) from some fine producers like Leon Beyer, Dopff & Irion, and Marcel Deiss.

In the past 10 years, the grapes have traveled to the New World. Whether the vino is called Pinot Gris or Pinot Grigio, American winemakers are putting their stamp upon this simple, pleasant grape. Bob Long of Long Vineyard is producing a Pinot Grigio as close to the Italian version as possible—we love it. And Oregon has embraced this grape, as well as Pinot Noir, as their own producers like King Estate, Duck Pond Cellars, and Rex Hill produce Pinot Gris at both the estate and reserve levels. Whether from California, Alsace, Alto Adige, or Willamette Valley, these are wonderful wines to share with friends and above all treat with some great food!

If you think about it, fire and spice in cuisine can pose a pairing conundrum with any beverage, really. The secret you've just learned here is that wine can actually be the best accompaniment around. True, there are some guidelines to follow—like, don't drink a tannic, full-bodied Cabernet with five-alarm chili, because the spice and the tannins will send you running for the closest bucket of ice. With some prudent selection, you can get the best of the fruit and the chili without losing any of the great qualities of both.

# chapter twenty-one

# Vintage Words: Interview with Michael Lomonaco

*I don't enjoy wine very much without food. I mean, I can drink a
glass of simple white wine and enjoy it, or I can drink a really complex aged wine that I'm just going to enjoy a glass of, but mostly
I really enjoy food and wine together because they both change.
They're never the same as they are separately.*

*—Michael Lomonaco*

Michael Lomonaco knows a thing or two about how to simultaneously
please the locals and tourists alike. After being at the helm of the kitchen
at Windows on the World—the beloved and much-missed sky-high restaurant that drew everyone from tourists, to Wall Streeters, to romance
seekers—Lomonaco, like most New Yorkers post–September 11, forged
on the best way he knew how. In his case, that meant to continue
bringing culinary joy to a down-but-not-beaten New York.

Enter Noche, the splashy, bright-as-a-Toucan eatery smack in the
middle of Times Square. The swirling, multi-level architecture makes
one think of the Guggenheim—if the Guggenheim were swept up by a
tornado and replanted in a full-on Technicolor Oz (well, if Oz was in,
say, Puerto Rico or Cuba or Rio). The atmosphere teems with South
American style: White leather banquettes are surrounded by curtains

the color of Caribbean waters, sunny orange walls peek through wooden-slatted wall hangings, and samba music syncopates from the speakers.

Ah, but the food—that's where Noche's real spice is.

We asked Michael to put together a few fiery dishes for our challenge of pairing wine with the spicier side of dining. Here's what we tried.

## Course I

Salmon ceviche marinated in lime, orange, and passion-fruit juices with red onion, shallots, chive, pickled jalapeño and jabanero peppers and cilantro
Lewis Chardonnay, 1999
Léon Beyer Gewürztraminer "Comtes d'Eguisheim," 1997

## Course II

Grilled chicken and vegetables with mustard and herb vinaigrette
Badia a Coltibuono Chianti "Cetamurs," 2000
Léon Beyer Gewürztraminer "Comtes d'Eguisheim," 1997

## Course III

Charred buffalo steaks with poblano-margarita sauce and South American sweet corn cake
Thelema Cabernet Sauvignon, 1998
Ravenswood Zinfandel, 1999
Montes Syrah "Alpha," 2001
Jean Luc Colombo Châteauneuf-du-Pape, "Bartavelles," 1999

## Course I: Take the Sweet with the Spicy

Sometimes the challenge of spicy food and wine pairing isn't just in the spice, but in the complexity of flavors within the dish. Michael presented us with a fantastic challenge—a salmon ceviche rich with a spectrum of flavor sensations: sweet, sour, pungent, spicy. What wine would tame the spice and yet marry all the flavors appropriately? Let's see …

**Michael Lomonaco:** So what we've got here is salmon ceviche—fresh salmon marinated with lime, orange, and passion fruit juices with jabanero, chives, red onions, shallots, pickled jalapeños, and cilantro. So it's a little spicy, but that comes more at the finish. I think it would be nice with a spicy white wine or a very minerally white wine, like an Alsatian white.

**Tony DiDio:** The first wine is a Léon Beyer, it's a Gewürztraminer, it's "Comtes d'Eguisheim." It's from 1997. Let's see how it goes.

> "Comtes d'Eguisheim" is a Grandes Cuvées, or blend, of grapes from the best slopes, primarily estates owned by the Beyer family. The majority of these grapes are from "Grand Cru" vineyards and the Cuvées is only produced from great vintages. For a 1997, the wine is incredibly mature tasting, with remarkable fruit overtones and a hint of spice. This wine is capable of aging into another decade, with proper cellaring conditions, and would reveal the depth of flavor that age gives to such a prestigious pedigree.

**Amy Zavatto:** Now, Michael, why would you immediately say that this is a good pairing for this dish? What is it about the flavor of the ceviche and the flavor of the wines that work together?

**Michael:** Well, the wine [Gewürztraminer] is dry but with lots of spicy fruit, and because of all the jalapeño and jabanero peppers in there you need something to cut through them. Something that can stand up to the peppers and that can stand up to the citrus juice, and that can stand up to the sweetness of the passion fruit.

**Amy:** Which is the first thing you taste in this—the sweetness of the passion fruit.

**Michael:** Right, the first thing you taste is the sweetness of the fruit in the ceviche—the sweetness of the passion fruit purée and the orange juice. Then the next thing you taste is a little of the citrus acid of the lime; then the next thing you taste in the ceviche is the onion—the red onion, the shallot, and the chives; you get the fresh chive, you get the greenness of the fresh chives. Then the next thing you get is the heat of the peppers.

**Tony:** Exactly! That's exactly what I went through when I just tried this. Well, you know, sweetness is always going to hit your tongue first—right at the tip of your tongue. And then the last thing is going to be the spice. And that's exactly how it went.

**Michael:** The Gewürztraminer on its own is a little unctuous. There's a little viscosity in it that's a little oily almost.

**Tony:** Right, right. It's a rich wine.

**Michael:** Right, but now against the flavors of the ceviche the wine loses that richness in a good way.

**Amy:** It tames it.

**Michael:** It mellows out the chili peppers.

**Amy:** It also really allows the salmon flavor to come through. I can still taste everything else in the dish, but the salmon doesn't get lost in the spiciness at the end when combined with the Gewürz.

**Michael:** Well, the salmon isn't overmarinated. It's only marinated for a few minutes before we serve it.

**Tony:** Oh really.

**Amy:** So it's not an overnight process?

**Michael:** Oh no, no, no. That would really transform it. You'd lose the freshness of the fish. You would lose the saline, you would lose the ocean quality of the fish if you marinated it overnight. That's not at all how Latin American ceviches are done.

**Tony:** I always thought that ceviches were marinated overnight.

**Michael:** Oh sure, I've cooked in kitchens where they marinate, for instance, scallops overnight and that transforms the fish so much. The acid of the marinade cooks it, it transforms it. And it does, it really does, and now it's not the same dish as a fresh, out-of-the-ocean ceviche, which is the Latin American, the Peruvian, the Caribbean style. Overnight marinated ceviche really changes the dish. The flavors have been tamed, the rawness has been tamed, even the acid of the marinade is flat the next day. It's not as sharp as it was. In a way, those ceviches are almost more wine-friendly because if you take ceviches that have lots of raw onion and peppers, like this, they almost call out for beer, or they call out not for an oaky Chardonnay, but for a very crisp sort of uncomplicated white wine. The Gewürz is almost a little complicated for this.

**Tony:** The mineral quality of a Pouilly-Fumé or Pouilly-Fuisse would probably work really well.

**Michael:** Another thing that would be great is Spanish Cava. Crisp, bubbly, a little on the tart side.

**Tony:** Yes, it's green. But what I want to do now, since I have it here, is to pour a glass of something that seems like an obviously incorrect match—just so we can taste it and see why. We might as well mix and match. What I took out was a Lewis Cellars Sonoma Chardonnay 1999—from my cellar to you! Michael asked me yesterday for a big, oaky Chardonnay to go with the chicken dish, and I thought of this. I figured since this is a Latin American restaurant, you're probably not going to have that many Alsatian Gewürztraminers on your wine list, but you do have Chardonnays, so let's see how this Chardonnay goes with it, if it goes at all.

**Amy:** I'm almost getting a little mineral flavor in this when I taste it on its own, but with the ceviche all of the traditional Chardonnay components are knocked out.

**Michael:** See, I think what happens is that all of the acid in the ceviche makes the Chardonnay unappealing.

**Tony:** For a great glass of wine, which this is, the food totally strips the flavor.

**Michael:** The Gewürz is much better for this.

**Tony:** I think it's the oak aging that changes it; I think it's the fact that it's a rich grape, whereas Gewürz is racy, spicy. This [the ceviche] overpowers the Chardonnay and the wine is underwhelmed by it, so it's totally a bad match.

**Michael:** Even the lighter-style Riesling would be great with this. A German Riesling. You see in Alsatian food and you see in German food a lot of vinegar, a lot of acid being used in the food. So that idea of pickled vegetables—and the ceviche is really the Latin American counterpart, there's acid, there's citrus—they really get balanced out by those kinds of wines better than the Chardonnay.

**Amy:** It almost seems counterintuitive really, if you think about it. If you think about the flavors that you expect to be in a ceviche and the flavors you would expect to be in a Chardonnay, it would seem that the ceviche would overpower the vanilla and oak in the Chard.

**Tony:** It's totally the wrong thing.

**Amy:** But it's great to try it for that reason—as an exercise to see why it doesn't work, instead of just saying, no, that doesn't work. Well, why? I just learned so much by doing something that I would normally overlook.

## Course II: Spice of a Different Color

When it comes to the "poultry with white" theory, there's nothing like a little spice—mustard, in this case—to turn an old piece of epicurean lore upside down. One of the principles we've been hammering home in this book is balance, so for this pairing, we brought in an underdog— a Coltibuono Chianti—and put it up against our Léon Beyer Gewürz- traminer. See how it all shook out.

**Amy:** Now, this is really going to be interesting—we have a red *and* a white here. I don't want to color anyone's final decision, but I can't help but hope that the Chianti is the winner with this chicken, simply to blow the "white wine with poultry" rule out of the water. And here, I think it might make sense. The chicken has a real earthiness to it that, in my mind, would really be complemented by a Chianti as opposed to a Gewürz.

**Michael:** This is a really earthy dish. You've got the grilled vegetables, which aren't grilled for too long, but just seared to the point where you have the flavor of the grill and vegetable together. Then there's the mustard and herb vinaigrette, which is very earthy. It's got thyme, oregano, basil, some balsamic vinegar.

**Amy:** I taste something sweet in here …

**Michael:** That would be the honey.

**Tony:** Michael, as a restaurateur who really gets to see the dining habits of so many people from all over the country, do you think that Ameri- cans are moving more toward wine in general?

**Michael:** Well, they're trying more wines. It's not just Cabernet and Chardonnay, it's not just Merlot. Sauvignon Blancs are selling, Pinot Blancs and Pinot Gris are selling. Pinot Noirs are selling a lot more. I think people are starting to get the differences between the varietals. And enjoying them.

**Tony:** Probably five years ago you didn't really see that kind of experimentation. Five years ago you probably wouldn't have seen Viognier by the glass, for instance, which I see a lot in restaurants now.

**Michael:** And also the old style of diner had one kind of wine that they drank. They drank Burgundies. They drank Bordeaux. Or the younger set went with the big Cabernets and Chardonnays from California. Now there's more experimentation and more diversity in their wine ordering. It's more, "What do I feel like tonight?" "Well, tonight I feel like a South American wine," or, "I want a Spanish wine," so I think people are ordering that way. They're more adventurous if the price is not prohibitive.

**Amy:** I think the variety of American restaurants and the popularity of dining as a hobby in the last few years has really allowed for that to happen. You can think what you want of Emeril, but he has almost single-handedly brought a more adventurous style of eating to middle America. I think that's great. And I think it leads to more curiosity about wine.

**Michael:** There's so much more that the average person can read about now—wines from all over the world. And you're more likely to find them in stores and restaurants. Not just French wines in a French restaurant, or Italian wines in an Italian restaurant. Although, I tend to want to stay regional with the cuisine I'm eating, simply because I know it's going to work better and it just seems more natural that the land where the food and wine originate marry well together.

**Tony:** You couldn't have said it better. That's exactly what I've been saying, that people should think regional when they're pairing wines and foods, and then experiment. I was out Thursday night with Patrick Campbell, the winemaker and owner of Laurel Glenn in California, and we went to I Trulli restaurant, which has a great, full Italian wine list. We sat down and told the chef just to make us a couple pastas, and then opened up a Barbaresco, and we were in heaven. These are wines that should be drunk with these foods. And thinking, well, should I be drinking a South African wine with this? Should I be drinking an Australian Shiraz? Well, maybe it does work but definitely the wine we picked was the right wine.

**Michael:** Well, I'll drink those wines that you just mentioned but in other contexts.

**Tony:** Exactly.

**Michael:** There are American restaurants where they have a very broad mix of flavors and styles of cooking. I think an American restaurant, like my kind of American restaurant, where they have a broad style of cooking, really works.

**Tony:** So let's get back to business here—what do you think, kids? What's working for you?

**Amy:** As I suspected, it's the Chianti for me. It's all about the earthiness in the dish and earthiness in the wine. And the spiciness of the Dijon mustard also is allowed to really take center stage with the mellowness of this wine. The Gewürz, while it worked incredibly well with the bright, bold flavors of the ceviche, is too high of a note for this chicken dish.

**Michael:** It's too green for the mustard and the grilled vegetables. The Chianti is the best match here.

**Tony:** Well, then it's unanimous—the Chianti and the chicken are great together.

**Amy:** And can we please note that it's a red, and not a white, that was the winner? So much for hard and fast rules. Again, it all boils down to not just the meat or the fish or the vegetable, but how it's prepared.

## Course III: One Margarita, Hold the Salt

We saved the big guns until last—a delectably rare buffalo rib eye steak drizzled with a poblano margarita sauce and served with a melt-in-your-mouth South American sweet corn cake. Only a bold wine could stand up to such a hearty, spicy dish—but which one? In the midst of figuring out the winner and bold champion, the conversation turned philo-sophical, as a good wine and a great meal can tend to engender …

**Michael:** This is the buffalo rib eye steak with poblano margarita sauce. And that means that it has all the elements of a margarita. There's tequila and cuantro and triple sec and lime juice, a little bit of honey, and there's three kinds of chili peppers—ancho, chipotle, and fresh poblano. It's rich meat, and it's not a traditional chili sauce that you'd find in Mexican cooking. There's a Southwestern influence to it, but really they're big flavors that I think Americans like in their big-red-meat category. I bet the Chilean Syrah will be really great with this, and we also have that Zinfandel ...

> Ah, the sin of Zin. Zinfandel is a fleshy and flashy grape that can be made into many different styles: (1) elegant, with great structure that is capable of aging, and (2) big and bold, with high alcohol and fresh berry aromas. Tony prefers the more elegant style, where the alcohol is tamer, and the wine is made almost in a Bordeaux style. When the alcohol is lower than some of those with 14.5 percent and 14.3 percent alcohol, the grape's spicier and berry aromas are allowed to unravel. Zins that are "too big" have too much fruit and too much alcohol to match with any pairing of food outside of some cheeses.

**Tony:** We're going to have four wines with this dish. This is fun, right?
**Amy and Michael:** Yeah!
**Tony:** We're using the Syrah from Montes, we're using the Châteauneuf, and then you have the Zin and a Cabernet from South Africa.
**Amy:** Tony, are there any particular qualities to a South African Cabernet as opposed to a California Cabernet or a European version that are distinctive?
**Tony:** I find South African Cabernets a bit more elegant—they're not as broad, they're not as fat. And also there's a little more green pepper to them. I look at a California Cab and South African Cab totally differently, as if the South African were more like a Bordeaux. So I find that, to me, they're a little bit more focused.
**Amy:** So Michael, following what we said earlier about Italian wine with Italian food, etc., do you think with South American food that people should be drinking South American wine?
**Michael:** Well, we have the Syrah on the table now, and we have a lot of South American wines on our list here, but what I was really getting at before was grape varietals. Most of the South American grape varietals are the European grape varietals. And Zinfandel is probably the only real American varietal that's not based on a European model.
**Tony:** Well, yes and no, it actually comes from a Croatian varietal but ...

**Michael:** … it's been here so long.

**Tony:** Exactly. It is the most American of all varietals.

**Michael:** Although American Cabernets and Merlots are different than the European versions. They're not modeled on European wines.

**Tony:** Okay, we've got four wines in front of us. They're all red. This is buffalo. So we're going to see what really works. We have only one American wine and that's the wine that's really indigenous to America—the Ravenswood Zinfandel—and we'll see how it works with the dish.

**Amy:** The chilies in the sauce are great.

**Michael:** Too spicy?

**Amy:** No, no! I love it.

**Tony:** Too spicy for what?!

**Amy:** What advice would you give to people who wanted to eat South American food that was very spicy, or spicy food in general? Do you have any guiding principal?

**Michael:** I always tell people to try to do what we've just done without the food. Try to taste four or five different wines with different characteristics. In other words, have a Syrah, have a Zinfandel, have a Cabernet, have a Merlot. Do it at the price you're comfortable with and taste them. Start to develop and educate your palate. Then next time, spend a little bit more if you want. But make it fun. Get to know the varietals because that's how to figure out what to pair. It's really simple to do. Within the price range of $10 to $15, you can find almost every varietal we've talked about today. Try to do this at home rather than in a restaurant where wines get to be more expensive. I think that the only rule is that if it doesn't taste good, don't do it. But you have to have some experience with it before you choose a wine with a poblano sauce. Educate your palate.

**Amy:** Hey, there's something sweet in this sauce.

**Michael:** That's the honey. This is great with the Syrah.

**Amy:** The Zinfandel is a little too big for me so far. It's overpowering. The Cabernet I like.

**Michael:** The Zinfandel is almost a little too fruity, too.

**Tony:** Really, this dish could go with a Zin, but this one is too big. The heat is intense. The Syrah I think is working for me, and the Thelema Cabernet is also working very well for me. The Cabernet is really singing.

Tony loves a good song, and sometimes judges a great wine as "singing." What he means by this is the wine to him is hitting all the notes: balance, fruit, acidity, and finish. When the right wine is matched with the right food, watch out—an aria is about to begin.

Thelema Cabernet did it for both of us with the buffalo rib eye. The balance of great mature fruit, hints of leather and spice, added another dimension to the buffalo. And brought out the spice in the dish.

**Amy:** It's really carrying the flavors for me.

**Tony:** Try the Ridge Coastal Range—it's a simple wine, it's not even really expensive. It's easy to drink. It's almost like a Châteauneuf-du-Pape, where it has more than five grape varietals in it.

**Amy:** I think the spices in the meat really bring out the spicy and fruity qualities of this wine. I'm getting a pepperiness, probably from the Zinfandel portion, that I didn't get tasting it on its own.

**Tony:** We've really been finding, Michael, that it's the food that draws the wine out and the wine that draws the food out.

**Michael:** I don't enjoy wine very much without food. I mean, I can drink a glass of simple white wine and enjoy it, or I can drink a really complex aged wine that I'm just going to enjoy a glass of, but mostly I really enjoy food and wine together because they both change. They're never the same as they are separately. This Coastal is good. It has tannins, probably came from the stems.

**Tony:** Like I said it's an inexpensive wine, but 22 percent Carignane, 20 percent Zin, 20 percent Sangiovese, 15 percent Mattaro, 8 percent Petite Syrah, 8 percent Barbera, and 7 percent Alicante.

**Michael:** It's a little acidic.

**Tony:** I just went back to the Thelema Cabernet and that's absolutely delicious.

**Michael:** I agree, it's the Cabernet and Syrah that work the best for this dish.

**Tony:** And if we need a third party, I'd go for the Ridge Coastal. Although it's a little bit too fruit-forward.

**Michael:** Well, the Ridge has an influence of raspberry fruit, and it's high in acid.

**Tony:** But it's not a shy wine, it's assertive. With this dish I think we're right, it's the Syrah from Montes, and the South African Cabernet, of all things. So much for my theory of eating and drinking regional! *[laughter]*

**Michael:** Well, when I was talking about that before I was really referring to being in a restaurant. If I'm in an Italian restaurant, I'm going to go for the Italian part of the wine list, which I also expect is going to be broader and more well chosen. I really think with wine and food pairing there's an issue of what to do in restaurants, but it's more about lifestyle; what you're doing at home. Has anyone had the guts to do hot dogs with you?

**Tony:** We should have done that with Daniel!

**Amy:** I read a great article in *Food & Wine* a couple of years ago about pairing wine with fast food. If you're having take-out Chinese, or you're having pizza, or you're having this or you're having that. They interviewed a sommelier and they did a very specific fast-food with wine pairing. That's the thing, we Americans don't really think of wine that way, the way Europeans do. For many of us, it seems to warrant a special occasion, so there's less occasion to try and experiment.

**Michael:** Wine every day. That's my theory.

**Amy:** My grandparents certainly drank like that and ate like that because that's what it was like in Italy. My grandfather made his own wine.

**Tony:** But Michael's got a point—if you are having hot dogs, what are you going to drink?

**Amy and Michael:** Beer!

**Michael:** But if I added sauerkraut …

**Amy:** That adds a whole new dimension!

**Tony:** I say go Riesling.

**Michael:** A New York State Riesling. They're nice and dry.

**Amy:** Michael, is there any general principal that you use at home when you're drinking wine and eating in?

**Michael:** I don't eat at home every day so I couldn't tell you what I would drink every day if I were home, because I'm not. So on the one or two nights a week that I'm home, I tend to be pretty diverse. Sometimes Spanish wines, sometimes American wines. I just enjoy wine from all over. I buy mostly American, Italian, and South American. I drink a lot of Spanish wines at home, mostly Crianzas from Rioja. I'm going to be as price-sensitive as anyone else depending on the occasion. But I never worry about the cost of wine if it's coming out of my cellar and what it will cost to replace it.

**Tony:** Wine is not to be worshipped. It is not to be put on a pedestal. Wine is for every day. If you're buying wine and you're saving it for a special occasion, you know what? That special occasion never comes around and you end up not drinking it. You know the other day I opened up a jar of caviar that I had from Christmas. We had it just hanging around. It's like, when are you going to eat it? When are you going to drink it? Forget saving it—it's for right now. The present *is* a special occasion.

# Try It for Yourself

Have your own spicy tasting with this kicked-up recipe from Michael Lomonaco. Although he used buffalo rib eye, this might not be readily available at your supermarket or butcher shop, so feel free to use prime (of course!) rib eye instead. Pair it with a Ravenswood Zin, a Montes Syrah, and a Colombo Châteauneuf-du-Pape, and you've got your very own *bueno* Noche experience.

## Charred Buffalo Steaks with Poblano-Margarita Sauce

1 TB. olive oil

1 TB. unsalted butter

4 (12- to 14-oz.) prime rib-eye steaks

Sea salt and freshly ground pepper to taste

1 small Vidalia onion, diced

2 poblano peppers, roasted, peeled, seeded, and medium diced

1 TB. New Mexico ancho chili paste

1 small chipotle pepper, re-hydrated, seeded, and puréed

½ cup orange juice

¼ cup lime juice

2 TB. honey

1 oz. gold tequila

2 oz. orange liqueur

1 cup veal stock

1 TB. orange zest

½ cup heavy cream

2 TB. salted butter

Heat olive oil and unsalted butter in a sauté pan large enough to hold two steaks at a time over high heat. Season steaks with salt and pepper, and add to the hot pan. Turn the heat up to high and char both sides of meat thoroughly, about 2 minutes each side. Remove steaks from the pan, place on a warm platter, and set aside. Cook remaining two steaks in the same fashion and set aside, covering to keep meat warm.

Add onion and poblano peppers to the same sauté pan you used for meat, spread out evenly, and cook until wilted. Add chili paste and chipotle purée and combine well to toast spices. Add orange and lime juices and honey, deglaze, and allow juices to boil for 2 minutes to reduce by half. Working carefully, away from the flame, add tequila and orange liqueur to the pan over low heat and allow to reduce before adding veal stock. Reduce stock by half over high heat and add orange zest. Cook for 2 minutes and then add heavy cream and bring to a gentle simmer (do not allow to boil) for 2 minutes before swirling in butter.

Uncover meat and pour sauce around it. Serve immediately.

Makes 4 servings.

# *chapter twenty-two*

# Dessert and Dessert Wines

*Prejudices, it is well known, are most difficult to eradicate from the heart whose soil has never been loosened or fertilized by education; they grow there, firm as weeds among the rocks.*

—*Charlotte Brontë*

Even the most sophisticated of diners may find themselves perplexed by the notion of pairing wine with sweet treats come meal's end. After heaving a smirking sigh of guilty resolution when the dessert menu or cart pops up, many diners will go right for the caffeine, opting for coffee or tea with their dessert. Or, if wine is still on their minds, they will ask for an after-dinner drink in lieu of chocolate and cream and raspberry couli.

There are a few explanations for this—but there's only one that we accept: You are simply not in the mood for any more alcohol and are still savoring the finish on that lovely Barbaresco you consumed with your main course. Any other reasons—like, say, you have NO idea where to begin with pairing wine and dessert—are from this point forward forbidden. Prejudice is never good in any realm, and food and wine pairing is no exception. It's a simple matter of getting over a fear. Take a tip from Ms. Brontë—educate yourself to eradicate such stubborn inclinations.

If you've learned anything in this book, it's that you've got to be a little brave, a little adventurous when pairing. You saw this in every single tasting we did—from Daniel Boulud to Rick Moonen to Michael Lomonaco. Even the most revered chefs of our time have to try things out. Sometimes a wine you think will work does, like the Qupé Syrah with Don Pintabona's beef tenderloin, and sometimes it doesn't, like the Zinfandel we had with the buffalo steak in Chapter Twenty-One. But you should not be intimidated if even the experts can get stumped.

It's true, dessert can be tricky to navigate. We'll allow that. Remember what we said in Chapter Four—when in doubt, pop the cork and give it a try. Just as wine can enhance, complement, and completely transform an appetizer or entrée, so it can for sweets. To shirk the challenge and skip it altogether means missing out on some truly sigh-inducing pairings. In the (paraphrased) words of Ernestine Ulmer, life is uncertain; eat dessert and drink wine first.

## To Pear or Not to Pair?

In Chapter Six we discussed how on your tongue, the first sensation and flavor you get is that of sweetness. With entrée pairings between food and wine, this can be just the first layer in an epicurean experience. One that may be followed by, for instance, savory, spicy, sour, salty, bitter, or a combination of all these. You want a wine that brings out each of these qualities. There are desserts that are one-dimensional: a rich, chocolate cake, for instance. But it's not really that often that desserts are merely one flavor and one flavor only. True, the predominant sensation you will get will be sweet in most cases. But a pastry chef and a county fair blue ribbon–winning baker alike could tell you that much more goes into the pudding than sugar, sugar, sugar.

Amy was at one time in her foodie career a bit of a professional pie baker, supplying restaurants with seasonally based tin-filled rounds of pastry and fruit. You might think to yourself, "Well, pie is a pretty simple dessert. It's just sugar and fruit, which in essence is more sugar. Right? That's pretty one-dimensional." Ah, young Skywalker, you have much to learn. What's in a pie? It depends. For Amy, pies can contain any or many of the following: fruit, sugar (white, light brown, or dark brown), cinnamon, nutmeg, citrus juice (lemon, lime, or orange), clove, anise, cream, vanilla, salt, egg, nuts, chocolate, rum, bourbon, ginger, and a slew of other secret things she will not reveal at this juncture. You'll have to wait for another book for that.

The point is, that's quite a spectrum of flavors. You've got sweet, you've got sour, you've got salt, you've got dairy, you've got spicy. Wouldn't it be nice to find a wine that made all of those flavors really come out?

We sat down at one point during the writing of this book with Johnny Iuzzini, the immensely talented, James Beard–nominated young-gun pastry chef for Jean Georges (as in, yes, Jean-Georges Vongerichten). Iuzzini, who trained under the watchful eye of Daniel Boulud, has a passion for pastry that, after one sampling of his multi-dimensional creations, would convince anyone that dessert is a course worthy of more attention than a simple "Mmmmm" provides.

In fact, take a look at what is referred to as the "Dessert Tasting" menu at Jean Georges created by Iuzzini, which we tackled one day, wine in hand:

**Chocolate**
Warm chocolate cake, vanilla ice cream
Chocolate caramel mousse, hazelnut success, salted peanuts
White chocolate tarragon millefeuilles, grapefruit
Chilled juniper spiced chocolate soup, Devon cream

**Exotic**
Chocolate passion soufflé, passion sauce
Roasted pineapple with cardamom, coconut sorbet
Soft Kalamanzi cream, matcha meringue
Mango soup, papaya, litchi ginger sorbet

**Citrus**
Milk chocolate and licorice cake, ginger and candied kumquats
Yuzu cream filled doughnut
Lime semi-freddo, sable Breton, warm blood orange and date stew
Yogurt vanilla soup, toasted almond tofu, mandarin sorbet

**Caramel**
Chocolate crepe suzette, Meyer lemon
Caramel-banana cake, sablé croquant
Pepper crème caramel, walnut nougatine
Apple soup, caramel gelée, Granny Smith sorbet

Granny Smith apples are an influence not only in desserts, but in wines as well. For instance, you may have whiffed the aroma of green apples in a Riesling. But who exactly was Granny Smith and how did she get a variety of apple named after her? Her real name was Maria Ann Smith and despite the down-homey sounding moniker, she was from Down Under, not down South. She found an apple seedling in her Sydney, Australia, garden one day in the spot where she'd dumped some rotten apples years before. This seedling grew to bear the tart green fruit we all know as Granny Smith apples.

With such a mind-boggling array of flavors (the man effectively uses cardamom and tarragon in *dessert!*), this was a pairing challenge worthy of addressing. We brought along six wines:

- ❖ Voss Botrytis Sauvignon Blanc and Semillon, 2000 (Napa)
- ❖ Muscat de St. Jean Minervois (nonvintage, France)
- ❖ Saracco Moscato D'Asti, 2001 (Italy)
- ❖ Cascinetta Moscato D'Asti, 2001 (Italy)
- ❖ Kracher Trockenbeerenauslese, Welshriesling 1998 (Austria)
- ❖ Graham's Six Grapes (nonvintage, Portugal)

Even with this varied selection of classic dessert wine—ranging in flavor from light and floral to weighty and jammy—we learned some intriguing tasting lessons. The most important, though, is that you absolutely can follow the same rules of complexity that you do with main courses (i.e., the more complex your dish, the more yin and yang you need between what you drink and what you eat).

For instance, the reason a dessert like the white chocolate tarragon millefeuilles with a grapefruit essence works so well with a Moscato D'Asti is that the delicate, floral quality of the Moscato allows the incredibly complex flavors in that dessert to find their way together. Also, the acidity of the wine stands up to the grapefruit. It doesn't compete—it complements. And how about the chocolate-and-red theory? Well, that all depends on what's with the chocolate. For instance, in our tasting, the Graham's Six Grapes did expectedly well with the chocolate cake, but with the chocolate crepe suzette with Meyer lemon?

That addition of citrus made the port bitter. Not a good match at all. In addition, as we will see throughout this chapter, whether you are matching your dessert to your wine or the reverse, use the main flavor influence to guide your choice.

Although we recommend using the flavors in dessert and nondessert wines alike as a parallel to the flavors in your dessert, you do need to be cautious about some exceptions to the rule. Chardonnay, for instance, is not the way to go with vanilla or white-chocolate. Although Chardonnays (California Chardonnays, most notably) tend to have an oaky, vanilla taste to them, they are way too overpowering for the simple flavor of, say, an angel food cake or a white chocolate mousse. However, with that said, there are late-harvest Chardonnays in which the strong fruit flavors are mellowed and meld with the oaky, vanilla flavors picked up from barrel aging. If Chardonnay is your weakness, then this might be an excellent dessert-wine choice for you.

# Chocolate

One of the wonderful things about pairing chocolate and wine is that many of the same wines that complement your dinner course can travel straight through to your warm Valhrona cake. Think about it—what are some of the main flavors you're going to find in a Zinfandel? How about a Syrah? A Cabernet? Berries, cherries, and plums. And have you ever met a chocolate cake that didn't taste good with those flavors? Not likely.

If you want to go with a dessert wine, however, here are a few things to keep in mind.

## Not All Ports Are Created Alike

Although it's widely assumed that port and chocolate pair well, there are different kinds of port and we don't think all of them are necessarily suitable with dessert. There are four main categories of port:

You may be familiar with the British love of port wine. Of course, port is a lovely thing to look at and an even lovelier thing to consume—but that's not the whole reason behind the Anglo affinity for the beverage. It has a little to do with the politics of war. Lisbon was a key port, and the Brits made sure to bring Portugal into their favor before war broke out between England and France. Of course, once it did, the English could no longer get their beloved Bordeaux, so Portuguese wine had to do.

❖ **Ruby.** Ruby ports are young, fruit-forward wines. They are a gorgeous hue—rich, deep red—and generally wood-aged about two years before they are ready for consumption. They are made from lower-quality batches of wine and are, on the whole, very reasonably priced. Ruby ports are excellent foils for basic chocolate desserts. Not as concentrated as a tawny or a vintage, this young wine tastes as fresh as the day it was bottled with an aroma of just-picked red berries. Try it with milk chocolate, dried fruit, or walnuts. We love the rich fresh fruit in the Quinta de la Rosa Ruby "601."

❖ **Tawny.** As you would suspect, the color of a tawny port is exactly as its name suggests—brownish, tan, caramel colored. It is made from a combination of several years' worth of grapes and is usually aged for 10, 20, 30, and 40 years (the bottles will state this; for instance, Graham's 20-year tawny). A tawny is usually a blend of the favorite wines of the producer, and tawnies, also known as "wood ports," develop into some great wines (of course, this depends on the quality of the blend). Tawny ports are also great with chocolate desserts, but they have even greater potential for pairing when the flavors start to get a little more complicated. For instance, if there are also bananas, cream, caramel, or spices (nutmeg, cinnamon, et al.) in the dessert, tawny ports are a good bet. We're particularly partial to the 20-year tawny from Graham's, which has a nutty, spicy aroma and takes on a brownish orange hue after sitting in the wood for two decades.

❖ **Vintage.** The good stuff. To Tony, vintage port is like a Barolo—it just doesn't get any better than this. Vintage ports are made from a single-year's grape that has been declared a quality year for that particular port grape. They have excellent aging potential (50 or more years) and can range in color from a surprisingly youthful red hue to deep brown. Now, as we've said, you can do whatever you like, but if either of us is ordering a glass of $40-and-upward port, savoring it all on its own is a heavenly experience. It's not just the price—it's that when you have a dessert wine of this quality, it's sort of nice to just taste what's happened to the grape over the years and truly savor the fleeting experience of the fruit. After consulting *Wine Spectator*'s vintage chart in Chapter Four we see that there have been some great years for port: 1963, 1966, 1970, 1977, 1983, 1985, 1991, 1992, 1994, and 1997—quite a great run of incredible wines.

❖ After a recent tasting of a Smith Woodhouse 1977, we found it to be youthful with its deep, rich purple color and a perfumed nose of sweet berries. Surprisingly, the color did not fade, as is the case of some older ports. The taste was mellow and elegant and matched to perfection the Stilton cheese and walnuts that we sampled.

❖ **White.** As you'd suspect, a white port is just like a red port, but is made with white grapes. Before the addition of a neutral brandy to stop the fermentation, white port is vinified dry. It is used primarily as an aperitif, not as a dessert wine. It has a nutty quality to it, and yet it's not as elegant as a sherry. We like it served cold, alone, or mixed with tonic water on ice on a balmy day. However, if you just can't get white port and chocolate out of your head, go for less-dense, lighter chocolate desserts, such as cream-based or whipped options (like chocolate meringue or mousse).

## Don't Ignore the Blush

Brachetto d'Acqui is a Spumante, meaning a sparkling wine that's fruity, light, and aromatic. That sweet nectarlike nose comes from the *Moscato* that is blended into the mix. We loved the "Rose Regali" by

Villa Banfi, which Johnny suggested to us. Oh yeah, Brachettos are red—don't let the Moscato fool you.

> Johnny Iuzzini likes to use Brachetto d'Acqui as his all-purpose fall-back dessert wine. "I tend to like fruitier wines; I really like the Brachetto a lot. I've tasted it with all the desserts, and it works really well. I like effervescent, sweet wines more than hard-core, thick wines. Those are too much—too heavy and syrupy. Like with my desserts, I want an essence of sweet, I don't want to leave the client with that extra sweet taste."

## White *Can* Work

And while we're on the topic of *Moscato* ... When trying to decide what wine goes with your chocolaty dessert, ask yourself (if you're preparing it), or your waitperson, as the case may be, what else is in it. Spices? Fruits? Cream? Licorice? Liqueur? You might find that, depending on what the main influences in the dessert are, a white dessert wine might pair very well. In particular, the Muscat grape is incredibly versatile and one that works well with just about every kind of dessert. This grape is grown in several places—Asti in Italy, Alsace in France, and Samos in Greece, for instance. The Alsace and Samos Muscats have more of an orange and tangerine influence, whereas the Asti Moscato frequently has a honeyed, floral aroma. While both make the leap over to chocolate desserts, the orange influence in the French and Greek versions are particularly complementary—orange with chocolate is a classic combination.

# From Fruit to Nuts

Desserts made with fruit or nuts, or a combination of both, are excellent foils for wine. If you think about some of the influences many white wines have—pear, peach, apricot, apple, pineapple, melon, lichee—it's nearly a no-brainer. More than that, matching the influence in a wine to your dessert is an excellent guide when you don't know where to go. For instance, say you've been drinking Riesling with your meal.

Along comes the dessert menu and, lo and behold, there's a lovely peach pie or melon sorbet on the list. There you go—the perfect match. Just as we were saying previously with chocolate, there's a good argument for keeping the same wine from start to finish, as more often than not, you'll find a complement for it from beginning to end.

However, we can make some other suggestions for dessert-wine pairings that are well worth traveling off your original path:

- For desserts with a fruit influence of apple, pear, or apricot, a Trockenbeerenauslese (or TBA) works very well. Also, the floral and honey flavors in a Moscato D'Asti allow these orchard fruit flavors to really stand out, as if they're practically gliding on the honey influence in the wine. Also, the floral and peach undertones in the same grape produced in France (a good example is the St. Jean Minervois Muscat we paired with Johnny Iuzzini's dessert creations) is a great pairing with pies, tarts, and cakes made with orchard fruit. Tony's favorite, Riesling, with its apricot and peach influence, also works incredibly well with this type of fruity dessert.

- For citrusy desserts, Canadian Icewine or the German and Austrian versions of the same (Eiswein), quell the high-acid taste of the citrus fruit. You also might want to try a late-harvest Gewürztraminer, as its bold fruitiness can have the influence of grapefruit and ginger.

- For exotic fruit desserts (those with a predominant flavor of pineapple, coconut, passion fruit, etc.), again, a Trockenbeerenauslese strikes a nice balance. The honeyed flavor of the sweet wines produced in France's Sauternes region are also an excellent foil for desserts that lean toward the exotic.

For desserts that are predominantly made of nuts, the Italians have the right idea. In a good Italian restaurant, you may have been presented with a glass of *Vin Santo* (meaning "holy wine") with a plate of nutty biscotti for dunking in the wine. For centuries, Catholic priests have consumed this amber-hued wine during Mass, but any proud Tuscan eatery or household serves this aperitif after coffee at the end of the meal. We are partial to versions produced by Badia a Coltibuono or Avignonesi. If rich, red grapes are what you favor, though, a tawny port is a lovely accompaniment as well.

Although Icewines, TBAs, and the like are well worth pairing with desserts as suggested earlier, you may want to enjoy them on their own. They are thick, sweet, incredibly delicious, an experience unto themselves. When pairing these wines at home for the first time, we recommend getting half bottles to try them out. Also, in the case of flavor-packed wines like these, you should consider going the route of finding a food to complement the wine instead of the reverse. In other words, go simple with the dessert pairing. Angel food cake, pound cake, and simple biscotti allow you to enjoy a confection but really let these wines show off their incredible qualities. If you find they're dessert enough for you, stick with the other options we've suggested in this chapter. Remember, you are your own sommelier, and in the end the proper choice is what tastes right to you.

## Light and Sugary

Some flavors seem easy as ... ah, no, we won't stoop to dessert cliché. But there are confections whose flavor is so easy-going it seems like they'd go with anything. With vanilla, you might not be too far from the truth. White chocolate is another fairly simple flavor to match. Whether you prefer the richness of a white port, the light, floral bouquet of a Moscato D'Asti, or the caramelized flavor of Madeira, the options are wide open. We particularly like the lush taste of a Semillon botrytis from Chalk Hill in Sonoma.

Caramel, however, we've found to be much trickier than you might assume. In our opinion, it's the most difficult dessert flavor to pair with wine. It's an odd phenomenon, but many a dessert wine seems to bring out the burnt quality of the sugar (after all, that's really what caramel is). When we did our tasting with Johnny Iuzzini, we found that all-around dessert-friendly wines like Moscato didn't do a thing for caramel and the floral nature of it was completely overpowered by the strength of the caramelized sugar. Ruby ports seem to bring out the worst in caramel, leaving only a burnt sugar taste in your mouth. The winner here is the wood-aging influence in a tawny port, which acts as a nice complement. Also, Trockenbeerenauslese strikes a good balance between the sweet and the bitter, as well as holding its own against those flavors. The caramel quality in Madeira also is an option that can hold its own.

Remember, as a seeker of great pairings, you've got to experiment—even when it comes to dessert. Use what we've given you here as a map—that is, start with the main flavor and look at what else is in the dessert, like citrus or spice or cream, to logically find the best wine for the job. Go back to our earlier chapters on sweet, salty, bitter, sour, and savory—you can apply these same rules to desserts as well. Is the dessert acidic? Is it creamy? Bitter chocolate or sweet? Packed full of orchard fruit? All of these aspects tell you something about what to pair. Don't be afraid to veer off the main drag to find your own great discoveries, though. There are no right turns or wrong turns—just a great big vineyard to explore at your leisure.

# Resources

If it's more information you seek in your plight as a Renaissance foodie, more information you shall have. Following is a list of books, magazines, and websites that offer important and entertaining information pertaining to food or wine (or both!). Happy reading ...

## Books

*Hugh Johnson's Story of Wine,* by Hugh Johnson (Mitchell Beazley, 1999). From Mesopotamia to Monticello, Johnson knows and tells all. Seriously fascinating stuff.

*The World Atlas of Wine, Fifth Edition,* by Hugh Johnson and Jancis Robinson (Mitchell Beazley, 2001). This 30-year-old tome has all you ever wanted to know about wine and so much more.

*The River Café Wine Primer,* by Joseph Delissio (Little, Brown & Company, 2000). An absolute must for your bookshelf. Delissio breaks it all down in a manner as easily digestible as the finest ... (oh, you know).

*Sip by Sip: An Insider's Guide to Learning All About Wine,* by Michael Bonadies (Main Street Books, 1998). Using a workbook format, Bonadies gets interactive with his readers. It's a fun, unintimidating way to learn about wine.

*Vino Italiano: The Regional Wines of Italy,* by Joseph Bastianich and David Lynch (Clarkson Potter, 2002). Respectively, co-owner and wine director of the Batali empire, their knowledge of Italian wine is unparalleled. Beautiful to look at, fun to read, great resource.

*The Oxford Companion to Wine, 2nd edition,* edited by Jancis Robinson (Getty Center for Education in the Arts, 1999). Just like its sibling book *The Oxford Companion to Food,* this heavyweight has information on history, wine diseases, wine-growing regions, lingo, and, of course, the wines themselves.

*Daniel Johnnes's Top 200 Wines: An Expert's Guide to Maximum Enjoyment for Your Dollar,* by Daniel Johnnes (Penguin USA, 1996). Tasting and wine-buying info from a great sommelier. Also information on how to set up your own wine cellar.

*The Wine Bible,* by Karen MacNeil (Workman Publishing, 2001). MacNeil's passion and enthusiasm are unrivaled on the page. Her witty, poetic way of describing a varietal and the land from which it comes is better than flash cards any ol' day.

*Windows on the World Complete Wine Course: A Lively Guide,* by Kevin Zraly (Sterling Publications, 2002). Just like taking the expensive class—only much, much cheaper.

*The Oxford Companion to Food,* by Alan Davidson (Oxford University Press, 1999). Is there any more comprehensive tome on the topic? We think not. The ultimate food resource, twenty years in the making.

*Vino: The Wine and Winemakers of Italy,* by Burton Anderson (Little, Brown & Company, 1980). An oldie but a goodie. Great info on the wine of one of the most prominent winemaking regions in the world.

# Magazines

### Food & Wine

Its monthly "Tastings" column is an excellent resource for the new, the old, and the up and coming. Often includes recipes for great pairings so you can actually try the match and not just take *F&W*'s word for it. Interactive—just the way we like it!

### Gourmet

Wonderful Ruth Reichl's monthly ode to great food and spirits often reads more like a novella, meandering from city to city, dining experience to dining experience, than a periodical to learn from. Ah, but you can. It's food and wine for thought in the most delicious way.

*Bon Appétit*

A pairing enthusiast's monthly dream come true. You'll always find something new to make or drink, or a place in which you can do both.

*Wine Spectator*

All that is new and noteworthy in the wine world. Packed with information, this mag has fantastic articles on wine, travel, and food, too, as well as their great vintage chart.

*Wine Enthusiast*

News you can use, plus fun stories to boot.

*The Wine Advocate*

A bi-monthly mag that offers advertising-free pages full of wine-tasting notes on what's new and noteworthy, with one annual issue devoted to Bordeaux and another to great wine values.

*Wine and Spirits*

Fair and reputable wine reviews and scoring. Also has great feature articles on wine trends, winemakers, etc.

*The Art of Eating*

Vermont-based quarterly magazine that believes the best edibles and drinkables are steeped in tradition and simplicity. We couldn't agree more.

## Websites

**www.epicurious.com**

The website of *Gourmet* and *Bon Appétit* magazines, it has a good, basic wine column that answers lots of questions quickly, provides ideas for pairings, and features news on the latest and greatest in viticulture. Wine and food dictionaries, and great recipes, too!

**www.foodandwine.netscape.com**

This site for *Food & Wine* magazine has a great wine column ("Ask Josh") that gives food and wine pairing advice, info on wine and food events, and great recipes and articles.

**www.egullet.com**

A.k.a. the Fat Guy, a.k.a. Steven Shaw. Sometimes controversial, always informative. The mantra of Shaw's site—"Read, chew, discuss"—says it all.

**www.winespectator.com**

The online arm of the powerhouse periodical. Free newsletter e-mailed right to your inbox tells you all that's new and interesting in the world of vino. Great way to keep up on trends and which wines are making a splash. Also has "What Am I Tasting?"—a fun way to test your wine knowledge online.

**www.slate.com**

Although their wine and food articles are few and far between, when they do have them they're incredibly informative and fun to read.

# Glossary of Wine and Food Terms

**acidity**   The backbone of a wine; acid gives wine structure and allows it to stand up to foods and their influences.

**aerate**   When a wine is exposed to oxygen, thereby unlocking its flavors and aromas.

**AOC**   Many European governments regulate the wine business by imposing standards to guarantee quality and uphold winemaking tradition. In France, the government wing that does this is the "Appellation Contrôlée" or AOC. You will find these words or letters on bottles of French wine that pass the AOC's strict standards.

**Arneis**   From the Piedmonte region, a white grape that produces a dry, fruity wine of the same name.

**astringent**   A tingly, lip-smacking sensation in the mouth caused by tannins (often in young wines). Too much astringency is distracting from the taste of a wine.

**balance**   The mantra of this book; the most important concept in food and wine pairing. Appropriate amounts of acid, tannin, fruit, terroir influences, as well as the flavors and sensations in the food.

**Barbaresco**   Made from the highly tannic red Nebbiolo grape from Piedmonte, this bold, powerful, spicy but elegant wine has great aging potential and a lovely dark color.

**Barbera**   The most widely planted grape in the Piedmonte region of Italy, it produces the acidic, earthy, bold wine by the same name.

**Barolo**   A product of the highly tannic Nebbiolo grape, this earthy, sometimes chocolaty wine has a beautiful floral aroma. The DOCG stipulates that this wine must age a minimum of three years.

**barriques**   Controversial, fairly new barrel-aging process that opponents of the method say makes the wine take on flavors from the wood, primarily a strong influence of vanilla, which tramples the natural fruit flavors and influence of the grape and the terroir and makes the wine overwhelming to almost all foods.

**Beaujolais**   From the Gamay grape in France, this wine is fruity, low in tannins, and has a lovely floral aroma.

**Beaujolais Nouveau**   Made from medium- to lesser-quality Gamay grapes, Beaujolais Nouveau is released the third Thursday of November and needs to be consumed immediately. This juicy, berry-flavored wine has absolutely no aging potential.

**bin number**   On a wine list, the number generally on the far left, which tells the sommelier where to locate that particular bottle from the wine cellar.

**Bordeaux**   Located in southwestern France, Bordeaux is one of the most revered and important wine-producing areas of the world. Major Bordeaux grape varietals include Cabernet Sauvignon, Merlot, and Sauvignon Blanc.

*botrytis cinera*   Also known as "the noble rot," this is a beneficial fungus that attaches itself to the skin of grapes in the form of a mold, perforating the skin, and removing the water inside. This strange procedure of Mother Nature concentrates the sugar that is left in the grape and helps to naturally create some of the most delicious, sweet wines available.

**botti**   The name of Italian barrels used to age certain wines, which are made of chestnut wood as opposed to oak.

**bouquet**   A wine's aroma.

**braising**   A manner of slow-cooking tougher cuts of meat in order to make them tender. Frequently requires the addition of wine.

**brix**   The measurement of the sugar level (i.e., ripeness) of a grape.

**Brunello di Montalcino**   Made from Sangiovese grapes in Tuscany, this complex wine has a deep, dark color and dark-fruit influences. Great aging potential.

**Burgundy**   Wine-producing region of France most well known for producing Pinot Noir (Burgundy) and Chardonnay (white Burgundy).

**Cabernet Sauvignon**   The grape that produces the wine of the same name. Cabernets are tannic, acidic, deeply hued red wines that have berry, plum, and currant influences. Fantastic aging potential.

**Cava**   Sparkling Spanish wine made in the style of Champagne.

**Chablis**   The area of northern Burgundy that produces Chardonnay grapes. Before Chardonnay became common parlance, this popular white wine was also referred to in the United States as Chablis.

**Champagne**   The wine-producing area of France that makes the famous sparkling quaff of the same name. In order to be called Champagne, a wine must be from the Champagne region. Otherwise, it is technically sparkling wine. Champagne is generally made from three different grapes: Chardonnay, Pinot Noir, and Pinot Meunier (the latter two are red).

**Chardonnay**   White grape that produces a buttery, golden wine of the same name that can have the influences of apple, pear, and pineapple. Chardonnay is rare among whites in that it is frequently (especially among U.S. winemakers) barrel-aged.

**Châteauneuf-du-Pape**   Robust, earthy, gamy red wine with infuences of leather and tar from the Rhône region of France. Although the principle grape in this wine is Grenache, it is a blend of several different varietals.

**Chenin Blanc**   Highly acidic white wine with a crisp, mineral qualities.

**Chianti**   Made from the Sangiovese grape, it is an earthy yet elegant red wine that can take on the influences of dried cherries, plums, leather, and even chocolate.

**clone**   Because grape varietals mutate due to viruses, they produce multiple versions of the original, which are called clones.

**Côte-Rôtie**   Made from Syrah grapes, this northern Rhône wine has a gamy, peppery flavor.

**Côtes du Rhône**   A complex, spicy wine made from several grapes with the primary varietal being Grenache.

**dessert wine**   Wines that have a higher sugar content and, often, a higher alcohol content as well. Examples of classic dessert wines are port, Trockenbeerenauslese, and the versatile Moscato d'Asti.

**diacetyle**   Produced in wines that go through malolactic or secondary fermentation. With the best results, diacetyle adds a buttery, sometimes vanillin flavor in a wine, as well as greater complexity of flavor.

**Dolcetto**   A grape from Piedmonte that produces a fruity, low-acid wine of the same name.

**DOCG**   Italian governmental regulations for grape growing and wine production. Stands for Denominazione di Origine Controllata e Garantita.

**earthiness**   A quality in a wine that gives off aromas and/or flavors of the very soil in which a grapevine is grown.

**enoteca**   Literally, "wine library" in Italian, this is an establishment dedicated to wine knowledge where, more often than not, you can taste as well as read about them.

**esoteric wines**   A single varietal or a unique blend, native to the region where it grows, and consumed mostly by the locals.

**estate**   A wine that is produced entirely in one particular area, or estate, from the growing of the grapes to the production of the wine to the bottling of the final product.

**fermentation**   Commences when the grapes are crushed and the skins come in contact with the mushy inside of the grape, or the pulp. Yeast is added to the mixture, carbon dioxide and heat are emitted, and the sugar of the fruit is turned into alcohol. How long this process occurs depends on how much sugar the winemaker desires there should or shouldn't be in the final product.

**finish**   The way and amount of time the flavor of a wine lingers in your mouth and the sensations it leaves. Very important concept in food pairing, as the flavor of the food also influences what the lingering tastes are.

**Friulia-Venezie Giulia**   Part of the Tre Venezie, the northernmost wine-producing region in Italy, this area is known for its production of Pinot Grigio, Chardonnay, and Sauvignon Blanc.

**fruit-forward**   Wines where the fruit influences in the aroma and taste are readily apparent.

**Gamay**   Grape grown in the Burgundy region of France. Used to make Beaujolais. Produces a lovely aroma of fresh strawberries and cherry.

**Gattinara**   A wine made predominantly of the Nebbiolo grape from the Piedmonte region of Italy. Similar to Barolo, but more tannic in nature.

**Gewürztraminer**   Spicy, fruity, low-alcohol, high-acid wine produced predominantly in Germany, Alsace, and northern Italy (where it is called Traminer).

**Grand Cru**   Grand Cru is what the French government designated over a hundred years ago as the best site in a particular area for the grapes grown for a particular wine.

**heirloom**   Ancient seed varieties that are untampered with by humankind.

**late-harvest**   Grapes that are purposely left on the vine longer in order to raise the sugar level and produce sweeter, dessert-quality wines.

**Merlot**   The grape that makes the wine by the same name that is low in tannins with a floral nose and easy-going flavor. Like Cabernet's shy little sister.

**microclimate**   An area in a particular wine-producing region that, due to the presence of various geographical influences, creates unique grape-growing conditions.

**Moscato**   Grape of the Muscat family, this Piedmonte grape is often used to make the delicious, sparkling Moscato d'Asti.

**Moscato d'Asti**   Short on shelf life, but big on taste, this low-alcohol sparkling wine from Piedmonte has influences of honey and orchard fruit.

**Montepulciano**   Grape commonly found in the central and southern regions of Italy.

**Montepulciano d'Abruzzo**   Made from Montepulciano grapes, this wine has a robust, rustic, fruity flavor that's not too high in tannins.

**Muscat**   Some say the grapes that come from these vines are the oldest that we know of.

**must**   The name for the mixture of pulp, seeds, juice, stems, and skins that forms during fermentation.

**Nebbiolo**   Piedmonte grape varietal producing the wine of the same name, as well as Barolo, Barbaresco, and Gattinara.

**Negroamaro**   From Apulia, this grape is often used to make Salice Salentino, an earthy, fruity wine.

**neutral spirits**   What is added to certain fortified wines such as brandy or port to sweeten the flavor.

**noble rot**   A mold or fungus that forms under certain (some say mysterious) conditions that attaches itself to grapes, piercing the skin and causing them to shrivel, deeply concentrating the sugar, acid, and flavor of the grape. Also known by its scientific name, *Botrytis cinera*. And yes, noble rot is a good thing.

**nose**   The distinct aromatic qualities of a wine.

**NV (nonvintage)**   When more than one year's grapes are used to make a bottle of wine.

**oak aging**   When a wine is stored in oak barrels to age for a prescribed amount of time. Usually, the wine will pick up flavors from the wood and this effects its flavor when bottled for consumption.

**phenol**   A chemical compound in oak that gives off the flavors of vanilla, tea, and tobacco.

**phylloxera**   *Phylloxera Vastatrix*, or phylloxera, is the name of a small plant louse that devastated European rootstocks in the mid-1860s.

**Piedmonte**   Possibly the most important wine-producing area in Italy next to Tuscany, Piedmonte is home to the Nebbiolo grape, which produces Barolo and Barbaresco.

**Pinot Blanc**   Grape that creates an easy-going wine with a light apple aroma and medium body.

**Pinot Grigio**   *See* Pinot Gris.

**Pinot Gris**   Alsatian grape that makes a clean-tasting, medium bodied white wine with a nutty, fruity aroma. Also called Pinot Grigio in Italy.

**Pinot Noir**   Grape that creates a wine that's fruity (think cherries) and earthy (mushrooms) at the same time.

**Pouilly-Fuisse**   Rustic white wine made from Chardonnay grapes in the Mâconnais region of France.

**Pouilly-Fumé**   Made from Sauvignon Blanc grapes in the Loire region of France, this is an elegant, smoky, racy wine.

**prädikat**   In Germany, this is the term used to define the style of a wine (i.e., sugar content, color, bouquet).

**Premier Cru**   A Premier Cru (or first cru) is the next step down from a Grand Cru, although in many cases they aren't too far behind their more esteemed siblings.

**Primitivo**   Made from the Negroamaro grape in the Apulia region of southern Italy, Primitivo is a spicy red wine similar to Zinfandel.

**Prosecco**   Sparkling Italian white wine.

**providence**   A wine's track record on the market.

**reserve**   Used in American wine labeling, sometimes can mean that the wine in question comes from a superior grape or blend of grapes, but it is not a legitimate term that has any actual real safeguards. However, if you see the word *riserva* on a bottle of Chianti from Tuscany, for example, it means the wine was by law aged in wood for a minimum of two years and then a further requisite bottle-aging time.

**residual sugar**   Sugar added to a wine to manipulate its final sugar levels and, thus, sweetness.

**Rhône**   Wine-producing region in southeastern France known for making great, rustic reds like Châteauneuf-du-Pape.

**Riesling**   A noble grape, the resulting wine is likely one of the most versatile made. It can range in flavor from dry to sweet, with excellent acidity and aromas of peach and pear.

**Rioja**   Spain's most important wine-producing region, most well-known for red wine of the same name.

**rootstock**   The root of a vine. Ironically, although Europe's winemaking culture is much older than America's, all European grapevines are grafted onto American rootstocks because of a virus brought over from the latter, which nearly killed off all European varietals.

**rosé**   While red wines get their color and tannic nature from the skins during fermentation, the skins are removed when making rosé wine so that the color becomes only a light pink and it is virtually tannin-free. Sometimes can be blended with white grapes as well.

**Sancerre**   Made from Sauvignon Blanc grapes in the Loire region of France, this wine tends to be crisp with chalky, mineral qualities.

**Sangiovese**   Grape used to make the wine of the same name, as well as the beloved Chianti and bold Super Tuscans. High in tannins with an aroma of leather and tar. Great aging potential.

**Sauternes**   Rich, fat wine with influences of apricot and peach. Made from a blend of Semillon and Sauvignon Blanc.

**Sauvignon Blanc**   Flexible grape used to make everything from rich, sweet Sauternes to dry, racy Pouilly-Fumé.

**Semillon**   Grape blended with Sauvignon Blanc to make Sauternes, a rich, fat, fruity wine.

**Shiraz**  *See* Syrah.

**sommelier**  A person with an incredible depth of wine knowledge (sometimes certified, sometimes not) who generally works in a restaurant and guides diners to the best choice for their tastes, their meal, and their budget.

**Super Tuscan**  Wines that are made outside of the laws of the DOCG. These wines introduced French grape varietals like Cabernet Sauvignon, Merlot, and Syrah into the Sangiovese wines of Tuscany.

**Syrah**  Used to make the wine of the same name (sometimes called Shiraz in areas other than Europe), as well as Châteauneuf-du-Pape. Herby and spicy with plum influences and a beautiful, dark color.

**tannins**  The slightly bitter taste produced by the skins of grapes. Red wines have the highest tannic nature; while whites do contain some tannins, they tend to be extremely low.

**tartrate crystals**  Little snowflakelike crystals that form after a white wine is bottled and chilled.

**Tempranillo**  The grape used to make the wine of the same name, as well as Rioja. Produces soft, elegant wines with hints of chocolate and cherry.

**terroir**  Not just the soil in which a grapevine is grown, but all the influences around it (such as what else is grown there).

**Traminer**  *See* Gewürztraminer.

**Trentino–Alto Adige**  Part of the Tre Venezie wine-producing region in northern Italy, these two areas are known for their production of Traminer, Pinot Grigio, Chardonnay, and Pinot Bianco. The lesser-known Lagrein is also produced here (see Chapter Eleven).

**Trockenbeerenauslese**  A form of Riesling wine that has a particularly high sugar content. Frequently consumed as a dessert wine, these tend to be very expensive as they are a product of *botrytis cinera*.

**unctuous**  Thick and syrupy in texture.

**varietal**  A particular grape and, sometimes, the name of the resulting wine (i.e., Chardonnay, Pinot Noir, Cabernet Sauvignon, Riesling, etc.). In most English-speaking countries, wines are named after the varietal. In Europe, wines are usually named after the region in which they are produced (i.e., Chianti, Burgundy, Bordeaux, Alsace, etc.).

**Veneto**   Part of the Tre Venezie (three Venices), the northernmost wine-producing region in Italy. Most well known for the production of the wines Prosecco, Valpolicella, and Amarone.

**Vin Santo**   Literally meaning "holy wine," this honeylike, creamy, sweet wine is frequently consumed after a meal in Tuscany.

**vinification**   The process of making wine.

**vintage**   The year the grapes in the wine were harvested. Usually printed on the label of a wine.

**Viognier**   Full-bodied, fragrant white wine with the influence of peaches and honeydew melon.

**viticulture**   The cultivation of grapes and the resulting varietals thereof for winemaking.

**weight**   The range of lightness to heaviness in wine and food (e.g., poached fish with a little lemon is light; steak topped in béarnaise sauce is heavy). With wine and food pairing, matching the weight of your food with the weight of your wine is a vital part of creating the proper balance.

**white Burgundy**   Another name for Chardonnay, as the grape grows in the Burgundy region of France.

**Zinfandel**   Grape that produces the wine of the same name. It's spicy and sweet, with black fruit and chocolate influences. Good aging potential.

*appendix C*

# Major Wine Regions of the World

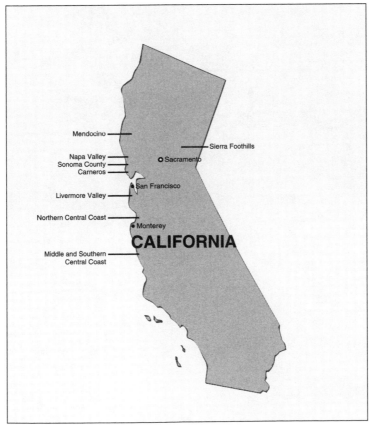

*California.*

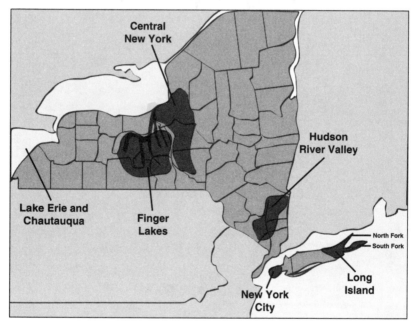

*New York.*

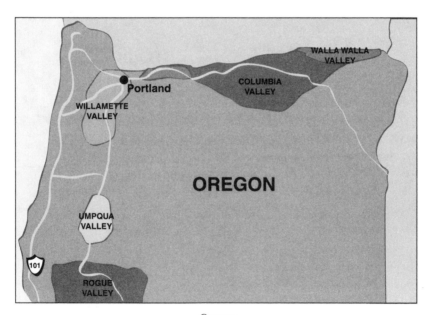

*Oregon.*

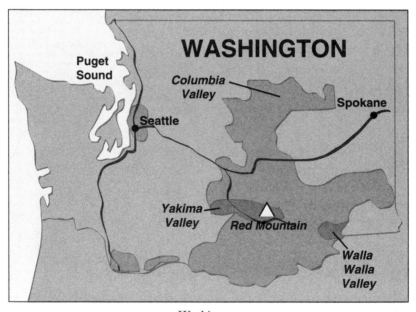

*Washington.*

*France.*

*Italy.*

*Germany.*

*Austria.*

*Spain.*

*Portugal.*

*Chile and Argentina.*

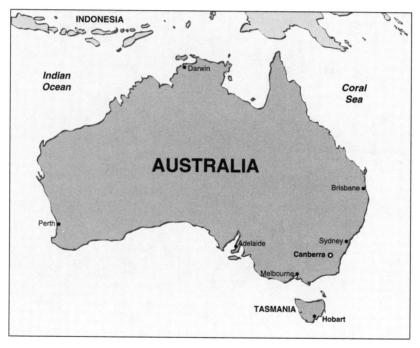

*Australia.*

*New Zealand.*

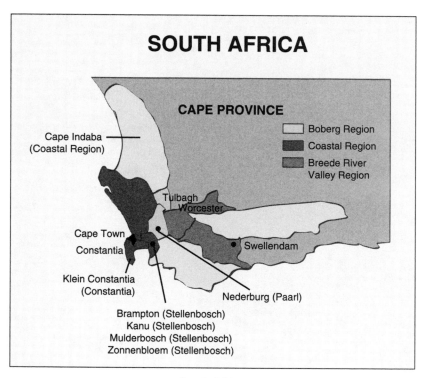

*South Africa.*

# Wine and Food Evaluation Chart

An excellent way to boost your sense memory is with a little old-fashioned note-taking. Following is a fill-in chart for you to photocopy and use each time you're having a tasting.

- ❖ In the first column, write the name of the wine and all pertinent information regarding it (grape varietal, producer, regional location, year).
- ❖ Next, make sure you smell and taste the wine *before* trying the food, and write down the main components you experienced.
- ❖ Then, take a bite of whatever food you are eating, and follow it with a sip of the wine. Write down your aroma and taste impressions *after* this.
- ❖ Next, breathe in a little through your mouth and exhale through your nose—what taste sensations are left for the finish on your palate? Write these down as well.
- ❖ Finally, jot down your overall impression of the wine and food pairing. Did one overpower the other? If so, did it work or was it too much? Did they parallel each other well? What flavors did they bring out in each other that, on their own, you might not have experienced?

| Wine | Main Flavors and Aromas (Before Food) | Main Flavors and Aromas (After Tasting Food) | Finish | Overall Impression |
| --- | --- | --- | --- | --- |
|  |  |  |  |  |
|  |  |  |  |  |
|  |  |  |  |  |
|  |  |  |  |  |

| Wine | Main Flavors and Aromas (Before Food) | Main Flavors and Aromas (After Tasting Food) | Finish | Overall Impression |
|---|---|---|---|---|
|  |  |  |  |  |
|  |  |  |  |  |
|  |  |  |  |  |
|  |  |  |  |  |

# Index

Windows on the World restaurant
Charred Buffalo Steaks with Poblano-Margarita Sauce recipe, 283
interview with Michael Lomonaco, 271-283
*The Wine Bible* (MacNeil), 57
*Wine Enthusiast,* 56
wine labels, 69
American, 72-73
French, 75-77
German, 69-72
Italian, 74-75
wine lists, 61
balance, 62
depth, 62
grouping of wines by weight, 63
I Trulli restaurant, 64
listing styles, 63-66
prices, 67
regions, 67
River Café, 65-66
size, 62
type of wine, 66
vintage, 66
*Wine Spectator,* 56
winemakers, 31
Clendenen, Jim, 45-50
Draper, Paul, 31-37
Lindquist, Bob, 37-39
Sessions, Bob, 39-45
winemaking, 15
fermentation, 17
filtering and bottling, 18
grape harvesting and pressing, 16-17
viticulture, 16

wineries
Au Bon Climat, Clendenen, Jim, 45-50
Benton Lane vineyard, 178
Chalk Hill, 187
Duck Pond Cellars, 269
Hanzell, Sessions, Bob, 39-45
King Estate, 269
Long Vineyard, 178
Mission San Gabriel, 11
Mission San Juan Capistrano, 11
Qupé, Lindquist, Bob, 37-39
Ravenswood Vineyards, 218
Rex Hill, 269
Ridge Vineyards, Draper, Paul, 31-37
start-up costs, as consideration when pricing wine, 55
winter savory, 116

## X-Z

Zemmer, Peter, 269
Zinfandel
pairing with
cheese, 244
lamb chops and roasts, 188
seasoned beef, 187
spicy foods, 264
Ravenswood Zinfandel, 272
Zraly, Kevin, *Windows on the World Complete Wine Course: A Lively Guide,* 57

# Wine Index

## A

Abruzzi region (Italy), pairing pasta and wine, 214-215

acidity, 103
  savory flavors, 110, 117-119
  sour flavors, 109-111

Agrigento (province of Sicily), 218

Amarone red wine, 219

American wine labels, 72-73

Apollonio Primitivo, pairing with Italian-style veal, 188

Apulia region (Italy), pairing pasta and wine, 215-216

Au Bon Climat Winery, Clendenen, Jim, 45-50

Auslese
  Kracher Trockenbeerenauslese, 288
  pairing with spicy foods, 266

Avignonesi Chardonnay, 221

## B

Badia a Coltibuono
  Chianti, 272
  pairing with stewed or simmered chicken, 178
  Trappolina, 221

Barbera wine (Piedmonte region), 25, 119
  pairing with burgers and meatloaf, 187

pairing with rabbit, 191

pairing with stewed or simmered chicken, 178

Barberani Vallesanta Orvieto, 221

Barolos, 260

barrels
  chestnut-tree wood, 18
  oak, 18

*barriques,* 233

Beaujolais, paired with
  cheese, 244
  grilled, seared, and seasoned fish, 153

Benton Lane vineyard, Pinot Noir, pairing with grilled chicken, 178

Bordeaux region
  Cabernet, 22
  Merlot, 23
  Semillon, 25

bottling wines, 18

Brachetto d'Acqui, pairing with desserts, 291-292

Brocard Chardonnay, paired with arugula, 112

Brunello di Montalcino (Tuscany), 187, 202
  Sangiovese, 220

Burklin Wolf Riesling, pairing with chicken with sauces, 178

# Food Index